Industrial Relations in Sch

The subject of industrial relations is intimately connected with the nature of schooling – in particular, the teacher trade unions have played and will continue to play a crucial role in shaping the school system – yet this subject has been virtually neglected in educational literature. Mike Ironside and Roger Seifert's book redresses this balance and unravels the complex issues surrounding the employment and management of teachers, setting them within the perspective of the historical development of and relationships between unions, teachers, managers and their employers.

The Education Reform Act and the introduction of LMS have had a dramatic impact on traditional industrial relations in schools and on the distribution of funding. The authors argue that there is now an urgent need for a well-funded and integrated education system operating on the principle of genuine equality of access, as opposed to the move towards re-introduction of a multi-tiered system of schools. Teaching unions, they feel, are the most consistent defenders of these principles, and indeed the only organisations capable of mobilising enough power from within a democratic base within the system. It is the fear of this power which Seifert and Ironside perceive as responsible for the Government's often open hostility towards the unions.

In order for schools to continue to function, industrial relations must be given priority, including the development of a proper framework for negotiation and resolution of conflicts. The book questions who controls or ought to control schools, focusing on the government, Department for Education, LEAs, head teachers, school governors, parents and teaching unions, and examining the balance of power amongst these groups.

Both authors work at the Centre for Industrial Relations, University of Keele, where **Mike Ironside** is Lecturer in Industrial Relations and **Roger Seifert** is Professor of Industrial Relations and Director of the Centre.

Industrial Relations in Schools

Mike Ironside and Roger Seifert

London and New York

First published 1995
by Routledge
11 New Fetter Lane, London EC4P 4EE

Simultaneously published in the USA and Canada
by Routledge
29 West 35th Street, New York, NY 10001

Typeset in Times by
Ponting–Green Publishing Services, Chesham, Bucks

Printed and bound in Great Britain by
TJ Press Ltd, Padstow, Cornwall

British Library Cataloguing in Publication Data
A catalogue record for this book is available from the British Library

Library of Congress Cataloguing in Publication Data
A catalogue record for this book has been requested

ISBN 0–415–08088–6

From Mike to Rachel.
From Roger to my wife Anne and to my children Sarah, Joseph, Rachel, Adam, Hannah, Judith and Miriam.

Contents

Illustrations

FIGURES

TABLES

Preface

The impetus to write this book came from our concern for the future of the school education system. While there is a huge volume of literature on education, there is almost total neglect of industrial relations in schools. We started with the view that the nature of industrial relations in schools is intimately connected with the nature of schooling, and that any attempt to restructure the school system will have profound industrial relations consequences. Within this view the trade union movement in general and the teacher trade unions in particular have played a significant and positive role in shaping the state school system.

In the course of writing this book these views have been strengthened, as we have tried to unravel some of the complex issues surrounding the employment and management of teachers in state maintained schools in England and Wales. We bring together much historical material not previously assembled into one book, locating into an analytical framework the findings of Keele University's two year ESRC funded programme of research. The structure of the book reflects our belief that to make sense of the responses of the teacher workforce, their unions, their managers and their employers to the reforms it is necessary to examine the historical development of those groups and of the relationships between them.

Discussion about education turns on a bewildering array of issues which, one way or another, stem from a view that somehow the school system is failing us. It is widely believed that schools and teachers are at least partly to blame for the perceived ills of economic decline, moral breakdown, social division and juvenile crime.

At the heart of the puzzle is the question as to who is in control, or who ought to be in control, of schools. Government, the Department for Education, local education authority (LEA) councillors and officers, head teachers, school governors, parents, and all six of the teacher and head teacher unions are among those who have an interest in running schools. What actually happens in schools is largely determined by the balance of power between these groups, a balance that has been radically redistributed by the reform programme.

We have assumed that the government has two main objectives. The first is to break with the principle of comprehensive education, reintroducing a multi-tiered system involving independent schools benefiting from government encouragement, government funded grant-maintained schools, a few well funded LEA schools, and a large number of under-funded LEA schools. The local management of schools (LMS) mechanism ensures the unequal distribution of funding between LEA schools while also enabling the delivery of the government's second objective of reducing state spending. The LMS system of delegated budgets based on pupil numbers forces school-based managers to cope with declining budgets by driving them into market competition with the managers of other schools. To aid the implementation of their programme the government has acted to drive the main opposition, the teacher unions, out of positions of influence, by dismantling advisory bodies, by ending national collective bargaining, by neglecting to consult with them, and by ignoring their views.

At the time of writing this book there is a view emerging from within the Labour Party, the liberal-minded press and the education establishment that, while the government has gone 'too far', there is nevertheless much merit in their reforms. These commentators see benefits in the LMS system, and they suggest that provision can be strengthened through the use of advanced communications technology, stronger assessment and inspection systems, and the introduction of unqualified workers to support teachers in the classroom. It is our view that these proposals raise the same issues as the government's reform programme – downgrading teacher skills, reducing teacher autonomy, and diluting the teacher workforce.

Any attempt to transform the job of teaching, to impose tighter control over teacher performance, or to restructure the skills profile of the teaching workforce, one of the most highly unionised groups in the country, will lead inevitably to conflict. If schools are to continue to function then the industrial relations issues must be given proper consideration, which means establishing a viable framework for negotiations and for resolving conflict. The panacea of the General Teaching Council is again being debated, apparently ignoring the lessons of repeated failures to establish such a body over the last hundred years and more.

The education system is in crisis. Its future direction hangs in the balance, with major implications for current and future generations of school pupils. We believe that there is widespread support for a well funded and integrated system that operates on the principle of genuine equality of access, not under the market but under democratic control. In moving towards such a system the views of parents, the policies of government and the actions of the teacher employers all have importance. But the most durable and consistent defence of these principles has come from within the teacher unions, which are the only permanent organisations capable of mobilising power from a democratic base within the system. The government's open hostility to the unions and to the NUT in particular gives some indication of their fear of union power.

Acknowledgements

This book draws from research funded by the ESRC. Jackie Sinclair did much of the fieldwork in connection with that project.

We are indebted to the teacher union officials and activists and to the local education authority officers who contributed to all aspects of our research.

Dave Lyddon has our gratitude for reading earlier drafts.

Abbreviations

AAM	Association of Assistant Mistresses (now part of ATL)
ACAS	Advisory, Conciliation and Arbitration Service
ACC	Association of County Councils
ACSET	Advisory Committee on the Supply and Education of Teachers
AEC	Association of Education Committees
AFL–CIO	American Federation of Labour and Congress of Industrial Organizations
AHM	Association of Head Mistresses (now part of SHA)
AMA	Assistant Masters Association (now part of ATL)
AMA	Association of Metropolitan Authorities
AMMA	Assistant Masters and Mistresses Association (now ATL)
ATCDE	Association of Teachers in Colleges and Departments of Education
ATL	Association of Teachers and Lecturers
ATTI	Association of Teachers in Technical Institutions (now NATFHE)
AWPU	Age-weighted pupil unit
BMA	British Medical Association
CBI	Confederation of British Industry
CEO	Chief Education Officer
CLEA	Council of Local Education Authorities
CLEA/ST	Council of Local Education Authorities/Schoolteachers' Committee
COPPSO	Conference of Professional and Public Service Organisations
DES	Department of Education and Science
DFE	Department for Education
EA 1944	Education Act 1944
EC	European Community
EIS	Educational Institute of Scotland
ERA 1988	Education Reform Act 1988
GCSE	General Certificate of Secondary Education
GMB	General, Municipal, Boilermakers and Allied Trades Union
GMS	Grant-maintained status

GNP	Gross national product
HMI	Her Majesty's Inspectorate
HRM	Human resource management
IA	Incentive allowance
IAC	Interim Advisory Committee on Schoolteachers' Pay and Conditions
IAHM	Incorporated Association of Head Masters (now part of SHA)
ILO	International Labour Organization
IPM	Institute of Personnel Management
JCC	Joint consultative committee
JNC	Joint negotiating committee
LACSAB	Local Authorities Conditions of Service Advisory Board (now LGMB)
LCC	London County Council
LEA	Local Education Authority
LGMB	Local Government Management Board
LIFO	Last in first out
LMS	Local management of schools
NAGM	National Association of Governors and Managers
NAHT	National Association of Head Teachers
NAS	National Association of Schoolmasters (now part of NASUWT)
NASUWT	National Association of Schoolmasters and Union of Women Teachers
NATFHE	National Association of Teachers in Further and Higher Education
NEA	National Education Association
NEOST	National Employers Organisation, School Teachers
NES	New Earnings Survey
NHS	National Health Service
NJC	National Joint Council
NUET	National Union of Elementary Teachers (now NUT)
NUT	National Union of Teachers
NUWT	National Union of Women Teachers
OME	Office of Manpower Economics
PAT	Professional Association of Teachers
PRP	Performance-related pay
RTA 1965	Remuneration of Teachers Act 1965
SATS	Standard Assessment Tests
SHA	Secondary Heads Association
STRB	School Teachers' Review Body
TPCA 1987	Teachers' Pay and Conditions Act 1987
TQM	Total quality management
TUC	Trades Union Congress
TUPE	Transfer of Undertakings and Protection of Employment Regulations

TURU	Trade Union Research Unit, Ruskin College Oxford
UWT	Union of Women Teachers (now part of NASUWT)
WIRS	Workplace Industrial Relations Survey
WJEC	Welsh Joint Education Committee
Burgundy Book	Conditions of Service for Schoolteachers in England and Wales

1 The crisis of change

INTRODUCTION

The main purposes of this book are to explain and describe the impact of the local management of schools (LMS) on the traditional institutions, procedures and outcomes of industrial relations. We are concerned, therefore, to show how the main parties involved – employers, managers and trade union representatives – have changed and responded in light of the legal, financial and managerial reforms based in the 1988 Education Reform Act (ERA). We are also interested in how two of the core elements of industrial relations, pay and performance, will be controlled and determined under the new order. This requires, *inter alia*, an analysis of the Burnham system and the reasons for its collapse, an account of the current national pay setting mechanisms through the School Teachers' Review Body (STRB), and some consideration of the role of trade unions in pay determination through the presentation of argument and the taking of action. In addition we need to consider the applicability of private sector managerial control systems associated with performance issues such as appraisal, performance related pay, discipline and more generally the introduction of human resource management (HRM) methods into schools. The book is a result of these concerns and outlines the traditional industrial relations system, and then examines the issues and changes associated with the introduction of LMS – a heavier workload, some de-skilling and limited school management autonomy.

The research for the book falls into two main categories. The first half relies heavily on secondary sources not previously discussed within a single book together with work from our previous research. The second half of the book depends upon our recent research into LMS. This was based on a two year project funded by the Economic and Social Research Council (ESRC) and based at Keele University's Centre for Industrial Relations. The field work for the project was through extensive and detailed interviews with trade union officials, personnel managers at the LEA level, and all teachers in our case study schools. Jackie Sinclair carried out this work and we are indebted to her for the high quality of research material produced. The rest of the research was based on a questionnaire to every head teacher in schools in three midlands LEAs to which we received a 64 per cent response rate. We also issued a questionnaire to every school based trade union representative from all the unions in all the schools in the same LEAs, with a similarly high response rate.

The organisation of the book reflects our attempts to compare the traditional system with the new emergent one. Chapters 2 and 3 offer evidence and discussion of the traditional institutions, especially the trade unions and the national pay determination systems. Chapters 4, 5 and 6 present material on the introduction of performance controls through HRM by school managers under the new employment circumstances; the emergence of issues previously unknown in schools such as redundancies and performance related pay; and the efforts to create new industrial relations mechanisms at school level to help resolve these new issues.

This opening chapter tackles two contextual matters. First, the meaning and relevance of industrial relations to the current reform of the maintained school service, and secondly, the centrality of work and wages (performance and pay) to this analysis of teachers' job regulation. The discussion starts with the dominant tradition in wage setting – the multi-employer, multi-union effective rate national bargaining through Burnham, and then proceeds to the nature of industrial relations through a brief account of the relevant perspectives. We then investigate the importance of a national rate for the job for school teachers in terms of the dominance of the National Union of Teachers (NUT) from 1919 to 1985 within Burnham. We also examine the type of arguments used to support national pay advancement especially that of felt-fair comparability, and how LMS might shift interest away from national wage setting systems towards business needs as defined by the performance and management of individual schools and the teachers within them.

THE MEANING AND RELEVANCE OF INDUSTRIAL RELATIONS TO THE REFORM OF THE MAINTAINED SCHOOL SECTOR

The reform of the state school education system since the 1988 Education Reform Act represents the greatest change in the provision of education in Britain since 1944. The main concern of this book is to examine its impact on industrial relations institutions, school-based management and trade union organisation.

Much of the reform programme is centred around new financial systems and structures which are founded in limiting resources and stimulating managerial controls. Industrial relations is an important element within the total strategic operation as it impinges on the fundamental issues of resource allocation: both the absolute level of resources and their distribution within the school system. Successive Conservative governments have sought to reduce public expenditure whilst maintaining the quality of provision and so, for them, the key issue has been the management of available resources rather than the level as a proportion of Gross National Product (GNP). This is the issue that has formed the basis of most of the relevant debates and struggles within education: the management of resources and their allocation as between staff, equipment and the employers' costs of the use of any given skill mix of labour. Thus the utilisation and cost of labour within a labour intensive service makes industrial relations a central concern.

The cost of employing teaching and non-teaching staff represents half of the vital new business equation. The other half, for employers and their managers, is the performance of individual employees and of the school as a whole. In contrast the staff, individually and collectively, seek to control their own total remuneration package, conditions of service and workload. Entry to and exit from thc labour market, both internal to the school and the external market, are increasingly important in a period of redundancies, increased differentials between classroom teachers and heads/deputies and with the unions reluctant to take national industrial action over pay.

The timing of the reform process has coincided with a deep and long-term recession in the wider economy, and this has greatly influenced the implementation and direction of the changes. In a recession private sector managers seek to reassert their authority over the workforce, and this is now happening in the public services. The most appropriate slogan for this process is 'more for less': more work and production for less pay and fewer rights. In the 1990s this formulation is being crudely applied to public service workers including school teachers (Seifert 1990). The implementation in schools of management techniques, more usually found in factories and offices, has come at a time when the national and regional institutions for the setting of pay and conditions of service and the resolution of conflicts are in crisis. So school teachers face four aspects of the wider crisis of the 1990s: first, the reduced funding in line with public expenditure controls; secondly, the implementation of private sector management practices in schools; thirdly, the abolition of national collective bargaining institutions; and finally, the increased powers of central government at the expense of the Local Education Authorities (LEAs). All of these developments impinge upon, and are influenced by, the level of pay of the teachers in the schools.

There are nearly half a million school teachers working in over 24,000 maintained schools throughout England and Wales. They teach the eight million children of school age the necessaries of formal learning. They constitute one of the largest professional groups in the country, one of the largest categories of public sector employees, a major employment type for women professional workers, and one of the most highly unionised groups of workers (see chapter 3). Their pay was determined, more or less, between 1919 and 1987 through their form of Whitley Council – Burnham. This opening section examines the major characteristics of that mechanism and its underlying assumptions (see chapter 2 for details). Such a dominant national system tended to limit bargaining at the level of the workplace and employer, but this is beginning to change (see chapters 5 and 6).

The Burnham Committee allowed employers' representatives and union representatives to bargain in a formal national committee over pay. This was a multi-employer/multi-union system which set effective national rates for all teachers employed in state schools.

There are three important aspects of this system: multi-employer, multi-union and effective rate. The first point is that the vast majority of teachers are still employed by their LEAs, although the powers and duties of the employer are now shared between LEAs and school governing bodies. The LEAs in England and Wales form two employers' associations: the Association of Metropolitan Authorities (AMA) and the Association of County Councils (ACC). Each is subject to change whenever there is a local election, and frequently the two associations are controlled by different political parties. This implies sharp division from time to time with respect to a united employers' position. Recently the two have formed the National Employers' Organisation for School Teachers (NEOST) for some bargaining purposes. The features of employer association bargaining are that industrial relations expertise need only be concentrated at national level in a few hands and that relevant data need only be held in one or two centres such as with the Local Authority Conditions of Service Advisory Board (LACSAB, now the Local Government Management Board, LGMB). The most important feature of multi-employer bargaining is that wages are taken out of employer competition and therefore each employer competes for labour on an equal footing with regard to pay levels. Therefore competition must be based on other factors, such as location, reputation and some conditions of service (Clegg 1972).

The pressure on employers to form associations was noted long ago by Adam Smith: 'We rarely hear . . . of the combination of masters though frequently of those of workmen. But whoever imagines, upon this account, that masters rarely combine, is as ignorant of the world as of the subject. Masters are always and everywhere in a sort of tacit but constant and uniform combination not to raise the wages of labour above their actual rate' (Smith 1776: 59). With the demise of the LEA and LEA employers' associations it will be interesting to see how individual schools go about the business of wage setting either as individual business units or in some sort of cartel.

The move to single-employer bargaining under LMS and grant maintained status (GMS) proposals will radically alter the ways in which pay is set. The school as prime determiner of pay and conditions of service as distinct from the LEA/Burnham model involves a move away from employer federation and that requires the development of bargaining expertise and relevant data at each unit of bargaining. Once employers break away from a single wage bargain then competition for labour can develop on a wage basis, which allows the better off to bid higher. The single-employer bargainer will, therefore, be forced to be more competitive and more expert, and to divert resources to both activities.

Single-employer bargainers are likely to bring alive the issue of management's 'right to manage' – a right based partly in law, partly in custom and partly in power relations within schools and LEAs. The restoration of the right to manage has been seen as part of the reform process, and it implies the restatement of traditional rights to make decisions free from 'restrictive' Department for Education (DFE) officials, 'incompetent' LEA planners, and 'overpowerful' trade unions. This emphasis on management has led to the introduction of human resource management (HRM) as the all embracing substitute for traditional personnel management and industrial relations. It has also raised the vital issue of the level at which management is exercised within schools and the rights of the managed (see chapter 4).

A key component of the right to manage and the move to single-employer bargainers is the need to raise labour productivity within the teaching and non-teaching workforce. We will discuss the definitions and measurement problems of this later, but for now it can be argued that higher productivity forms a major part of the total reform process. The search for higher productivity develops management's awareness of the need for the simultaneous application of incentives, control mechanisms and flexibility. These come in various packages: incentive allowances and promotions; discipline and appraisal; and more flexible hours, staffing levels, skills and remuneration packages including individual performance related pay arrangements.

Each new employer and governing body must make a series of policy decisions with respect to collective bargaining. These include three particular aspects of bargaining: the level at which it takes place – through some residual national forum, LEA-wide, or school and department based; the units that it covers – teachers, senior teachers, technicians, clerical staff, or all staff together; and its scope – for example pay, conditions of service, redeployment, equal opportunities. All this assumes that the employer will continue to recognise the unions for bargaining purposes, rather than for individual representation only or not recognise them at all.

The other side of this coin are the multi-union bargainers. This situation was created by the unusual ability of the Secretary of State to unilaterally change the trade union composition of the staff side of the Burnham Committee. The traditional literature on industrial relations suggests that multi-unionism is a bar to effective management and efficient representation (Clegg 1972). For school teachers this was not a real issue until the early 1960s, and not decisive until the mid-1980s. From 1919 to 1961 the NUT held the overall majority on the teachers' panel of Burnham, and therefore whatever the pressures to accommodate the views of other unions the NUT could, and often did, decide the issue for all unions and therefore all teachers. In the early 1960s the NAS agitated successfully for representation on Burnham and began a formal campaign to whittle away the NUT's majority. It was not until the 1980s, however, that government antagonism and the changing balance of teacher union membership created the circumstances for the removal of the NUT's overall majority in 1985. As soon as this happened, the other unions settled the 1985/6 teachers' strike, and the government abolished Burnham (Seifert 1987).

The third point was the existence of an effective rate national pay agreement negotiated at Burnham. The importance of a rate for the job which is nationally determined and applied in all schools cannot be overestimated. The central unifying issue within the NUT and among the majority of teachers was the desire for a rate which held in every school, and for all teachers irrespective of sex, age, qualification and sector. It was particularly important that the national rate applied to all LEAs since their individual budgets, political disposition and labour markets varied. If such variation had been reflected in pay then fundamental aspects of teacher education, training and professional development, as well as the schooling of millions of children, might have been quite different.

The rate for the job is fundamental to British trade unionism and a commonplace among public sector employees. Its significance will be examined later, but for now it should be noted that the current changes in the education system will remove the nationally determined rate as the effective prevailing rate. The most likely outcome of all the reforms will be a national minimum rate set by either a Review Body or incomes policies. In either case the national pay settlement will become less important, setting a low minimum rate increase which will be the effective rate in schools with tight budgets where teachers' bargaining power is reduced. In other LEAs and schools where teachers are in a stronger bargaining position then the national minimum rate will provide a starting point for locally determined higher rates. The disintegrating impact of this change on the profession needs to be assessed and later we will turn our attention to local patterns of pay determination and their consequences for teachers, the unions, and the managers/employers.

This debate on the main changes in the industrial relations in the school system resides within a wider debate in industrial relations in general. The main elements of industrial relations with which this book is concerned include the basic assumption explained by Flanders (1965) that job regulation (work and wages) should be through formal and joint rule making processes such as collective bargaining. This dominant pluralist tradition concerns itself with the making and implementing of the rules that allow for a controlled conduct of labour relations. These rules are divided between the 'how' procedural rules of recognition, discipline, grievance and redundancy – the managerial rules; and the 'what' substantive rules on pay and conditions of service – the market rules. On this view the best way to achieve any set of organisational goals is through joint regulation as embodied in the institutions of collective bargaining and the institutionalisation of conflict. Such a general set of propositions underpinned the two most important practical versions of the British tradition: the Whitley Council reports (1917) and the Donovan Commission report (1968). Their prescriptions were widely accepted by trade unionists, employers and governments until the late 1970s.

The main issues remain, however, even for the pluralist, those associated with pay and performance. For those adopting a *unitarist* perspective the school as a business is seen in terms of a 'team' with managers/heads as team leaders/captains whose task is to motivate, lead by example, set objectives and encourage team work. Team members/other staff are required to work hard, be loyal to the team/school, and share the set goals of the leadership. Opposition to management is seen as disruptive, unacceptable and creating discontent and inefficiency. Such a management ideology prefers unilateral rule-making and shuns, in theory at least, trade union representative activity (Fox 1966). In its most modern version it is presented as HRM (Storey and Sisson 1993) which, during a recession, becomes an important part of re-establishing managerial definitions of performance standards and 'excellent' education/schools, and of emphasising the individual's contribution to the success of the school rather than wider notions of bargained comparability within a national system.

In contrast the *pluralist* perspective accepts the legitimate interests of trade unions as long as they are confined within orderly and reasonable limits and that they ultimately share in the objectives of the school (Flanders 1965). *Marxists* consider both these ideologies, unitarism and pluralism, as variants on a dominant managerial perspective, and contrast it with a worker-centred theory (Hyman 1975). Here conflict and exploitation are put at the heart of the employment relationship, and the task of trade unions is to organise workers to both protect their interests and further their demands (Allen 1966). The emphasis is on direct and indirect challenges to the exercise of managerial control, and its substitution with the central concern for all staff *qua* employees and the process of deflecting the educational process away from any simple reproduction of dominant bourgeois values (Carlson 1987).

The importance of differing perspectives is that they allow us to judge more objectively the proposals about the future methods of regulating the job of the school teacher. There are three possible options: the first is based on the pluralist perspective and is supported by the NUT and NASUWT along with some Labour LEAs and heads. This position prefers a reformulation of the post-war consensus in which there is some national pay bargaining, limited LEA-wide negotiations and that school industrial relations remains largely concerned with individual staff issues. The second option is the application of unitarism through HRM practices. In this model the unions' role would be reduced to case presenter nationally, spectator at LEA level and nothing at school. This would be the position of the ATL and NAHT, officials at the DFE, most managers and the majority of Liberal Democrats and Conservatives. The third option is really a radical variant of HRM supported by the government and their allies in the educational establishment and the business world. There would be no role for unions, and the managerial process would be driven by market forces built around the pursuit of 'quality' management (Seifert 1991b).

Whichever perspective is adopted the parties involved in industrial relations remain the trade unions as the representative organisations of the vast majority of employees in schools, and managers (heads, deputies and other designated teachers) as the agent-representatives of the employers (the governing body/LEA). When Burnham met, therefore, it was the representatives of the main parties who participated in negotiations, and this provides an important clue as to the nature of the collective bargaining processes and the strengths and weaknesses of the Burnham system itself.

Once the relevant parties – the unions, managers and employers – are recognised and agree to interact then the nature of that relationship needs to be clear: it is normally all of the mutually interdependent set of communication, consultation and negotiation. Even before any interchange takes place there are two essential factors which prefigure much of the bargaining: the real objective power of the parties, and that each side is committed to a set of rights and interests which often conflict. Such rights include the right to manage, the right to dismiss, the right to assess performance and the right not to recognise trade unions. On the other hand there are other rights such as the right to strike, the right to work, the right not to be discriminated against and the right to fair reward.

So when the parties meet in a 'good faith' bargaining session they do so from positions already prefigured by the relevant exercise of power. For example, the global amount available for pay increases from the employers is determined mainly by government allocation of funds to the education service, and this in turn is decided by an overall government view of public expenditure. Such 'pre-bargaining' bargaining within the government–employers axis is part of intra-organisational bargaining (Walton and McKersie 1965) and its outcome draws the boundaries within which the employers must operate. This is not to say that the final agreement between the parties is over-determined in this manner since in extreme circumstances, such as 1969, 1974 and again 1984, industrial action and/or arbitration/pay inquiries might alter the original settlement from government. None the less, the bargaining process under Burnham was important and illustrated the main elements of any future bargaining at whatever level pay becomes settled.

In terms of employer-based industrial relations we find that managers want to *communicate* with their subordinates in order to achieve controlled consensus over decisions and actions. In recent years managers have been sent on hundreds of different courses to improve their communication skills and have been subject to a welter of management consultancy reports and management books. The majority of these concentrate on the competencies involved and assume the beneficial qualities of improved communication skills. Few define and/or explain what communication means and fewer comment on the importance of the content. The key virtue, it is suggested on this model, is that better communication between managers and their subordinates leads to greater trust, more loyalty and ultimately higher performance through greater motivation. The practicalities of these motivation theories are found in quality circles, employee participation schemes and team briefings. Such is the stuff of HRM. It is essential to bear in mind, however, that the introduction of HRM and TQM practices threaten to

disestablish collective bargaining (Purcell and Ahlstrand 1994), and their successful implementation is highly dependent upon the wider conditions of recession and the demobilisation of the social democratic consensus.

The emphasis on the benefits of good communication is itself predicated on elements of unitarist ideology and rarely based in evidence. The meaning of communication in this context slides around according to need, and has been increasingly extended to embrace payment systems. So the reward policy of the school, as with more increments for higher pass rates in examinations, is considered to be message-bearing information. Equally, the message to all staff when a teacher or a secretary is made redundant should be clear. The ideology provides a simplistic explanation of conflict at work as abnormal, and is blamed on the lack of understanding by employees of the motives, reasons, reasonableness and rationality of management decisions. This lack of understanding is itself blamed on poor communications and lack of trust within the organisation. The trade union representatives and members may approve of management efforts to improve communications and may be very interested in the content of such communication, but do not see good communications as a substitute for joint decision making through good faith bargaining.

The second mode of traditional interaction between staff representatives and school/LEA managers has been *consultation*. It is what it says it is: the seeking out of opinion without any obligation to act on the views of others. In some cases the process has some force, and the timing of the consultation process often provides a central element of the decision-making round. In times of change and of trade union retreat consultation may become an attractive toe-hold to provide representation through unions rather than through some works council and/or school staff forum.

The third method of interaction, and traditionally the most important at national level, is collective bargaining through representative *negotiations*. Negotiations are what the trade union representatives want to do most, and do best. It is one of the main purposes for trade union formation and existence. Managers may resist genuine negotiations since 'good faith' bargaining requires the bargainers, such as the managers, to make concessions from their 'ideal' position. Whatever its outcome an important aspect of the bargaining process is the determination of what is negotiable and what is not negotiable. This negotiability of issues has been described as the 'frontier of control' which separates the two parties, but moves over time and workplace according to the balance of power (Goodrich 1920). Such a frontier provides two useful insights at the present time: first it reminds us of the dominant metaphor of traditional industrial relations, namely the clash of interests and the thinly veiled threat of conflict. Secondly, it provides us with a tentative hypothesis about the future of school-employer based industrial relations – that it will be extremely variable and that the variation will matter in the determination of the total remuneration package for all staff and in the performance of individuals and the school business as a whole.

The outcomes of any formal bargaining process are usually contained within collective agreements. These tend to be divided into *substantive* agreements on issues such as pay and conditions, and *procedural* agreements on matters such as dismissal and dispute. The latter represent the institutionalisation of conflict through 'impasse resolution mechanisms'. The substantive issues correspond with Fox's expression 'market rules' and indicate market forces as part of the determination of pay and conditions. In contrast, procedural matters are akin to Fox's 'managerial rules' and focus attention on control mechanisms and conflict avoidance (Fox 1974).

So far we have summarised the issues central to industrial relations, and we have outlined the great changes taking place in the national system of collective bargaining. For those who work in schools pay will no longer be determined through Burnham and effective rate national bargaining – for teachers it will be through the Review Body setting minimum rates and for non-teaching staff it will be through NJCs which are also moving towards a national minimum with local supplements. The traditional national system embodied the immensely influential post-first world war settlement with Whitley Councils in 1919, with its central quality of a multi-employer/multi-union representative system setting effective national rates of pay for all state employed school teachers remained intact until 1987.

In this book we take the view that both the education reform programme and the responses of the employers and the unions to it are rooted in the tensions within the traditional system. The system has evolved since 1919, with five major changes in pay determination. In 1944 the system was extended, renewing the dominance of the National Union of Teachers (NUT). In 1965 the Remuneration of Teachers Act (RTA) removed certain staff side complaints, introducing both retrospection and arbitration, and bringing the DES onto Burnham's management panel through the secret deal known as the Concordat. In 1985/6 the Concordat was ended and the NUT's majority on Burnham's teachers' panel was removed after the national strikes. In 1987 the Teachers Pay and Conditions Act (TPCA) abolished Burnham and introduced the Interim Advisory Committee (IAC). In 1992 the School Teachers' Review Body (STRB) was established.

These changes have themselves been part of wider and deeper themes taken up in this book. In chapter 2 we examine developments in national bargaining arrangements. We discuss the debates about bargaining arrangements, and we indentify the importance of industrial action in driving change in the context of successive governments' failure to establish an effective policy for teachers' pay. In chapter 3 we look at the origins of the teacher trade unions, at the growth in their size and influence, and at competition between them. In chapter 4 we deal with the employers, examining the impact of reorganisations and the introduction of HRM into schools. In chapter 5 we identify the reform and recession-driven search for higher productivity, and for greater value-for-money based on affordability and demand (the market) in place of customary pay comparability and consensus (the public service). In chapter 6 we consider the emergence of a local system of industrial relations.

This book is written against the background of the deregulation of state schooling, the removal of the influence and power of LEAs, the overall relative decline in funding and the recreation of a two tier state school system. The power of central government has increased and with it the policy making functions of the renamed DFE. These changes represent a profound shift in the delivery of school education and in the trading of the education of children as a commodity in a government-regulated market. The forces that such a market unleashes remove the basis for traditional centralised national pay bargaining. They also result in a redefinition of performance, among both individual teachers and whole schools.

In a labour intensive industry with thousands of small businesses and millions of potential users the formation of a new set of relationships as between teachers and their trade unions, the unions with each other, individual staff with school managers, school managers with governors and residual LEA services is emerging. The destabilising influences of the reforms have been immense and with a power vacuum over the setting of pay, and no clear authority for the control over performance the future pattern of school provision appears uneven at best and unworkable at worst.

None the less, the industry has certain important features which it will carry forward throughout the 1990s. A large number of teachers will remain in state employment and most schools will still employ state qualified teachers to teach. The vast majority of teachers will stay in membership of one of the six teacher unions. The two largest classroom unions – the NUT and NASUWT – will stay in the TUC, take industrial action, and maintain an impressive organisational base at national and regional levels. Nearly all staff still have their pay determined through some centralised national system – in 1992 the STRB, in 1993 government incomes policy, and in 1994 STRB with a frozen pay bill. Individual employers and senior managers at school level will get weaker in labour market and bargaining terms with the corollary that the emphasis will remain on administrative functions (some carried out through residual LEA service agreements) and the development of HRM. Finally the government's ideological impulse to secure greater central control over state education through regulating the financial reward systems, through deregulation of advisory and inspection functions, and directly through DFE powers to intervene in school life (examinations, tests, national curriculum) will continue to represent a severe example of controlling the twin purposes of any educational system – the cultural transmission of dominant values, and the value-for-money level of quality required to feed the labour markets of the 1990s.

WORK AND WAGES: THE DOMINANCE OF THE TRADITIONAL SYSTEM

The struggle to establish a national pay bargaining system was fought through the NUT by its members in various elementary schools. Before and after the first world war there was considerable strike action by teachers alongside that of other workers, and these disturbances allied to acute labour shortages and the changing nature of international competition and the pattern of demand for skilled labour created a centralised drive to improve education and therefore the status and remuneration of the school teachers (Seifert 1987).

The fight for the national effective wage was central to the NUT, the profession and the government, but it was not greeted with equal enthusiasm by some local authorities and some sections of the teaching force. After the establishment of the Burnham Committee in 1919 some areas refused to apply the going rate and there was further industrial action, but the government and local opinion allied with the teachers' own efforts finally achieved the national implementation of the Burnham agreements. This was more likely to stick when the recession of falling prices and wages left school teachers relatively better placed to withstand unemployment and poverty in the 1920s and 1930s.

The consequences of a national rate that embodied equality across the spectrum of the teaching force within the NUT and the profession was more important. Certain teachers felt that their status, qualification and professionalism was better served through the pursuit of sectional interests rather than united teacher organisation, and in 1922 the NAS was formed as a splinter from the NUT (Latta 1969). At the time, and for many years after, this had little impact on the NUT, on wages, on Burnham or on the profession, but it demonstrated the tendency of teachers, like other groups, to fragment. It also shows how skilful employers and governments can use divisions to further divide and weaken the teachers as a whole.

The triumph of Burnham for school teachers was the triumph for both organised labour in its trade union form and for the centralising tendencies of both the left within the profession and NUT and the right within the civil service and government. Towards the end of the first world war the threat of social revolution at home and the reality of Bolshevism in Europe prompted the Lib-Labs to fall in line with the modern Tories in an early escape from laissez-faire monetarism and in favour of a centralised military-style state command. At the same time the command economy in the USSR became a model for British socialists within the teaching profession and the NUT.

Once Burnham rates and methods had been accepted there was a period of consolidation. To characterise the years from 1924 to 1944 as ones of simple peace and profound quiet would be to mistake the political battles within the profession and the NUT, and also the significant struggles between teachers and the government to upgrade education and to utilise it as an instrument of social engineering and economic growth. None the less, in terms of industrial relations the main features of the period remained the dominance of the NUT on the teachers' panel, the compliance of the employers' associations, and the government pleased to contain control at arm's length.

The period after 1944 saw twenty years in which the numbers of teachers and schools rose dramatically, and in which attitudes to change, authority and state sponsored full employment slowly altered until it reached a crescendo of activity in the late 1960s. In the early 1960s the death throes of the Conservative government saw moves to curtail the power of the NUT and the first awareness that full employment might need to be checked by reductions in public expenditure through pay policies. The steady rise in inflation and the surge in public expenditure created the conditions for an early crisis of Burnham. The events in 1963 were the start of the process which with many interruptions led to the end of Burnham in 1987.

By the late 1960s the NAS was gaining ground as more male secondary school teachers felt that their status and therefore pay was being held back through the importance the NUT placed on its female members in primary schools. The left within the NUT was taken up with a more general resurgence of socialist and militant ideas which spread throughout the student and labour movement and merged with the cultural movements among women, blacks and young people. Such disturbances of the post-war settlement were acutely felt among school teachers with their proximity to the young, and with the large influx of student radicals linking up with more traditionally minded trade union socialists within the NUT. A Labour government and more left-wing labour councils shifted the balance of forces towards the NUT and after a false start the union launched and won the first national pay strike in 1969. This coincided with action by other groups which lends weight to Kelly's (1988) main thesis supported by Ozga and Lawn (1981) that teachers, as with most groups, tend to take action when a sustained number of other groups also take action.

The years 1970 to 1979 saw the triumph of the left in the NUT and the triumph of the NUT and many other unions within public policy areas. Thus the comprehensive education movement fed into and was strengthened by the NUT as were elements within the Labour government of 1974–9. But at the same time serious challenges to this triumph of the left emerged: the use of incomes polices as part of macro-economic controls to influence economic indicators rather than to secure the needs of the education industry and its staff undermined the relative pay of teachers; the rise of the newly created NASUWT and AMMA as contenders for NUT membership threatened Burnham's stability; the reduction in public expenditure led to many local disputes, raising issues of managerial control and the use of the employment contract; and the new right mobilised increasing national pressure to centralise decisions over educational content and practice.

Central themes throughout the 1970s and 1980s include: first, the restatement of the paramount importance of *comparability* in pay determination as supported by Houghton (1974) and Clegg (1980), but smashed by Margaret Thatcher and Keith Joseph in the 1980s and its replacement with *affordability*; secondly, the government removal of arbitration as an option to settle deadlocked disputes in 1981 (although this was used in 1984); thirdly, the development of appraisal and the beginning of the debate on performance related rewards; fourthly, greater control over what is taught and how it is taught as a result of the backlash triggered by the William Tyndale affair; fifthly, the sustained reduction in public expenditure as a proportion of GNP and finally, the erosion of LEA powers in favour of central government. All of these changes fuelled the crisis within the schools, but whatever important educational issues were involved the dominant industrial relations issues remained those allied with the pay and performance of the school teachers themselves.

Work and wages are the most important elements of industrial relations and combine to form the basis of a central definition of the subject – job regulation. The work people undertake helps explain differences in 'morbidity, mortality, fertility, social outlook and political allegiance' (Routh 1980: 1). A consequence of this is that those who follow a common occupation will tend to form together to protect and advance their common interests. Such joining of common interests comes with the formation of trade unions. Teachers have been members of trade unions for over 120 years. The importance of union membership and union influence should not be underestimated. In the search for a higher intensity of labour utilisation managers need to control the work effort and direction of their subordinate workers. In this imperative for greater managerial controls the managers themselves need to deal with the trade unions involved.

Hence unions remain the organisations through which managers, employers and reforming governments have to reach a balance of interests and influence. As Routh noted: 'The British Medical Association was established in 1832, the National Union of Teachers in 1870, and somewhere in between there grew the associations of skilled craftsmen that formed the basis of the modern trade union movement' (Routh 1980: 1).

Routh's main starting point was the role of trade unions in any account of differences in occupational pay during this century. His central concern with collective bargaining and the institutions and processes involved in collective bargaining places him in the mainstream of political economists involved with the practical understanding of wage determination. This tradition is best expressed in the works of the Webbs and Thorold Rogers. The latter's views will have a familiar ring for today's trade unionists: 'the evidence of the present and the example of the past appear to prove that labour partnerships are the remedy for low wages. They undoubtedly put the employer in a difficulty. They claim a greater share for labour in the gross profit of industry' (Thorold Rogers 1884: 566).

The themes which concerned the Webbs and Thorold Rogers have been taken up in recent years by Routh and Phelps Brown. The latter has shown the long-term impact on wage differences of trade union activity, government policy and the power of custom. These factors alter the workings of the labour market and therefore create additional pay differences. Our book puts trade unions at the centre of the pay determination system, and therefore the policies, influence and rivalries between the teaching unions are of vital interest.

Internal relativities within teaching and constant external comparisons play a major part in trade unionism, collective bargaining and management policies. Customary bargaining practices and worker perceptions of the fairness of the wage-effort bargain are important. Much of the subtext of the reforms since 1988 deals with management's concern for achieving higher levels of productivity through controls over performance at lower labour costs. Current industrial relations within education, therefore, is concerned with the interaction of national and local bargaining outcomes, and with the institutions and traditions associated with those outcomes. As Phelps Brown concluded, where there is an effective labour market then the relative pay of occupations varies with ability, education and training, experience, responsibility and status. Customary pay differences, however, become much more important for those occupations 'whose pay, within limits, is insulated from the forces of the market' (Phelps Brown 1977: 142).

This proposition is worth further analysis. The thesis is that where the 'free' market prevails then rewards are distributed according, *ceteris paribus*, to certain features such as level of qualification (graduate/non-graduate), performance, and responsibility. These are the characteristics, it is argued, that require more pay in order to motivate, recruit and retain the best mix of staff at the best value. Many teachers, some teacher unions, some employers, and the government favour such developments. But they divide the profession, exploit temporary criteria for deciding between their merits, and create complex internal labour markets. The rest of the proposition suggests that when the market is limited by government policy and union practice then customary differences within the profession usually prevail. This itself raises issues of the changing nature of the profession and the job, its ranking, and control over union practices (Carlson 1987).

The main point at which teacher-managers in schools will need to 'manage' teacher-colleagues and non-teaching staff in schools will be over the ways in which their individual effort, performance and behaviour *qua* employees is monitored and directed towards the short-term market-led needs of the school business. As Routh notes of the workings of the internal labour market 'so it is that, within the employing organisations, where the decisions are made, we at last witness the assertion of sentiments and beliefs, hopes and convictions, of what is right and proper, just and fair, with the meting out of some sort of rough justice' (Routh 1980: 219). Such a management function will not be entirely centred on heads and responsible deputies but will be shared with governors and some residual LEA staff. Whatever the combination of sources of decision-making the thrust of decisions will be towards reducing unit labour costs and intensifying labour productivity. Such business objectives will be achieved through the use of, on the one hand, management techniques to measure and reward such as appraisal, performance related pay and promotions, and on the other, familiar recession driven devices such as performance related redundancies, zero pay rise for average performance, and weaker contractual duties on the employer. The impact of this package of

HRM with its more professional approach to labour markets and its more ruthless approach to individual rights will include a renewed emphasis on quality through flexibility. These developments will tend to find support among many teachers at first as many believe they will benefit from the new reward systems and feel that perhaps the new market changes cannot be worse than the old LEA corporatism. The role of the trade unions will be vital in pushing up the costs of flexibility, restating the importance of a national system peopled by a national teaching force, and re-establishing collective bargaining over reward and punishment systems.

The HRM debate has only been partly understood in the school management world. It has tended to be taken at face value and reproduced uncritically as a set of related practices which together add up to something more than the amalgam of past personnel activities. In fact, the emphasis tends to be on quality, leadership and flexibility. None of these, in and of themselves, either establish a new approach or raise new problems, but the partial introduction of some of the practices that are derived from these general propositions in schools at this precise moment of LMS/GMS does have real consequences for school industrial relations.

The debate on leadership is often linked to the notion of 'excellence' and what makes an 'excellent' business. In most discussions, both academic and among teachers, the view of leadership is a conventional belief that an individual, or a small group of individuals together, make the main decisions that determine the performance of any organisation, and that these include decisions on style and culture as well as on costs and products. Chapter 4 deals with this in more detail but for now we should note that much evidence and argument ignores concepts such as power, the real limitations within which decisions are made, and that most books, including that of Peters and Waterman (1983), are *ex post facto* rationalisations and are deeply flawed as evidence of anything let alone excellence.

The apolitical and ahistorical approach to the study of excellence and its concomitant notions of leadership and quality have spawned an industry of get-excellent-quick management texts and advice centres, including private management consultants. Some address the issues of flexibility. So Beare *et al.* (1989) ask for the 're-conceptualisation' of the school which would allow, *inter alia*, for a more flexible school week with variable hours of opening and closing. As they suggest: 'the freeing-up of the school day, and therefore of the school week, creates greater opportunities for a much more diverse and creative approach to curriculum design and to school operation' (Beare *et al.* 1989: 55). As part of this they note that 'a more flexible deployment of teaching staff becomes a necessary part of the notion of a flexible school day' (1989: 57). In their book *Creating an Excellent School* there is no mention of costs let alone labour costs. There is no mention of finances, and there is no mention of how teachers might be rewarded. Yet the authors tell us that a fundamental change in conditions of service is a 'necessary' consequence of flexibility. The trade unions are not mentioned and the rights of individual staff are not mentioned. The book, like many others, acknowledges that to create excellence and quality and success in schools the willing co-operation of staff is required, but it does not discuss how this is to be achieved.

Flexibility itself comes in several forms and has been well documented for other industries (ACAS 1987a). It is often broken down into numerical flexibility concerning hours, types of contract and subcontracting of certain functions; and functional flexibility associated with job territory, qualifications and skill mix. This is not some neutral scientific device which in all circumstances creates a positive sum game with everyone a winner. The exact conditions under which its elements are introduced will determine the precise impact such schemes have on jobs, performance and professional unity. It matters whether the changes are imposed unilaterally on a top-down basis or whether there is some joint regulation through bargaining with the unions.

When all the management techniques have been exhausted and all the ideological exhortations explained, the remaining hard fact of business life for schools will be the pay bill. Any payment system will have to come to terms with the deeply held views of the majority of teachers that in some way and to some extent their pay should be based on felt-fair comparability. In labour intensive industries, such as teaching, the relevant pay issues are central to both the management of the service and the behaviour of the workforce.

The main pay issues include pay determination, levels, make up, and bargaining structures. All parties are greatly concerned with the pay outcomes and the arguments used are of great importance in winning support and influencing the decision-makers.

Comparability in the public sector was to be replaced by the principle of affordability. This market concept fitted well within the government's ideological approach to economics and public services, but was difficult to implement and determine. The main mechanism used was arbitrary cash limits which set a global sum for pay to local authorities and then left the employers to argue that this was all that was affordable. They behaved *as if* the government could not change this amount and indeed that the amount was set on any rational and/or fair basis.

Whatever government intention and whatever the economic realities, the fact remains that comparability is still the most powerful pay argument put forward by the teachers' trade unions and the one that receives most support from the teachers themselves. Comparability, whether with a specific external group or with the average earnings index, is essentially a moral and social argument associated with fairness. This was famously expressed by the Priestley Commission (1955): 'We believe that the State is under a categorical obligation to remunerate its employees fairly, and that any . . . [arrangement] . . . which does not explicitly recognise this is not adequate' (Priestley 1955: 23).

Some general points can be made about customary pay differences and the workforce which apply to teachers as to other groups. Throughout the Burnham years the Teachers Panel, dominated by the NUT, put its claim to the Management Panel and couched it in a variety of arguments supported by evidence. This process of presentation of the case did not change as such when the IAC and later the Review Body recommended pay settlements to the Secretary of State. The teacher unions tended to support their case with a set of related arguments which have formed the basis for all pay negotiations. These include the two most familiar to public service workers with a national pay system: comparability and the cost-of-living. Then there are arguments about the labour market – the ability of the industry as a whole or units within it to recruit, retain and motivate the required quantity and quality of staff. More recently other arguments have come to the fore such as affordability as the public sector equivalent of bottom line profitability, and finally some notion of pay rising with performance/productivity/workload. These arguments represent the rational basis upon which pay campaigns are based. It is not suggested that pay claims are met because of the rationality or correctness of the case, but that for groups such as teachers the case plays an important part in mobilising trade unions and their members to put pressure on relevant decision-makers, winning wider community support, and attacking the position of the employers and government.

The teachers expressed their cases and their fears in traditional bargaining terms so well analysed by Wootton. Trade unions, she observed, carry the burden of proof when they ask for any advance in wages and/or conditions of service. In contrast the employers are 'under no pressure to produce any specific arguments at all for rejecting particular wage claims' (Wootton 1962: 125).

She contended that in the post-war era the most popular argument for a pay rise had been increases in the cost of living. She emphasised that the issue is not whether wages have kept up with prices but the assumption that they ought to. The next most popular argument is that of comparability: the proposition is that any occupation in which wages have not kept up with average earnings have at least a *prima facie* case for a pay increase. Wootton believed that most chosen pay comparators are not well founded in fact, but again reveal a moral imperative of fairness. She was only impressed by the economic arguments surrounding labour market considerations, and rejected as clumsy and inadequate measures based on performance and productivity which she saw as pseudo-scientific at best.

The demand by teachers, expressed through their trade unions, for some kind of fair pay level, fairly determined and fairly distributed will remain as a central theme in the industrial relations of schools. We argue that the traditional industrial relations institutions designed to set pay levels and avoid disputes are in disarray and have not been replaced by acceptable alternatives. This is to suggest that there is a deep crisis at the heart of the school system and one not likely to be resolved by the government. The government has no serious view of what or how teachers should be paid, and leaving it to a mixture of market forces and performance rewards is as meaningless as it is dangerous.

The traditional national bargaining system for pay served the profession and the schools well. It allowed for public awareness and debate of the relative wages and worth of teachers; it allowed employers to plan employment policies without the uncertainty of wage setting, and it allowed teachers through their unions to participate in the wage determination process knowing that any settlement would normally embody the three main principles of fair comparison, inflation indexation and the rate for the job.

This chapter has set the scene for a more detailed discussion of recent developments in schools on the main issues facing all teachers within the area of industrial relations. The main themes remain the importance of pay and pay determination and in particular the rivalry and role of the different trade unions in establishing a rate for the job and curtailing the internal differentials within the profession. The concern of government with performance is not new, but in the 1990s it has taken a more severe form in terms of pressures on individual teachers and schools and this has resulted in the short term in school-based managers trying to adopt human resource management practices to control teacher performance outside of the normal professional methods of standard assurance.

Most of the evidence in the rest of the book is based on a two year research project at Keele University financed by the ESRC into the industrial relations consequences of LMS. Our main findings include that the unions are still well supported but are seeking ways to accommodate the loss of national bargaining (chapters 2 and 3). We found a reduced relevance of the LEA personnel function and the enhancement of management authority at school level (chapters 4 and 5). We observed that the employers are still working out the exact nature of the new employment relationships as between LEAs and governing bodies, and that school-based managers are seeking to benefit from the introduction of explicit HRM practices (chapter 4). These union and management endeavours are taking place within an overall financial framework in which the main cost (wages) is linked to the collapse of the pay determination system. Our evidence suggests that the future is bleak when pay is caught between Review Body recommendations, pay bill freezes and the faltering attempts to introduce performance-related pay (chapter 2). Finally our research showed how heads and other school managers are responding to the new financial regulations and national controls by intensifying teacher workload, tightening supervision over teacher activities, and disturbing traditional professional relationships within the authority structure of the schools (chapters 5 and 6).

2 Pay and pay determination

INTRODUCTION

The system of centralised collective bargaining for school teachers was established in 1919 and remained largely unchanged until 1987. The Burnham Committee settled the pay of teachers, although conditions of service were determined through CLEA/ST. This system can be characterised as centralised national pay bargaining in which the parties agreed an effective rate for teachers through multi-employer/multi-union negotiations. If, and when, no agreement was reached then the parties resorted either to arbitration or to industrial action. In some years the bargaining was suspended through incomes policies and this use of macro-economic policy instruments to set pay rates within a given industry helped dent the relevance and credibility of the Burnham system.

This chapter provides a summary of the Whitley system with its Burnham variant, followed by a discussion of what happened to pay when Burnham failed. This concerns the use of three measures to deal with such failure – first arbitration, secondly industrial action and thirdly pay inquiries and pay review. In the process it provides some detail on the main events since 1964 in order to trace the development of the shifts in power and concern among the relevant parties. The imposed peace settlement by the DFE in the 1990s has resulted from the victory of one strand within the educational establishment aided by confused and divided opponents.

The final section of this chapter deals with long-term trends in teachers' pay and the basis for any future national and local pay system. The traditional institutions for pay setting for teachers are in crisis and have not been replaced by any widely accepted alternatives. This is crucial given the central role of pay levels, structures and settlements for all concerned in school education. Our view is based on the general proposition that successive governments have not been very interested in either the level of teachers' pay or the methods of determination as long as neither caused serious political embarrassment. If this is the case then the dominant determinants of any settlement have been in the hands of the teachers themselves. Hence the Burnham system itself and the original 1919 pay scales were born out of widespread and largely successful struggle, as were the 1944 settlement, the 1974 Houghton inquiry and the 1980 Clegg exercise. The defeat of the NUT's position on pay and pay determination in 1985–86 heralded both the end of the Burnham system and the abandonment of the rate for the job. The current situation is one in which teachers' pay may drift to locally agreed levels based on the ability to pay of any given school through its position within the market competition under LMS.

This crisis in pay determination has its roots in the developments of the 1980s. These include the Conservative government's efforts to move away from the national bargaining system based on comparability, the employers' eagerness to introduce flexible working practices and payments, and, according to Simon (1991), years of muddled neglect by Keith Joseph. These in turn allowed the New Right to dominate education policy in the second half of the 1980s, and this domination in general led to 'the arrogation of centralised powers, in defiance of traditional "partnership" systems' and was seen as having 'a clear social purpose': namely, to educate people to know their place (Simon 1991: 504).

The wider educational crisis reflected the main themes of the 1980s – deregulation of public services, privatisation, the removal of intermediate tiers of governmental control such as LEAs, and the centralising tendencies of the New Right. In industrial relations this meant, in general, efforts to curtail the activities and bargaining power of trade unions, fragmentation of professions, atomised workforce, making employers more accountable for their actions to central government, making managers more responsible for their own efforts, and destabilising the national pay bargaining mechanisms through cash limits and refusal to use arbitration and/or pay inquiries to resolve deadlock. This has been summarised elsewhere:

> The New Right argues that schools should become private, independent self-governing charitable trusts with control over their own budgets and their own pupil enrolment policy. Their income would be derived from education vouchers and from cash paid to parents as 'top-up' fees. At the same time the New Right regards the removal of teachers' national pay scales, the rewriting of individual teacher contracts and the break up of teachers' capacity for trade union activity as necessary to the provision of an improved educational service.
>
> (Demaine 1993: 35–6)

As was argued in chapter 1 a main part of both the economic theory and the practical politics was the attempt to move away from comparability as an argument for wage advancement. It was considered by the Conservative leaders of the late 1980s that the educational reforms they required alongside the reduced levels of expenditure could only be achieved by the removal of the powers of the trade unions and the LEAs. The former were perceived as gaining influence from national bargaining and therefore decentralised bargaining was a mechanism to both weaken trade union opposition and drive down unit labour costs.

It may be that the dismembering of the national pay bargaining system is a prelude to the end of bargaining itself. The essence of collective bargaining is the recognition that the best way to determine pay and conditions of service for groups of employees is through joint regulation, bilateral rule-making, as between managers representing the employer and trade unions representing employees. This was the position of the Donovan Commission and the dominant pluralist ideology.

It is this set of propositions that the New Right have challenged. Their position is that corporate objectives of, for example, profit maximisation and/or market share and/or high performance, should dictate the industrial relations objectives. In this model the main purpose of industrial relations in a labour intensive industry must be to raise productivity and increase management controls at the point of production. In order to achieve such objectives many employers and head teachers are embracing the new industrial relations of human resource management rooted in traditional business performance concepts which now include total quality management and control.

This general position relates to educational performance in terms of the labour market usages of the educated pupils – education as primarily a traded commodity. This line was powerfully represented in the late 1980s by, among others, Lord Young. He argued, with support of leading business people, that 'schools were failing industry' and, as Simon persuasively shows, 'the strategy was now becoming clear – to shift the blame for what government policy had done to the schools onto the schools themselves – the teachers, administrators, even local government as a whole' (Simon 1991: 527). He could have added trade unions to this list. This triumph of the New Right in education was finally secured through the 1988 Act and the use of assessment for all children as requested by Rhodes Boyson and the Black Paper authors in 1975.

This position, foreshadowed by Hayek (1984), hides a simpler truth which is that once education is treated as a traded commodity in a market then the purchasers of the product, the employers of labour, play an increasingly dominant role in the determination of the product itself. The service providers, the teachers and managers, are driven to create a product whose quality is defined in employment use terms only and therefore the performance of the providers is measured in such terms. Both traditional definitions of professionalism and labour movement concerns with employees' individual and collective rights are squeezed.

A central part of the disestablishment of national bargaining and efforts to deflect attention away from wage bargaining at any level through HRM is the major push to rid the industry of comparability pay arguments. One important staging post in this strategic set of objectives for schools is the removal from school teachers of the felt-fair system of pay determination. All the teacher unions continue to use comparability in their presentation of cases to the IAC and STRB, and this includes both internal and external comparisons. The strength of the felt-fair pay levels should not be underestimated for teachers, and has played a major part in their industrial action. The 1985–86 strike, for example, resulted in the setting up of the IAC which explicitly took account of comparability.

In contrast the first report of the STRB made clear its commitment to affordability as the main basis for pay increases and that this would be in line with business needs such as quality of performance and labour market issues. It rejected comparability firmly stating that: 'Some of the teacher unions asked us to start restoring teachers' pay to a relative position established at some previous date. Although we have taken note of recent movements in teachers' pay against the retail prices and average earnings indices, we do not accept that indexation is an appropriate mechanism for determining future pay levels or that any single year is necessarily an appropriate starting point for comparisons' (STRB 1992: 6). Yet such a rejection fails to provide a serious basis for pay determination. For example, in its recommendations the Review Body says it is 'desirable to have a reasonable level of basic pay for all classroom teachers' (STRB 1992: 17). What constitutes a 'reasonable' level in 1992, 1993, 1994 or 1995?

Behind much of the debate is the assumption that trade unionism and collective bargaining are incompatible with efficient management practices and professional teaching services, and that a more effective future for schools will be one in which trade unions play no part in wage setting. Johnson tested the general proposition that trade unions and bargaining inhibit good management and asked some interesting questions: 'Do teacher contracts reduce teacher services or enhance professional commitment? Are routine school practices more adversarial or simply more equitable as a result of collective bargaining? Do teacher unions undermine administrative authority and divert teacher loyalties or ensure better management and promote teacher participation in policy-making?' And she suggests, quite rightly, that 'the answers put forth have been shaped more by dogma than by data' (Johnson 1984a: 3). We too seek to answer some of these questions in the following chapters.

WHITLEY AND BURNHAM: THE BASIC HISTORICAL MODEL

When Whitley presided over the committee bearing his name it was part of a threefold effort to modernise the British state and in particular to fend off social and political revolution through the accommodation of labour interests into the national interest. The year 1918 saw the great democratic advance with votes for women, the first major efforts to establish a welfare state, and the model for industrial peace through union recognition and bargained agreements.

Clay took the view that the Whitley reports were far from innovative, but simply reflected the conventional wisdom of industrial relations practitioners based on long-term developments. These included the growth of trade union membership, the spread of collective bargaining, and the increased nature of state intervention. The Whitley Committee itself was a subcommittee of the Reconstruction Committee set up by Asquith in 1916. Its rather vague terms of reference led to five separate reports, of which the first report was the most important. Clay argued that the first report on Joint Industrial Councils was based on traditional attitudes and that: 'its importance consisted in three things: it asserted the principle of trade union recognition, it embodied the outlines . . . of any effective conciliation scheme, and it made a case for widening the scope of conciliation organization' (Clay 1929: 153).

Whitley used collective bargaining as the basis for industrial relations, and noted the importance of any conciliation scheme being permanent. The schemes would be national in scope but local in action. The extent to which Whitley represents the triumph of collective bargaining is stated by Clay: 'Collective bargaining, for which organized labour has been fighting for over a century, was authoritatively pronounced normal and necessary, and was extended, potentially if not actually, over the whole field of wage-employment for the market' (1929: 177).

When Whitley was applied to schools under Burnham in 1919 Clay's three conditions had been met: high levels of union membership, growing collective bargaining and increased state intervention both as an employer and as policy-maker. His argument that such a scheme would help reduce the number of disputes and create a smooth application of the principal practices of industrial relations, and his stress on national agreements locally implemented allied with conflict avoidance procedures, was well based. After a few stormy years when local employers resisted the Burnham blanket there was a remarkable period of stability in industrial relations in schools from about 1924 to 1964. It seemed to hold the situation in recession, war and post war expansion, but began to creak with the general crisis in economic prosperity and control over state expenditure which has dominated British political economy ever since the early 1960s.

In September 1919 the Standing Joint Committee on a Provisional Minimum Scale of Salaries for Teachers in Public Elementary Schools was formed with Lord Burnham in the chair (NUT 1972). Its main objective 'was to secure the orderly and progressive solution of the salary problem in public elementary schools by agreement on a national basis' (Tropp 1957: 212), and that 'the problem should be settled if possible by agreement' (letter from Hal Fisher to Lord Burnham 25 November 1919). The actual settlement, as with Whitley in general, was born out of a coming together of opposites. On the one hand the government was faced with social revolution at home based on widespread industrial action by large numbers of organized workers including school teachers. It also embraced the centralising tendencies developed during the war and associated with dislocated labour markets and the demands of new industries for better educated entrants.

On the other hand the socialist and labour movement was inspired by events in Russia, and was able to form a broadly based protest movement which demanded centralised solutions to ownership and the public services. Hence the left in the NUT was able to force through a policy that supported the establishment of national scales through national bargaining and this coincided with Hal Fisher's needs as President of the Board of Education. The militancy which swept up many NUT activists was partly located in the high levels of inflation at the end of the war, the use of diluted/untrained teachers, and the renewed power of trade union action (Ozga and Lawn 1981). As has been argued elsewhere:

> The capitalist state buffeted by post-war recession, the threat of communism abroad and socialism at home, and faced with renewed international competition required three things: greater central government power whose foundations had been laid by Lloyd George during the war, a better educated workforce, and a new economic strategy which incorporated state finances and services into the authority structure of political control needed to maintain social reform without social revolution.
>
> (Seifert 1987: 32)

The basis of the final settlement of the Burnham constitution was that pay for all teachers would be determined through bargaining between representatives of employers and employees. This principle was extended in the 1944 Act with the development of secondary and tertiary education, and ran unmolested until the early 1960s. The 1965 Remuneration of Teachers Act represented the compromise based on the first major crisis of the traditional system – benefits to the trade union side from the introduction of retrospection and arbitration were matched by more direct government intervention at the bargaining table. After the 1985–86 strikes Burnham was abolished and replaced with the Interim Advisory Committee (IAC) under the 1987 Teachers Pay and Conditions Act, and in 1988 the Education Reform Act created the basis for the reduction in influence of both the unions and LEA employers. The 1991 Act set up the School Teachers' Review Body which after one year has twin threats to its functions: a 1993–95 incomes policy in the public sector, and the development of school-based pay determination.

In one sense we can talk of a twenty year crisis between 1965 and 1985 during which time the Burnham variant of Whitley came under steady attack from various governments. There is no doubt that the trade unions and the vast majority of their members both favoured and benefited from the centralised national system of pay bargaining. The government was the greatest loser: the traditional cost–benefit analysis that government could control total wage costs through such central methods and avoid damaging national disputes was eroded by both the strength of the union position and the weakness of the government's economic hold on public expenditure.

These twenty years saw endless attempts to secure control over public sector wages through some form of incomes policies (Clegg 1971 and 1979;

Allen 1966). None worked and all alienated the victims. The efforts needed to secure incomes policies helped bring to political importance the two central bodies of the main protagonists: the CBI and the TUC. It also unleashed the greatest wave of strikes in the post-war period especially among public sector workers (Durcan *et al.* 1983). In the process the long term expansion of education provided the teachers with the confidence to adopt more pragmatic and oppositional policies which helped form part of the move to affiliate to the TUC (Coates 1972b; Sigurjonsson 1976), take strike action (Seifert 1987) and demand fairer pay settlements.

The crisis in 1965, therefore, represents the start of the process which in turn generated the 1969 national strike, the 1974 Houghton pay inquiry, the 1980 Clegg pay commission, the 1985 national strike, and the abolition of Burnham in 1987. All these landmarks will be discussed below, but for now a brief account of that first public crisis sets the scene.

In 1965 the Remuneration of Teachers Act (RTA) brought the DES directly into Burnham, as Ministers sought to control bargaining outcomes more directly. In 1963 the AEC produced its account of the crisis in Burnham and observed about the muddle in the government's mind that the Minister had to decide 'whether he wishes to abandon negotiated agreements and impose settlements himself or devise independent arbitrators or review bodies to do the job for him' (AEC 1963: 28). The key issue as noted by Coates (1972a) was the role of the Minister in the determination of teachers' pay.

In 1961 David Eccles, the Minister of Education, wanted to be involved in negotiations by limiting the scale and scope of the settlement and by reserving the right to reject it outright. Later Quinton Hogg for the Conservatives and Michael Stewart for Labour arrived at a compromise whereby the LEAs had twenty-six votes and the DES fifteen on the Management Panel of Burnham, but the global pay figure remained subject to ministerial veto. Under the agreement, arbitration become subject to reference if either party requested it. An important variation was that the independent chair of Burnham could arbitrate on the terms of reference should the parties disagree. (This was changed in 1981 to allow reference if, and only if, both parties agreed.) The unions were delighted by the introduction of retrospection for pay awards. The key weapon, however, remained with the Minister: the ability to alter unilaterally the staff side composition of Burnham. Thus the 1965 Act gave far more to central government than the unions understood and the employers showed an abject approach to the loss of their powers.

The NUT, however, did learn some important lessons from the protracted negotiations from 1961 to 1965 which lead to the RTA. As Manzer comments:

> the confrontation between the Ministry and the teachers arising out of the negotiations of 1961 was the most serious in negotiations from 1944 to 1964. The first phase of the dispute during the summer was touched off by the consequences with respect to teachers' salaries of the government's measures to defend the value of the pound. The second phase was the result

of the Ministry's effort to exploit this first dispute to get a more efficient structure of teachers' salaries.

(Manzer 1970: 129)

The 1965 reforms had changed little in terms of the main issue of pay. The NUT in particular urged fair pay rises in line with other groups such as the local government workers, opposed incomes policies and argued the special case for education: 'now was the time to demonstrate the reality of statements that education was fundamental to economic growth and to a just, humane and civilized society' (*The Teacher*, 8 September 1967). This echoed earlier left views as stated by Labour leaders such as Arthur Greenwood: 'education, in the view of the labour movement, stands so high in the scale of social values that the wildest lashings of the storm of "economy" would never reach it' (*The New Leader*, 8 June 1923: 7). Both statements seem to represent the central theme of the 1993 Education Commission as summarised by Claus Moser (1993).

The four years between the reform of Burnham in 1965 and the first national pay strike by teachers in 1969 proved that the system was unable to deal with either incomes policies or industrial action. It also showed that arbitration awards that fail to reflect the power reality of the parties cannot restore the balance of peace, and create a rightful cynicism with respect to the independence from government of arbitration systems. This then was the start of the crisis which staggered from strikes to pay inquiries and from more strikes to pay review bodies, and which dealt the fatal blow to Burnham and has left a dangerous vacuum at the heart of pay determination policy.

The strengths and weaknesses of the Burnham system can be seen at a glance in the composition of the Teachers' and Management Panels. Its power and authority lay in the representativeness of the teachers through their organisations and in the acceptance by the employers of the national rate for the job. Its weaknesses became apparent when the government through the DES gained direct representation on the Management Panel in 1965 and when the NUT lost its overall majority on the Teachers' Panel in 1985, shown in Table 2.1. These two changes allowed both the divisions among the teachers and the weakness among the employers to combine together to make Burnham unworkable.

Table 2.1 Composition of Burnham Teachers' Panel, selected years

Union	*1944*	*1965*	*1981*	*1985*
NUT	16	16	16	13
NASUWT	0	3	7	7
AMMA	4	4	4	4
SHA	2	2	1	1
NAHT	0	1	2	2
PAT	0	0	1	1
NATFHE	4	2	1	0
Total	26	28	32	28

The trade union side bargained with the employers as one. This meant fierce bargaining within each union and between the unions and this again led to intense rivalries and strange alliances. The dominance of the NUT for most of the period of Burnham, however, meant that it was able to control the teachers' panel more or less effectively when it mattered. This was not the case with the equally divided employers. They too had to bargain as one, and they too were often bitterly divided by political loyalties and regional antagonisms. Table 2.2 illustrates the formal membership of the management panel.

Table 2.2 Composition of Burnham Management Panel, selected years

Management group	*1944*	*1965*	*1981*
ACC	9	9	13
AMA	6	6	10
WJEC	2	2	2
AEC	6	6	0
LCC	3	3	0
DES	0	2	2
Total	26	28	27

The national representatives of the local authorities are divided both within and between their employers' associations. So the Association of County Councils (ACC) and the Association of Metropolitan Authorities (AMA) dominate, but frequently disagree. The Welsh Joint Education Committee (WJEC) is more stable in composition, but both the AEC and the LCC have disappeared. The crucial point is that this panel, unlike the teachers' panel, does not determine its position through a simple majority vote based on representation. The DES representatives had fifteen votes as secretly agreed in the 1965 Concordat between local authorities and the government.

Each panel held formal meetings to decide their own position, and then came together under the auspices of an independent chair. The RTA 1965 allowed for the domination of the DES on the Management Panel, but did allow outside arbitration in the case of deadlock. Thus the 1965 reform fatally wounded the Burnham pay system even though it took another twenty-two years to die!

The crisis of 1965, which so accurately reflected the wider crisis of economic policy and political commitment to public services, had created the conditions for future failure. As Coates has argued,

> the restructuring of the Burnham Committees marked a crucial stage in the demise of what might be termed the 'old order' in the English system of educational administration .... It marked the rise of the Department of Education .... a rise paralleled by the declining ... influence of the local authorities.
>
> (Coates 1972b: 203)

This shift in policy-making itself represented another shift within government which was the increasing subordination of departments to overall economic requirements. These two shifts, embodied in the 1961–65 crisis, helped to strengthen those elements within the NUT and NAS in favour of a more forceful policy towards collective bargaining and industrial action.

The determination of teachers' pay levels, structures and make-up remains one of the central issues which dominates the power and conflict relations within the education system. The purpose of institutions such as Burnham is to provide orderly and formal mechanisms by which the power conflicts between the parties can be resolved without recourse to actions such as strikes, mass lock-outs and/or the failure to recruit, retain and motivate teachers of the required ability to staff the school system. From time to time Burnham and its equivalents elsewhere in the public services have failed to provide such a cover against overt disruption. Sometimes this has been the fault of government, sometimes the fault of the parties to Burnham, and sometimes it has been rooted in the inadequacies of Burnham itself. The next section examines the three main alternatives to orderly collective bargaining that were used when Burnham failed – arbitration, strikes and pay inquiries/reviews – and thereby examines the difficulties involved in setting teachers' pay and the crisis of the pay determination system in the 1990s.

WHAT HAPPENED WHEN BURNHAM FAILED TO DELIVER?

Deadlock in negotiations among public sector employees, especially professionals in the public services, presents real political problems to those involved. Whatever the collective bargaining mechanism in use, deadlock suggests a failure of both the structures and the political balance behind the structures. In such circumstances the main tendency in the UK this century has been for either the employees to take industrial action or for the government to instigate some form of pay inquiry and/or change in pay mechanism. Failure to resolve major industrial relations issues, such as pay levels and union recognition has tended to result in industrial action, and that action has ended with either one-off settlements or more permanent changes in the ways in which teacher pay is decided. The determinant factor, therefore, in the choice of collective bargaining mechanism for settling pay has been industrial action by the teachers rather than the decisions of government, the DES or the employers.

There have been three historic turning points in how teachers' pay was to be settled. First was the 1918 settlement rooted in the industrial action by teachers; second was the 1974 Houghton inquiry which restored comparability to teachers' pay in the aftermath of the 1969 national strike; and third was the abolition of Burnham in 1987 based in the defeat of the 1985–86 national strike. The outcome of each was partly determined by the unity, or lack of it, within the teaching profession.

One of the most important features of the profession in terms of its trade unionism is the divisions which always existed but which became increasingly acute after 1979 (see chapter 3). 'Inter-union conflict between teachers' unions is deeply rooted in differing conceptions of status, professionalism, and the legitimacy of industrial action' (Winchester 1983: 162). These divisions have been discussed elsewhere but are frequently perceived as being based on the characteristics of the teachers themselves: men and women; secondary and primary; graduates and non-graduates; by subject; by seniority and by age. While some of these factors are important some of the time it is our view that the more important divisions are based on teacher identification with various elements of the wider labour and trade union movement. Sometimes these associations are linked with the personal and/or work characteristics of individual teachers.

Much depends on the ideological disposition of some active teachers and the general identification with such positions of the inactive majority. The vital dividing issue is the extent of awareness of the teacher as employee of their own employment condition in terms of economic weakness in the labour market, however much protected, much as for other employees in modern Britain. Those teachers who see themselves in a labour market in which supply and demand form a major determinant of pay, conditions of service and job security will tend to both identify more closely with traditional trade union activities, and seek means to reduce the power of the employer and/or government and to control the supply of labour as well as its price. On such a view teachers would wish any pay determination mechanism to allow for relative pay rises when demand was strong and protection when it was weak – no sliding scale, basic mandatory national agreements and some say over supply and demand.

From the beginning of the century until the late 1970s the vast majority of organised teachers belonged to the NUT. The NUT for most of its history contained teachers in favour of the above propositions, although the exact practical application of such general positions was subject to often bitter internal strife. Much of the battle within the NUT was contained but represented more than just debate over detail: NUT members and leading activists were divided as between identification with mainstream trade union activity, such as industrial action, and influence through enhanced professional status which in turn could be used to put pressure on ministers and the DES. These divisions are not hard and fast, but as school teacher numbers grew and as individual status within the profession became more important than unity of professional interests so these divisions took on more rigid organisational forms.

This analysis corresponds with Beatrice and Sydney Webbs' views expressed in their series of articles in the *New Statesman* during the first world war (for an application of their position for NHS professional unions see Burchill and Seifert 1993). The key point is the tension between different 'methods' of trade union operation: collective bargaining, mutual insurance, and legal enactment. As they argue 'voluntary associations of brain-workers use, though under other designations, the method of collective bargaining, with its corollary of the strike; the method of mutual insurance . . . and the method of legal enactment'; and these methods are enforced by 'imposing restrictions on the entry into the occupation . . . maintaining restraints on output . . . and disciplining disloyal fellow professionals and recalcitrant employers' (Webb and Webb 1917: 46). The analysis then provides further insights into the blurred distinction as between professional and union objectives. As the Webbs explain:

> we see in operation the creative impulse, or the desire to advance the science and perfect the art of the vocation. We see also the fellowship impulse, or the yearning for comradeship, social intercourse and mutual assistance among persons of one's own kind. . . . Along with these two impulses towards creation and fellowship, and heightened by them, there arises what we have called the possessive impulse, or the desire to secure for the members of the group all the remuneration and status that the community can be induced to accord for the performance of a particular service.
>
> (Webb and Webb 1917: 46)

It is the potential for division, and for unity, which the Webbs have sought to analyse and which has dogged attempts to develop common interest policies and organisations of teachers. In 1915 Beatrice Webb noted in her account of all organisations of teachers that 'besides the head and class teachers in elementary and secondary schools engaged in teaching the ordinary subjects, there is in England an ever-shifting personnel of teachers of special subjects, or teachers using methods adapted to particular kinds of pupils, whether these are taken individually or in schools of various grades, or in university, technical, or normal colleges' (Webb 1915: 1). We return to the Webbs' analytical framework in chapter 3. Right now our concern is with the one issue of great potential for unifying the profession around policy and organisation – the rate for the job (the Webbs' 'standard rate'), in the form of a basic scale of payment for all teachers. The development and understanding of this is central to the underlying unity of the profession and to its strength in bargaining with employers and the government. In efforts to maintain unity around this norm the NUT in particular stood out for pay rises based on price inflation and the earnings of other comparable groups. As Saran noted in her detailed study of Burnham negotiations in 1956 and 1971 the NUT concentrated their pay demands 'on cost-of-living and comparability issues' (Saran 1985: 2). One consequence of the forced competition between schools and the abandonment, *de facto*, of national pay setting is that school is set against school and teacher against teacher in a free market rumpus which attacks the root of unity and therefore undermines the strength in numbers needed for national collective bargaining.

By the late 1980s the NASUWT and AMMA had grown rapidly and for the first time threatened the NUT's dominance of both teacher politics and trade union bargaining. The NASUWT increasingly represented groups of teachers who wished to use their market place strength for their own benefit – first men and later professional career teachers in the secondary sector. The AMMA appealed more and more to those teachers against overt trade union activity and hence opposed to industrial action. In other words the NUT failed to hold together the broadly based alliance of teachers committed to a national labour market strategy, and fell prey to those who sought to abandon collective bargaining (AMMA) and those who sought to narrow the base of the bargain in classic craft fashion (NASUWT).

These divisions, both when within the NUT and when more formally outside, provide part of an explanation about why teachers have only been involved in national pay strikes twice (1969 and 1985) although they have been involved in many local struggles. The current three-way split of most classroom teachers into competing trade unions should not mask three important points. First is the general success of the profession in the post-war period. Second is the role of heads and deputies within their own organisations. Third is the reappearance of the reality of market-determined pay and conditions; ideological dispositions with regard to acceptance of or reaction to this reality are deeply embedded in the teacher workforce, manifested in current debates not only within the NUT but also within the NASUWT and, to a lesser extent, within AMMA. The reforms of the 1990s will increase the market basis of pay determination, conditions and security and therefore sharpen the debate as to how to avoid market solutions and how to cope with them.

The history of the profession and the unions indicates that there has always been an important minority of teachers willing to take industrial action to protect their interests and that the best predictors of this have tended to be ideological disposition, the nature of job regulation, and the role in the wider educational reform movement. For most of the time pay levels and the mechanisms that formally determine them have often been allowed to drift by default. This may be due to a general satisfaction with the system as operated, but for school teachers, as with other employees, tends to reflect ignorance of the forces that determine their pay and organisational control by those that favour such mechanisms. These periods of complacent acceptance tend to give way to periods of action and change, and such changes for school teachers have been at times when other groups of trade unionists have also been active because both the cause of the activity and the consequences are shared or perceived to be shareable (Kelly 1988; Hyman 1989).

Ordinary teachers begin to stir when they feel relative losses in pay, conditions, status and security. These feelings feed into the ideological patterns and theories of those within the union closer to the realities of market forces and government power who in turn seek to turn popular discontent into union policy and practice. Such moves from below can and have led to widespread and intensive industrial action with the demands of the active majority usually winning the day. The employers, the government and the DES have tended to react at the last minute to the political crisis based on both teacher action and teacher exposure of related wider educational failings. Rarely, despite the cosy partnerships, have the DES and government acted early enough to stave off crisis, and frequently some employers have sided with the teachers and their unions to force the hand of the DES and ministers.

The final decisions when teachers have taken action as to the future of pay levels and pay determination have been largely moulded by the teacher unions and not by government and the DES or their advisers. This indicates two points: first, that government has no strong view on teacher pay and pay mechanisms; and secondly, that government has no interest in strategic decision-making in this area. Our argument as to the nature of pay levels, structures and determination has been set within a political and institutional framework shaped by industrial action. Strikes shift the balance of power within the system so that when they are successful as in 1969 they create new acceptable pay criteria, and when they fail as in 1985 they let in opponents of the rate for the job basis of teacher trade unionism.

In an attempt to prevent industrial action the government introduced Pay Review which represents a form of permanent and compulsory arbitration operating within cash limits imposed by the government. The government stumbled onto Pay Review for teachers and considered it very much a second best solution since it hampers the move away from national bargaining and provides some protection in the short run for trade unions shy of taking action. Its use therefore further supports the contention of Brown and Rowthorn that 'Britain has entered the 1990s with a public service pay structure in disarray. This will breed short-run problems' (Brown and Rowthorn 1990: 8).

The point at issue is the continued desirability of collective bargaining as the most favoured pay mechanism for any group of employees. As the Webbs understood, and as Clay and later Clegg elaborated, collective bargaining depends on recognised trade unions: 'moreover, it is the trade union alone which can supply the machinery for the automatic interpretation and the peaceful revision of the general agreement. To collective bargaining, the machinery of trade unionism may bring, in fact, both continuity and elasticity' (Webb and Webb 1897: 179).

The vital industrial relations aspect of the current reforms in schools is to raise labour productivity through management controls: over a more flexible labour process and over the costs of employing any given mix of staff. The modern employer in schools, whether LEA or governing body, is driven by competitive financial pressures. These must inform operational decisions on the main costs of the school – labour costs. These in turn will be subject to increased human resource management (chapter 4). The sum total of these efforts will be to reduce unit labour costs, and the industrial relations issues will be whether this is achieved unilaterally without trade union and/or staff power sharing, or bilaterally with some degree of formal collective bargaining. If employers seek the unilateral path, whatever the HRM content, it may, as elsewhere, lead to bitter disillusionment as promises are broken, targets not reached, and expectations dashed. In such circumstances teachers will either quit the school, stay but reduce effort, and/or take action through trade unions to regain a voice in decision-making.

Arbitration was the main historical method used to reduce open conflict at times of trouble – 'the extensive provision of arbitration machinery throughout the public sector provided further support for the peaceful settlement of conflicts' (Winchester 1983: 163). When in the 1980s government abandoned the principle of arbitration then industrial action was more likely, and as a result of the 1985–86 strike government was forced to reinstate a form of arbitration through the IAC and later through Pay Review, even though this reduced managerial controls over the most important element of costs – labour costs – as desired in other aspects of the reform process.

It remains unclear how Pay Review will fit in with other pay determination models buzzing around the schools and LEAs. The most likely solution is that Pay Review will set national minimum rates of pay and/or that public sector pay will either be limited or frozen altogether, and that schools will be able to add to these through some form of discretionary 'performance' allowances, labour market adjustments and phoney regradings. The following sections on arbitration, industrial action and pay inquiries provide a brief description of the decay of the Burnham pay determination system through government expedient and teacher militancy.

Arbitration

Arbitration remains an important option when there is deadlock in pay negotiations. It allows for both the public hearing of the arguments and for explicit government defence of government policies without disruption in schools. The Webbs defined the essential feature of arbitration as: 'the decision is not the will of either party, or the outcome of negotiation between them, but the fiat of an umpire or arbitrator' (Webb and Webb 1897: 221). The parties agree beforehand to be bound by the arbitrator's decision and then present a series of formal arguments and evidence. Where arbitration is like collective bargaining is that the decision usually applies to all those involved and therefore establishes a standard rate for the relevant workgroup. In this form arbitration can be seen as part of collective bargaining rather than opposed to it. ACAS certainly takes that view and pointed out in its summary of the 1980s that there had been an increase in ACAS arbitration activities and 'the significant contribution made by this type of third-party assistance to the resolution of several complex and long-running disputes in the public sector' (ACAS *Annual Report* 1989: 25).

Both the 1965 and 1967 teacher pay claims were settled by arbitration. In 1965 the NAS took limited action for a pay inquiry and this was one factor that pushed the conservative leadership of the NUT along the road to militant action. As Manzer notes, the NUT's demands were 'stretched by competition with the NAS and stretched again by militant elements inside the Union' (Manzer 1970: 142). The failure of the 1965 arbitration award to satisfy the teachers created the conditions for a more militant NUT conference in 1966. The aim was for a higher basic scale and to reverse the ever-widening gap between primary and secondary earnings. The government's pay freeze halted negotiations until April 1967, and the NUT was furious when the employers used their right to unilateral arbitration when the pay talks had only just begun. The NUT characterised the employers' action as 'an act of escapism' (Gibberd 1967: 78).

This combination of the Labour government's use of incomes policies and employers refusing to negotiate fuelled the general movement within both the NAS and NUT towards more traditional trade union and bargaining activities. As part of this the NAS affiliated to the TUC in 1968 and the NUT in 1970.

The 1967 arbitration award was again considered totally inadequate by the teachers' unions. The NUT argued to the Arbitration Tribunal for fair comparisons (after better awards for seafarers, bus workers and local government officers) and the need to recruit and retain the best quality teachers. In particular the unions argued that if education was vital to economic growth, as the Labour government agreed, then it should not be subject to economic vagaries and incomes policies.

This explicit trade-off between arbitration and industrial action further illuminates the importance of the way in which the government in the 1980s battled against the use of arbitration and comparability. This link of industrial action and arbitration appears strong: in 1969–70 teachers did strike for more pay and when they threatened to strike again in 1974 a pay inquiry was called. Teachers took action in 1978–79 and in response a pay inquiry was held. Arbitration was changed and then abandoned officially in the early 1980s under the specific instructions of Keith Joseph, and yet in 1984 when the teachers took industrial action to force arbitration the government gave in. When the teachers took action again in 1985–86 the government held out although it altered the staff side composition of Burnham and then called in ACAS and three arbitrators to help end the dispute and settle the pay issue. The government then set up a pseudo-arbitration body with the IAC which has now become a Review Body.

It is therefore industrial action that forces the setting up of pay inquiries and pay reviews rather than government policy. There is no evidence of any government strategy on the issue of teacher pay – rather than strategic planning we see *ad hoc* responses to strikes.

Among many public service workers arbitration, and/or one-off pay inquiries, and/or commissions have been the acknowledged mechanisms to prevent industrial action and to ensure elements of fairness in pay. When in the 1980s these became politically and economically eschewed, one consequence was industrial action on a large scale, which shifted the focus of trade union activity and strike action to the public sector (Edwards 1992). When school teachers were involved pay bargaining was abolished and replaced with pay review. The importance of industrial action by teachers in forcing the pace of change in pay bargaining and in holding back some aspects of government reforms in other areas is at the centre of the recent and current debates over the future of teacher trade unionism and teacher pay determination.

Industrial action

Teachers have taken industrial action nationally to enforce pay settlements and locally to fight against cuts in resources and to protect their version of professional autonomy. Despite the general reluctance of teachers to take industrial action they have still been the most militant of all professional workers within the public services. It is possible to talk about a strike tradition among teachers in ways which would not apply to nurses, lecturers or civil servants. What follows is a schematic history of teacher strikes concentrating on the two national pay strikes in 1969 and 1985, but with some reference to non-pay action as part of the tradition. The purpose of presenting this historical profile is twofold: first to provide a convincing case for the strike tradition and therefore of the likelihood of strikes in the near future over pay and jobs, and secondly to illustrate the dangers of the vacuum at the heart of pay determination policy.

The first teachers' strike was in Portsmouth in 1896 (Seifert 1987: 16–18), and ever since teachers in England and Wales have taken strike action more frequently than either other professionals or their colleagues in countries such as Scotland and the USA. The two most important descriptive issues are the level at which strikes take place – national, LEA or school; and the form of industrial action – for example stoppages of work, no cover for absent colleagues or at lunchtime. The importance of concentrating on these aspects is that they express the tensions and causes in a direct way. Throughout the 1970s and 1980s there have been large number of local episodes of industrial action. Many have been at the level of the employer, the LEA, and aimed at expenditure cutbacks. In these cases the teachers and their trade unions have been at pains to develop community support and put pressure on Labour councillors in particular. This aim tends to require a minimum of disruption to children and their parents and concentrates on hampering school administration and LEA duties.

In addition there has been important specific school-based action over a range of issues associated with central concerns of decision-making on educational/professional matters. One of the more famous was the 1975 strike at William Tyndale school in London which focused national attention on 'modern and progressive' teaching methods but which was also about the struggle within the NUT between the Broad Left and the Ultra-left trotskyists

(Seifert 1987: 132–4). This was not just unofficial action over teacher rights to teach a certain way, but as Simon has noted:

> The Tyndale issue raised, in a very dramatic form, a number of issues of key importance. One of these, of course, was pedagogical – what was meant by 'progressive' education? What was the relation between freedom and authority in the classroom? . . . Tyndale procedures were identified with progressive 'child-centred' approaches . . . the teachers themselves were identified with militant left-wing groupings. So a relationship was made, in the public eye, between 'progressivism' and the left.
>
> (Simon 1991: 445)

Other school-based industrial action raised major matters. These included the strike at Poundswick school in Manchester in 1985 over the reinstatement by the LEA of boys expelled for writing obscene graffiti about teachers. As one account noted: 'It has become a heated debate about who runs Manchester schools, how decisions are taken on matters of discipline, the powers of the LEA, and the role of governing bodies' (*Times Educational Supplement*, 18 October 1985: 6). Another case involved the suspension of a Bradford headmaster for commenting in public against his LEA's multi-cultural educational policies. Ray Honeyford had chosen the right-wing journal, *The Salisbury Review*, to make his views known. His suspension, reinstatement and later agreed retirement (Brown 1985; Seifert 1987: 216) led to local action by some teachers and further raised the question of the division of power as between the LEA, governors, the head, and classroom teachers.

There are obviously many more such cases. Their interest is twofold: first that so often they lead to industrial action which is not the case when professional matters of this type arise elsewhere, for example, with doctors; and secondly that they indicate the varied and complex power relationship between the parties which was rarely tested due to a national power brokerage system in which the unions played a full part. Under LMS and GMS it is unclear how such disputes will be resolved, although we would predict a sharp increase in them.

The other main type of action by teachers has been national strikes. These have really only happened twice: in 1969 and in 1985. In both cases the main cause was a perceived fall in relative pay, although both disputes were fuelled by a variety of other secondary causes. In both cases action was taken on a rotating basis with extensive balloting of members. The 1969 strike was dominated by the NUT, while the 1985 strike was characterised by an uneasy alliance of the NUT and NASUWT which finally fell apart.

The important surge in teacher strikes around the first world war created and set the Burnham system and the dominant role of the NUT. It was not until the mid-1960s that that system began to flake and with it teacher militancy re-emerged. As Coates said of the 1960s:

> The pattern of teacher militancy that characterised the decade was a direct

> response to the teachers' experience of these successive incomes policies; and the move by the larger associations into the TUC reflected their desire to participate in the formation of national economic policy in general, and incomes policy in particular, that so affected negotiations within the Burnham Committee.
>
> (Coates 1972b: 41)

The unions were faced with a series of policy choices: an alliance for educational advance, and/or professional unity and a teaching council, and/or an alliance with organised labour, and/or militancy. These were neither mutually exclusive nor driven simply by factors internal to the unions. As the Webbs had noted fifty years earlier professional associations of teachers would always be faced with a choice of methods as to how to pursue their objectives, and these objectives would be set according to the balance between the professional, creative and fellowship impulses.

The years from 1961 to 1967 had seen a deepening of the crisis and by 1967 the NUT was ready to start a sanctions campaign over the joint issues of pay, the use of unqualified staff, and the supervision of school meals. The beneficial experiences of this dispute persuaded members, local activists and national leaders of the efficacy of national action and developed some of the organisational and political skills needed. This was the training ground for the first national strike in 1969.

It appears that 1969 was a watershed in post-war strike activity in which the teachers played their part. As Durcan *et al.* argued:

> the choice of 1969 as a turning point was determined by a number of factors. During 1969 the number of stoppages rose very rapidly, the number of workers involved passed the million mark for the first time since the war . . . and the number of days lost exceeded five million for the first time since 1957
>
> (Durcan *et al.* 1983: 133)

The teachers and their unions responded differently at first to the government's 3.5 per cent pay norm. The NAS went straight for action, but the old guard at the NUT linked with strong Labour Party ties managed to stutter and stumble over an early acceptance and later rejection of the proposals. The key was the way in which other groups of workers breached the guidelines with the threat of industrial action in the run up to a General Election. Hyman argues that at this time there was a strong 'demonstration effect' – 'then the successful struggles of groups of workers with little record of militancy encouraged others to take action' (Hyman 1989: 226). And this is a faint echo of the more important arguments proposed by Lenin (1902), Luxemburg (1906), and Gramsci (1920) that strikes, in certain circumstances, advance beyond economic demands to political contests with the state, and in so doing raise the political consciousness of those participating in the action (Kelly 1988). This certainly seems to have been the case among some sections of teachers in the early 1970s.

The action got under way properly in the autumn and received wide support from teachers – on 1 December for example, 4,000 teachers in 250 schools in 81 LEAs went on strike for two weeks (Seifert 1987: 100). The government authorised an increased offer which the unions rejected. The employers called for arbitration and the chair of Burnham insisted the claim went to arbitration, but the unions rejected this and refused to be party to the arbitration procedure. With massive membership support the NUT was able to escalate its action in the early months of 1970, and this decided the government to settle in March after Ted Short directly intervened in Burnham talks.

The 1969 strike was the most important event for industrial relations in schools in the post-war period (for more detailed accounts see Seifert 1987; Price 1970; Coates 1972b; Burke 1971; Griffiths 1970). It represented the triumph for the coalition of the left in the NUT leadership, it laid the foundations for TUC affiliation of the NUT, and it provided the run up to the Houghton pay inquiry. It illustrated that trade union activities were open to teachers and that teachers could utilise them effectively – determined and united action could change the policy of the government. It also provided a touchstone for political and professional divisions of later years and fuelled the divisions on the left of the NUT which dogged it throughout the 1970s (Seifert 1984). A key part of what it illustrated was that neither the Labour ministers of the day nor the mandarins in the DES had a clear view of how to determine teachers' pay. In fact not only did they not think in strategic terms about the impact of pay on teacher labour markets and on departmental expenditure but furthermore they did not seem very concerned. Such indifferent incompetence runs through policy in this area frustrating the union leadership, bewildering the employers, and generating divisions and low morale amongst the teachers themselves.

The important lessons of this strike were not lost on commentators. So Margerison and Elliott found that the 'evidence clearly indicates that discontent lay deep amongst the teachers . . . the subsequent action has indicated that the reservations teachers may have had about their status being infringed by industrial action have been removed' (Margerison and Elliott 1970: 417), but as Coates noted there was more to what had happened: 'the militancy of the teachers in the second half of the 1960s reflected not just changing attitudes to industrial militancy within the profession, but was also a measure of the new relationship of power within the Burnham Committees that the 1965 restructuring occasioned' (Coates 1972b: 192). What else can be said of this momentous strike? The causes were clearly rooted in falling relative pay, and this was triggered by a series of related necessary conditions – the compositional change among teachers with the growth of the profession and the impact of the student radicals, the rise of the left in the NUT, the importance for the first time of the NAS as a militant alternative to the NUT, the widespread use of industrial action among other groups of workers, and a government increasingly concerned to control public expenditure.

There is perhaps one further point worth making which draws upon parallels with disputes in the NHS in the 1970s: how the disputes alter power and work relations at the workplace. NHS staff were not only subject to pay freezes and falling relative pay but also according to Carpenter: 'two things were happening: first, the work was often becoming more remote from the point of patient-contact, and second, those doing it were becoming subject to a more impersonal and "functional" style of management' (Carpenter 1988: 333). Another study on the impact of disputes by Morris and Rydzkowski (1984) showed that those employers which took tough measures against strikers and used 'volunteer' labour suffered from a severe deterioration in industrial relations after the end of the dispute. This evidence suggests a common theme: that changes in labour process (work and authority relations at work) both fuel other strike causes and worsen industrial relations. For teachers, there is important evidence that heads and some governors are becoming more managerial in the traditional sense especially in secondary schools. This is a function of both tighter financial regulation and tighter central control over standards and curriculum. As with hospitals this reflects the significant increase in average size of workplace (school) as between 1950 and 1986. In the primary sector in 1950 there were five or six teachers per school, and this had risen to eight per school by 1986. For secondary schools the figures rose from fifteen to forty-six. While these still remain small workplaces the rise in size has a consequence for the management of industrial relations and trade union organisation.

In the 1970s, then, the principle of comparability ruled supreme with first the Houghton Report and then the Clegg Commission. The need to revert to such *ad hoc* pay inquiries meant that Burnham itself, as Whitley elsewhere in the public services, was under attack. The attack was composed of an odd selection of bedfellows. The main group were the New Right with their market forces and born again managerialism. This overstated the importance of 'good' management and the importance of management freedom to set pay levels and motivate staff based on the needs of the business and its markets. No room for national pay bargaining here. This view, which particularly strengthened in the early 1980s, was supported by some sections of managers themselves. Here then the NAHT and some heads saw an opportunity to increase the status, power and pay of school-based managers. Other Tories, not the New Right, saw the possibility of weakening the trade unions and the LEAs through decentralised bargaining systems while maintaining highly central educational controls. Such would be the myopic view of the DES leadership. Individual teachers disillusioned with central pay determination and trade union tactics perceived hope in new localised systems in which excellent teachers in excellent schools in prosperous areas would outperform their colleagues and therefore deserved some additional reward. Some Conservatives at LEA level also favoured the breakup of Burnham as did those seeking to expand the private sector.

All in all, too many of this group believed the sunshine stories of the free marketers and management consultants, and many have since retreated from their support for LMS. This issue will be taken up again in chapter 5. For now we need to note that the main pay legacy of the 1970s was a stronger commitment than ever among teachers and their unions to fair comparison as a pay principle.

Despite the recession of the early 1980s, and because of the attacks on teachers and education, by 1984 the teachers were again facing a major collision with a government which had no clear pay policy and no clear principles with which to settle the educational future. The 1984 pay claim went to arbitration and the resultant low award fuelled the teachers' sense of unfairness.

In 1985 the teachers of Britain began what was to be their longest and largest national dispute. It was characterised by a high degree of unity across the teacher unions for much of the time, strong membership support, weak and vacillating policies of employers, and a hostile and intransigent government. The costs to the country, the pupils and the teachers were high, and the consequences bitter. It ended in an unsightly debacle with the unions defeated and divided, many teachers disillusioned and weary, and government victorious but with no idea what to do with such a victory. The employers remained in the middle caught between increasing managerial instincts to manage at whatever level of resource government provided and traditional yearnings for peace and plenty. (The details of this strike can be found in Seifert 1987: 196–229.)

From the perspective of the unions, especially the NUT and NASUWT, this was another 1969 – a strike over the fall in relative pay caused by governmental neglect and cutbacks. The unions called a series of one day and three day stoppages on a rotation basis and linked these with various school level actions such as no cover for absent colleagues and at lunchtimes. The general pattern was one of the greatest inconvenience to the employer and embarrassment to government at least cost to teachers and the unions. This worked very well. Most action was supported by ballots which indicated strong support. But this time the unions were confronted with a Secretary of State and Prime Minister more concerned with defeating unions, weakening local government and reducing teacher influence in education than with a traditional approach to settling the industrial dispute with the minimum of disruption to the *status quo ante*.

Indeed Keith Joseph chose to flag up other issues throughout the dispute. These included linking pay to classroom and management performance. The results of his emphasis are with us today in the Citizen's Charter and the implementation of performance-related pay throughout the education world. This tied in with wider objectives to remove pay from Burnham, to secure codified conditions of service, to reduce the influence of the teacher unions and the NUT in particular, and ultimately to set schools free from local authorities. A world in which a thousand schools might bloom!

The unions and majority of teachers failed to see these as realistic government aims and fell foul of further internal divisions and doubts. Worse was to come from employers – divided and hopelessly at odds with both their employees and paymasters. As the dispute dragged on government announced further cuts and job losses. As John Hughes said 'schools and education have become scapegoats for the broader failings of government policy. Education has thus become an easy prey for expenditure cutbacks and has laid itself open to the introduction of specious tests of effectiveness and performance' (Hughes 1985: 4). Was Hughes expressing clear prescience or just old fashioned prejudice? The extent to which government forged policies from the heat of struggle will emerge later, but Hughes certainly was right to question the scientific and ideological basis for the claims of the New Right.

The dispute ended in the spring of 1986 by which time the NUT had had its majority on Burnham removed by the Secretary of State for the first time and allowed the other unions to vote for a settlement under the confused stare of ACAS officials. Such a solution fell short of the teacher demands and was too dependent on government promises and employer acceptance of the ACAS botch. In the end the defeat hastened the relative decline of the NUT and stopped the advance of the NASUWT. It ushered in the day of the AMMA. It also meant the end of Burnham.

In 1987 the government passed the Teachers Pay and Conditions Act which ended Burnham and introduced the IAC. For the next three to four years successive ministers promised a return to collective bargaining, but finally and rather surprisingly ended up with a Review Body. The years of this enforced arbitration reflected in industrial relations what was happening elsewhere in education – tremendous increase in the powers of the DFE and Secretary of State at the expense of teachers, their unions, the employers and the education establishment.

Pay inquiries and reviews

The 1987 settlement reflected government determination to stop teacher strikes and reduce the influence of the NUT and NASUWT. The abolition of Burnham and invention of the IAC were created from a lack of clear policy on pay other than the Treasury's desire to keep tabs on the pay bill. The use of *ad hoc* pay inquiries such as with Houghton in 1974 and Clegg in 1979–80 served to emphasise the breakdown of orderly formal collective bargaining through Burnham. This itself happens when teachers believe that they are no longer in any sense negotiating with their employers but with the government. Incomes policies and constant interference with global sums available for pay meant that teachers and their unions felt the need, as did other public sector unions, to deal politically and publicly with government. The main ways in which this was achieved was through more public campaigns and industrial action. It is the use of industrial action which drives the pay determination process forward and/or backward. The success of such action depends on several intervening variables, but both the internal organisation and unity of the teachers and their unions and the political position of the government in terms of public expenditure and electoral security rank high as important factors.

It was the strike of 1969 and subsequent threat of strikes in the early 1970s which played a major part in causing the government to agree to a pay inquiry in 1974. Again it was industrial action and its threat that persuaded a different government to agree to the Clegg Commission on public sector pay. The final stage was that the 1985–86 strikes determined the government to abandon Burnham and after a dithering hiatus turn to a Review Body – a permanent pay inquiry. The ultimate irony is that since the STRB was formed the government has decided to prevent its work through a pay norm of 1.5 per cent in 1993–94 and a pay bill freeze in 1994–95.

Pay inquiries, whether *ad hoc* or permanent, require the main parties – trade unions and employers – to present a reasoned case with evidence for their positions. This statement is in effect a public document. It also allows each union to present separately, although they may choose to put in a single claim. The inquiry may take evidence from interested bodies such as the DFE, governors' organisations and others. The inquiry then summarises the arguments of all groups and presents written recommendations to the Prime Minister who can set them aside. What is important is that there is more public information about the cases and the decisions, and that a notional rationality creeps into debate.

If Whitley was criticised for being remote and incomprehensible to most teachers so Pay Review is worse. If Whitley was criticised for the muddled role of government, so Pay Review is worse. It is extraordinary that managers and employers who have clamoured for so long for greater freedom to manage should participate in such a system which removes from the employer any vestige of control or authority over pay.

The strangest element of the whole Pay Review system seems to be its acceptance on face value of the rationality of pay systems and arguments. The staff side present a set of interlocking arguments based on the cost-of-living, comparability and labour supply. The management prefers concepts such as affordability and productivity. The arguments are important but not decisive. The outcome of the review process is based on a complex interaction between ministers, department chiefs, employers, the unions and the mood of teachers themselves. Pay review bodies ape aspects of other bargaining structures and methods and are more under central control than Burnham ever was.

The STRB was established as a direct result of a lengthy pay dispute as with the nurses (Seifert 1992b), and its operation is supposed to be linked to a future without national strike action. Such a process is also designed to strengthen those unions, such as AMMA, which is less a trade union and more a political pressure group, and to strengthen those forces within the NUT and NASUWT which favour a lower trade union profile – who wish in the Webbs' analysis to downgrade their reliance on collective bargaining.

The Review Body operates in similar fashion to that for nurses, the armed forces and senior civil servants. It is serviced by the Office of Manpower

Economics (OME) which provides a secretariat and research. The body consists of seven members appointed by the Prime Minister for limited but extendable periods. Each year both sides submit written evidence and in addition other interested groups may provide information. Meetings take place between Review Body members and the staff and management sides, and the members then submit their report which may be implemented in full, or phased in, or partly phased or rejected.

It is clear that government has several bites at the pay cherry. It appoints the members of the Review Body, it presents the management side's case within its own pay guidelines, and it decides whether to implement and/or fund the recommendations.

The political benefits to government from this system remain its ability to distance itself from pay bargaining. For Pay Review to succeed, however, in its prime purpose of avoiding industrial action by school teachers it must meet certain objectives such as reasonable level of settlements acceptable to the staff side and the staff. In order to achieve this some weight must be given to comparability despite public disclaimers.

The government can blame pay review bodies for wrong-headed arguments and the Review Bodies can blame government for inadequate funding, but both survive and there is no national industrial action over pay by teachers. It is the new employers and managers who are most frustrated by Pay Review: it limits the ability to vary pay to accord with the needs of the school and its budget. Ways around this include higher levels of Incentive Allowances, new gradings, and local flexibility. So the mood is to combine national agreements with local supplements.

When Ken Clarke, the then Secretary of State, announced the setting up of the STRB in April 1991 he made several crucial points about its real function. First the timing of the proposal came after several weeks in which the government was preparing the way for the reintroduction of some form of national collective bargaining along the lines suggested by ACAS after the 1987 strikes. The main issue taken by the government was that this was a device, above all other considerations, to prevent industrial action. As Clarke claimed in the opening to his statement: 'The work of the interim advisory committee has, we believe, been of great importance in encouraging teachers' professionalism by avoiding conflict about the level of their pay. . . . Previously, the Government took the view that a review body for teachers could not be established because of the emphasis teacher unions had placed on their ability to take industrial action.' The core of Clarke's statement reads:

> I now propose that teachers' pay and conditions should in future be determined by an independent review body reporting to the Prime Minister, alongside the review bodies for the health service, the armed forces, and senior civil servants and the judiciary. This proposal is made on the basis that teachers fully recognise and accept their professional responsibilities, and will not in future take industrial action about matters within the review

body's ambit. The Government, for their part, will undertake, as in the case of the other review bodies, to implement the review body's recommendations unless there are clear and compelling reasons to the contrary. The recommendations will apply to teachers in maintained schools, except grant-maintained schools that choose to make their own arrangements.

(*Weekly Hansard*, 17 April 1991 col. 433–4)

The questions and answers which followed this announcement centred on the abolition of bargaining rights in breach of a previous government pledge, and the apparent removal of the right to strike from teachers. Labour MPs Jack Straw, Martin Flannery and Derek Fatchett were mainly concerned about this threat to the trade unions, and Dennis Skinner and Bob Cryer saw the STRB as the mechanism to impose wage restraint on the teachers. Ken Clarke was forced to repeat his view that recommendations would only be ignored if there are 'clear and compelling reasons'. In his final comment he acknowledged that the legislation setting up the STRB would not contain the duty on teachers not to strike, although he also took the view that any strikes on issues covered by the STRB would lead the government to 'review the remit' (*Weekly Hansard*, 17 April 1991 col. 445).

Pay review body reports are, therefore, best seen as versions of previous *ad hoc* inquiries such as Houghton in 1974 and Clegg in 1980. This is because they are explicitly used by government to try to prevent industrial action as a short-term solution to an immediate political difficulty rather than as part of any strategic considerations about teacher pay. As long as the pay inquiry stops the action and provides a rational gloss for any settlement then government ministers can move on to the next crisis!

When the government initiated the Houghton inquiry into teachers' pay in May 1974 it was responding to the substantial threat of strike action. The NUT was clear as to its concerns: 'the central issue dealt with by the review body was the decline in teachers' pay, for it was this which was having disastrous effect on recruitment to the profession, retention of teachers and the high staff turnover which schools were suffering' (NUT *Annual Report* 1975: 133). The NAS took a different line, emphasising 'the need for the maintenance of an effective career structure' (*New Schoolmaster*, September 1974: 175). Houghton remains important since it both set levels of relative pay acceptable to the teachers of the day and provided support for the pay arguments that have subsequently been abandoned by the government – comparability and labour markets, rather than performance and affordability.

Paragraph 14 of the Houghton Report says 'we see our task not merely to remedy an anomalous situation, but also to review . . . the pay levels and salary structures in the teaching profession'. So some twenty years ago the key issue in teachers' pay was that of comparability, and, as *Education* noted, 'as compared with general movements in salaries' (27 December 1974). The committee was not impressed with the NUT's case on teacher supply, nor by the NAS's concern with status, but more with the messy salary structure and recent relative loss in earnings. The NUT spent much time and space arguing that pay increases should also reflect the changing nature of the job – the greater time and responsibility encountered with pupil-centred learning and continuous assessment (NUT 1974).

A rare academic analysis of Houghton's award to the teachers by Way *et al.* (1981) suggests that teachers were able to gain what they see as beneficial treatment, not because of the genuine exceptionalness of their case, but more to do with the ability of the teachers and their unions to put pressure on government through mass campaigns, industrial action and some joint initiatives with employers. Way *et al.* refute the NUT's labour supply arguments with the view that pay rises do not simply improve the recruitment issue, and that Houghton achieved its real purpose which was to buy off teacher strikes. Way *et al.* follow the argument that Winchester supports, namely that in the public services when Whitley failed then arbitration was used to prevent industrial action. And that this remained the policy of all governments between 1945 and 1980. What Way *et al.* did not develop is the further point that the reason for this was the lack of government strategy in this area, and that one consequence of this was that power to decide teachers' pay levels and structures largely passed to the dominant group in the NUT. So in the years 1967 to 1979 the Broad Left leadership of the NUT was able to secure their formulations on pay and to some extent on wider issues such as comprehensive education and equality through the dominance of the NUT in teacher politics and the inability of any government to deal with public sector pay and expenditure in strategic ways.

The NUT was in no doubt that the Houghton award was a 'major victory for the Union' and was 'a result of the Union's powerful salaries campaign over the last few years' (NUT *Executive Report* 1976: 46). As Seifert noted 'the lasting significance of Houghton is the political recognition by all those involved of the prime role of central government in wage determination, and the prime role of wage determination in the politics of teacher trade unions' (Seifert 1987: 129).

A mere five years after Houghton the Labour government's education policy was in disarray. They had lost control of public sector pay and paid a high price for that, but they also lost control over the education high ground through the sad debacle of the Great Debate. Undoubtedly the correct assessment about the Great Debate comes from Max Morris, former President of the NUT:

> the 'Great debate' has focused attention on the alleged shortcomings of everyone in the service except those responsible for organizing, administering, paying for it, and for deciding policy at top level. The whole operation was skilfully designed to divert attention from the massive cuts imposed on the schools and further and higher education by all governments from December 1973 on.
>
> (Morris 1978: 127)

The Clegg commission was set up in 1979–80 to examine a range of public sector occupations with a view to setting some form of comparability linked within government notions of cost. Its importance was not so much in its greatly praised efforts to be professional about the calculation of pay, but in retrospect as a work of monumental irrelevance to the future conduct of public sector industrial relations. It was Houghton but this time at the start of a Tory government's term of office. As John Hughes noted 'this is the second time in five years that a major comparability report has had to rescue the teaching profession from a major deterioration in relative pay' (Hughes 1980: 4).

The 1979–80 pay round settled in May 1979 for 9 per cent with £6 a month on account of a future award from the Clegg Commission due in 1980. The unions only agreed to this on the understanding that the reference to Clegg should explicitly mention the Houghton settlement and the principle of fair comparison. The Clegg Commission was in the shadow of Houghton and despite efforts to make itself appear more modern the end result was similar analysis based on similar assumptions.

The employers in general wanted Clegg to recommend that pay rises should be tied to extra duties, and that comparison with other groups of professionals was a better way forward than any protection linked to inflation. Much of the union case was based on changes in the nature of the job: more complex, more stressful and more changeable. In response they wanted pay restored to the 1974 levels and better promotion chances. The NASUWT refused to participate in the inquiry on the grounds that it only worsened the pay bargaining crisis. In the end the Commission made rather a hash of their recommendations. They neither satisfied the teachers nor helped the employers, and they owed more to government pressure than to rational calculation. An editorial in the TES thought it was 'only fairly good, fairly difficult to pay, and just about fair to an underpaid profession which is expected to maintain and improve standards in the face of increasing public and financial pressures' (*Times Educational Supplement*, 18 April 1980: 2). Seifert has summarised the situation thus:

> The Clegg Commission marked the end of an era in public sector pay inquiries and shambled off stage right with consensus politics and a commitment to the financing of state education. The times had changed. The teachers suddenly became aware of the darkness that had fallen: cuts in funding, threats to create a merged pay and conditions negotiating body, rejection of arbitration, and a seat on Burnham for the anti-strike union PAT.
>
> (Seifert 1987: 156)

Between the Clegg commission and the next industrial action by teachers there were severe cutbacks in expenditure and several crucial public sector strikes. In April 1984, just as the famous miners' strike was under way, the NUT and NASUWT both announced limited industrial action to force the employers, and ultimately the government, to accept arbitration on the pay claim. This was of course anathema to Keith Joseph and the Prime Minister who both wanted a settlement based on cash limits and not decided externally to the system.

As Keith Joseph said: 'the arbitrator may not make the ability to pay the crucial concern, and he cannot provide more money' (*Weekly Hansard*, 18 May 1984 col. 132). This type of comment tended to unite the opposition and so all six teacher unions, the Labour Party and the head of the largest LEA all now wanted arbitration. In June the management panel of Burnham changed its mind and agreed to arbitration despite government protests. One aspect of this particular arbitration was that the management case was very poorly presented and failed to deal with facts. It rejected traditional settlement arguments based on comparability and strongly supported free market nostrums. In addition the employers went out of their way to attack teachers and their commitment to the profession. The teachers, in contrast, based most of their case on restoring Houghton and Clegg. Rarely can the two sides have been further apart in terms of approach and argument – even if the sums involved in this case were fairly small.

When the arbitration award was announced of 5.1 per cent the teachers and their unions were furious, and condemned the outcome. Two consequences followed: that next year the teachers' would have to take strike action to secure their pay rise and that neither the government nor the teachers would accept that kind of arbitration again. As with pay so with pay structure – the employers charge for conceding improvements in structure included stricter forms of teacher appraisal and worse conditions of service – the NUT pulled out of negotiations and the employers lobbied government for an end to the vague contractual terms of teacher work.

When the 1985–86 strike ended the government abolished Burnham and set up the IAC. The first IAC report in 1988 noted that the 1987 Act both altered the statutory basis upon which teachers' pay was decided and also that it replaced the multi-scale pay structure with a single scale and incentive allowances. As the IAC argued 'the changes thus introduced came in the wake of a period of unprecedented industrial disturbance in schools. In 1985–87 a total of 910,000 teacher working days were lost. The relationships between teachers, employers, central government, and of course parents and the public were affected by this period of turmoil in schools' (IAC 1988: 1).

The prime method of working was to accept written evidence from all parties and to behave as if the IAC members were independent of government. The report's main conclusion was that teacher morale was low. The main remedy was an across the board pay rise with some more flexibility in application of existing provisions. The report showed its credentials when it further argued that 'good management could do much to improve motivation of teachers' (IAC 1988: 3). The IAC in reaching their views were obliged by the 1987 Act to consult LEAs, governors and the unions. They received evidence from two employers' groups – the WJEC and the NEOST; from seven teacher organisations – the six unions (AMMA, NASUWT, NUT, PAT, NAHT and SHA) and the National Association of the Teachers of Wales; and from six organisations representing voluntary schools. They also received written evidence from the DES and other bodies. The job of the IAC was to report to the Secretary of State on pay, pay differentials, duties, London allowance, and on the social priority allowance. The point to note for now is how similar it sounds to Houghton and Clegg, and therefore the important lasting quality of the real issues.

The key elements in pay determination for teachers remain in place now as before: a largely homogeneous occupational group well represented by trade unions, even if they are frequently in disagreement; a national labour market with local variations; a pay budget controlled ever more precisely by the Treasury and implemented by the DFE; the labour intensive nature of the school education service; and the deep commitment of the profession and its representative bodies and its employers to an overall pay system based on fair comparison. It is this last matter, which itself arises from the previous factors, that dominates the entire debate. The government from the early 1980s rediscovered the policy of replacing comparability with affordability, but it has been thwarted at every turn by both organised teacher opposition, practical limitations and even its own creations – the IAC and STRB.

So the first IAC report concluded that 'in the Committee's view, perceptions of pay comparability are relevant to teachers' motivation, and hence also to recruitment, retention and quality' (IAC 1988: 64). In their next report the IAC was concerned about the implementation of the National Curriculum and Local Management of Schools following the 1988 ERA. It felt that 'the financial constraint on our recommendations was widely considered to be too restrictive in the light of rising inflation' (IAC 1989: 1), and that the 6 per cent recommendation may be too little in view of the IAC remit on motivation, recruitment, retention and quality. The line of the IAC was that ultimately all teachers needed to keep pace with inflation, but more importantly needed to keep pace with competitive occupational groups on a comparability basis. In addition, and in response to government pressure, the IAC members also supported higher levels of and more spread for incentive allowances and the development of a separate set of salaries for deputies and heads. Thus internal differentials would shift in line with local requirements while the basics would be covered by national comparability increases.

The third IAC report in 1990 repeated the problems of staffing the changes derived from the National Curriculum and LMS. The report reminded government that their reforms could not succeed without properly paid teachers and enough of them. Once again the labour market arguments were to the fore. The IAC argued in favour of 'appropriate' levels of pay (IAC 1990: 3). Again the term 'appropriate' means comparable to attract similar qualified people. This time the IAC appeared bolder in its critique of government policy and practice. Some emphasis was put on the need for higher quality management information on the teaching force, but the main thrust was a hotchpotch of ideas aimed at plugging holes in local labour markets while retaining some national strategy. Increasingly the recommendations looked like a return to a main scale with subscales and with endless additions. This is the inevitable outcome of a move away from the multi-scale nationally determined pay system. The pride of both government and IAC in the new 1988 salary structure looks misplaced when put next to the critical comments of the STRB in 1993 when discussing the new simplified structure!

The fourth and final report of the IAC in 1991 was the same again. Each successive report was more critical of government and more concerned that lack of funds and therefore lack of quality staff would destroy the 1988 reforms. As they say 'it is vitally important for education and for the future of the country that teaching becomes increasingly attractive as a career. Though not the only factor, pay is a central consideration' (IAC 1991: 3–4). This was to be achieved through the double device of a reasonably fair national pay rise for all and increasing, as the IAC saw it, opportunities for schools to pay teachers according to local needs – recruitment, retention, quality and performance. The IAC seemed to think that more and more attractive incentive allowances would be used to reward performance. The STRB and others found that in practice this was not the case, hence the enforced introduction of performance-related pay.

So after four reports from 1988 to 1991 during a period of exceptional educational change and reform, the central and dominant issues of pay and performance remained unresolved. The government showed less and less interest in any form of national pay bargaining, and the divisions within the unions made them unable to present a common front on pay, pay structure and pay machinery. In addition the LEAs were increasingly squeezed and reduced to watchers rather than players. In 1992 the IAC was replaced with the STRB – the form, the working methods, the arguments and the conclusions remained similar even if the personnel changed. None of the IAC members sit on the STRB. Of course the STRB work has been largely wiped out by a public sector wages policy of no increase on the pay bill for 1994–95. None the less the arguments raged and the STRB has, like its predecessor, tried to combine some continuation of national comparable rates with increasing local discretion.

The STRB differs from other review bodies because it is a statutory body under the 1991 Act and it also recommends on conditions as well as pay. In addition, unlike the other review bodies, the pay bill is met partly by the LEAs and some of the money therefore comes from local taxes. The first report was implemented in full with the 7.5 per cent pay rise for all and an increased number of incentive allowances. Once again in 1993 the remit from government was to look at overall pay levels and conditions, the introduction of performance-related pay, and a new pay structure to enable the easier use of performance-related pay. The emphasis on the good management of resources reflects wider debates and again is increasingly pushing aside the importance of adequate resources themselves.

The STRB members are selected by the government, it works under specific legislation passed by the government, it recommends on the basis of a government directed remit, and its recommendations to government can be altered. Even with some independence and some degree of open minds the overall impression is that little the STRB says or does contradicts government wishes outright. The detail is sometimes challenged and that can be important, but the main principles of government policy are embraced. These include the endless efforts to move away from comparability as the main basis of the annual pay rise, the substitution of national cost-of-living rises with local business and performance and labour market rises, and the illusion that pay determination is a rational process in which unions argue with employers and independent minded STRB members. All this takes place, apparently, in a conflict free world in which teachers abandon all previous methods of settling pay: collective bargaining, arbitration and industrial action. The temporary nature of this situation will surely be exposed once pay levels fall relative to others and with the mounting evidence for the failures of performance-related pay and local supplements.

PAY

As was suggested in chapter one the heart of industrial relations in a labour intensive service such as schools lies with pay and performance. Both are of interest to teachers, managers, employers, the pupils and their parents, government, and ultimately the nation as a whole. The reforms of the late 1980s required teachers to work harder in more supervised ways, and allowed schools to implement more flexible pay and conditions of service. In this process both LEAs and the teacher unions played a much smaller part than previously, and their loss of power and control was matched by the growth in power of the Secretary of State and central government. In 1994 the total pay bill for teachers covered by STRB was about £10.6 billion, and this was paid to nearly 450,000 whole-time equivalent school teachers. A great deal of public money was going to a very large occupational group.

Pay, of course, is more than just money going to individuals. It represents all kinds of messages within the organisation and to those outside. It also represents about 80 per cent of school operating costs. The central issue then is what should be the basis for teacher pay and what mechanism should be used to determine it. The answer may come later, but to some extent a retrospective glance at pay movements over time might help to elaborate the main concerns of the parties.

Pay before 1974 and Houghton

We can only provide a brief summary of the history of teacher pay from the inception of the Burnham scales in 1921. As with most pay data there are some problems of comparability over time as the methods of collection and definition vary. There are also problems associated with comparing teachers' pay with that of general movements in pay and with the cost-of-living index.

Again there are issues of definition, but in the latter cases also of comparing like with like. So in an era of unequal pay as between men and women and of falling prices and rising unemployment as in the 1930s we can see the difficulties. None the less, we have to make do with the figures as they exist and they do provide some general pointers as to the pay situation.

In general, then, between 1921 and 1940 teachers' pay was in line with that of other wage earners and strengthened slightly with falling prices, compared with the cost-of-living. For example, if 1924 is taken as an index base year of 100 for wage rates, cost-of-living and teachers' pay, then by 1937 the wage rates were 102, cost-of-living 88, and the pay of certificated teachers 101. But, as an article in the *Times Educational Supplement* for 1950 concludes, 'in the years 1925–1940 all classes in full employment, both teachers and wage-earners, were in a relatively better economic position than they had been in the years immediately after 1918', but the argument continues that 'it must also be assumed that the standard of living of the certificated teachers at 1924 was adequate, and there is ample evidence to argue that this was very far from being true' (*Times Educational Supplement*, 10 March 1950: 179).

The period of the war and after saw a sharp deterioration in teachers' pay. Using the 1924 index again, remembering that by 1937 all was relatively well, then by 1949 wage rates in general had jumped to 201, the cost-of-living risen to 160, and the pay of the certificated teacher to only 154. The pay of the graduate teacher fared worse with their index at 129. As the same *Times Educational Supplement* article makes clear 'the weakened and still weakening position of the graduate teacher is obvious'. To give a further indication of the plight of teachers we can see that from 1924 to 1949 the pay of coal miners more than trebled, shipbuilders more than doubled while that of teachers had risen between 29 per cent and 54 per cent.

An extension of this analysis in the post-war years provides some even tougher comparison problems due to the extensive use of allowances and the changing nature of the scales especially in 1951 and 1956. An attempt to analyse teachers' pay between 1920 and 1963 was made by Greenhalgh using four types of teacher (assistant teacher in primary school; headmaster of a primary school; assistant master in secondary school; and headmaster of secondary school). Greenhalgh concluded 'it is clear that before the war all four examples made real gains relative to the downward movement in prices'. This corresponds with the material above. From 1939 to the mid-1950s the main issue was the worsening overall position of teachers and also 'a considerable narrowing of the pre-war differentials between the graduate grammar school assistant and the non-graduate primary teacher' (Greenhalgh 1968: 30). This trend was sharply reversed in 1956 and again in 1959 when graduate teachers' pay rose much faster than non-graduates'.

So the somewhat egalitarian post-war settlement within the profession lasted about ten years by which time the pressure from labour market forces, the new increased number of graduates, and the expanding secondary sector created the objective circumstances for a breakdown in the dominance of the basic grade. The NUT fought to maintain the earlier position but the need to pay graduates in secondary schools more fitted well with the Conservative government's overall policies on public pay and enabled discontented NUT members to drift eventually to the NAS.

None of this, however, really deals with what teachers ought to be paid, as measured by some society-wide and/or economic model of their worth. In 1953 the World Organization of the Teaching Profession commissioned Hammer to examine teachers' pay because, as he said, 'such a study . . . is needed to verify the general assumption that teacher salaries typically are below the level they should be expected to maintain' (Hammer 1953: 1).

This study examined teachers' pay in twenty-five countries and used a series of ingenious methods to compare their relative worth. One table provides the relative economic status of teachers compared in each country with ten other occupations – in England teachers were ranked 6th and 7th for secondary and primary. In only one other country were secondary teachers ranked lower and that was 7th in the USA (Hammer 1953: 19). Hammer concluded that 'not only are salaries too low. The criteria on which they are based sometimes bear questionable relation to the degree of proficiency in teaching' (1953: 21). So by the early 1950s not only were teachers falling behind the pay of others in the UK but worldwide there seemed an increasing lack of confidence in the profession which was reflected in both pay levels and pay determination mechanisms.

Two further studies by Conway analysed teachers' pay from 1945 to 1965. As she argued 'increases in the basic scales during the years 1945 to 1959 have generally been justified by the rising cost of living and the general increase in wage and salary rates . . . changes in the allowances were intended to increase the differentials between various groups of teachers' (Conway 1962: 157). The actual pay of any given teacher was determined by three factors: salary scales determined through Burnham, the school organisation in terms of children, and the qualification and experience of the teacher.

Conway concluded after considerable skill in adjusting the official statistics to fit a real pattern of earnings that 'since 1945 teachers' salaries appear to have followed prices though usually with a time lag' (1962: 174), and it was also the case that teachers' pay kept up with like groups in the civil service. Conway did not compare teachers' pay with any private sector group. In a later study she tried to refine her use of comparative indices through age-standardisation of earnings and concluded that 'estimates of the differentials between teachers in different types of school naturally show greater differences than estimates of the differentials between men and women teachers' (Conway 1967: 77).

We now have in place some information that concentrates our general concerns: the level of teachers' pay as a profession against the pay of others and the cost of living; the differentials within the profession based on three main factors – gender, qualification and type of school; and the mechanisms and criteria used to determine teachers' pay. All of these points came together in the late 1960s with a major national strike and the subsequent build up of pressure explained above which created the conditions for the Houghton Report.

Houghton

In 1974 there were 416,325 full time and 33,879 part time teachers employed in LEAs in England and Wales. As we have suggested above by 1974 the pay determination system for this very large group of public employees had fallen into crisis as evidenced by the use of arbitration in 1965, 1967, 1968 (on London weighting), 1971 and 1972. The Houghton Committee felt that:

> the pay of teachers in Great Britain has thus been susceptible to government influence even when no formal statutory incomes policy was in operation. Teachers were also one of a number of groups in the public sector which felt that the operations of the counter-inflation programme and previous incomes policies had prevented them from attempting to restore their position.
>
> (Houghton 1974: 4)

The evidence taken from all interested parties led the committee to conclude that 'the pay of all groups of teachers had fallen behind and needed to be increased' (Houghton 1974: 6). The main evidence for this view came from a detailed examination of certain key areas: the supply of teachers, teachers' pay compared with general movements in pay, teachers' pay compared with other occupations, work and status of teachers, and the simplification of pay structure (allowances, grades and scales).

The main findings were that there was a need for higher quality staff since the number of graduates had fallen due to falling relative pay. This was also blamed for the high turnover and wastage rates. Using 1965 as a base year the committee calculated that the shortfall in comparable pay was about 17 per cent using NES averages. The report recommended a 27 per cent rise for classroom teachers and 32 per cent for heads based on both the comparability arguments and the changing nature of the job. There were also important changes to the pay structure in line with the some of the male only union's strongly argued case for a better career path (NAS 1974; AMA 1974).

Finally the committee felt obliged to comment on the pay determination system itself in terms of retaining the current bargaining methods but pleading for higher quality information and more use of the New Earnings Survey data (*Education*, 27 December 1974). As the committee noted:

> Another suggestion made to us was that a standing Review Body might be established to consider the pay of teachers on a continuing basis. Review bodies are independent bodies appointed to advise the Prime Minister on levels of pay in fields where there is no negotiating machinery or where

> negotiation is not regarded as appropriate for settling pay. Their recommendations are not subject to negotiation, and they have been assured that their recommendations will not be referred to any other body and will be accepted by the government unless there are clear and compelling reasons for not doing so. We think it unlikely that any part of the negotiating bodies would wish to surrender their negotiating powers in this way. Nor, indeed, do we think it desirable in the case of teachers that the normal bargaining processes between the two sides should be abrogated.
>
> (Houghton 1974: 66)

Houghton contained ninety-eight separate recommendations and represented the most detailed and scrupulous attempt to assess teachers pay in light of the previous post-war history of Hammer's concern with relative worth. As with previous studies the driving force of rational argument rested with change over time. So Houghton's basic position, whatever else was said, remained the relative worth of teachers' average earnings compared with the cost of living and average earnings of others.

The period 1974–79 and Clegg

In 1979 the teachers' unions were again arguing for a catching-up settlement. The NUT provided a detailed submission to the Clegg commission running to nearly 130 pages. The case was split between the facts of pay erosion (Figure 2.1) and the reasons for catching up. The NUT stated that there had been a 35 per cent erosion in pay since Houghton in 1974. The unions wanted a return to Houghton because:

> it stressed the importance of the teachers' role in our society. Second, because it acknowledged that teachers' pay had fallen badly behind over a decade and sought to put that right. Third, because it gave the profession a new pay relativity with other sections of the community and recommended that the Salaries Index should be used when making future settlements.
>
> (NUT 1979a: 1)

As the NUT's official submission says:

> the Panel is seeking the re-establishment of the levels of external salary relativities established by the Houghton Committee in 1974 . . . it is the view of the teachers' panel and of the union, that the report of the 1974 Houghton Committee of Inquiry represented a correct and proper assessment of the levels of salaries to be paid to teachers relative to the pay of other employees.
>
> (NUT 1979b: 120)

The Clegg Commission used an elaborate comparability study to reassess the Houghton analysis, and ended up by recommending pay rises from 17 per cent for scale 1 qualified teachers up to 25 per cent for the most senior heads

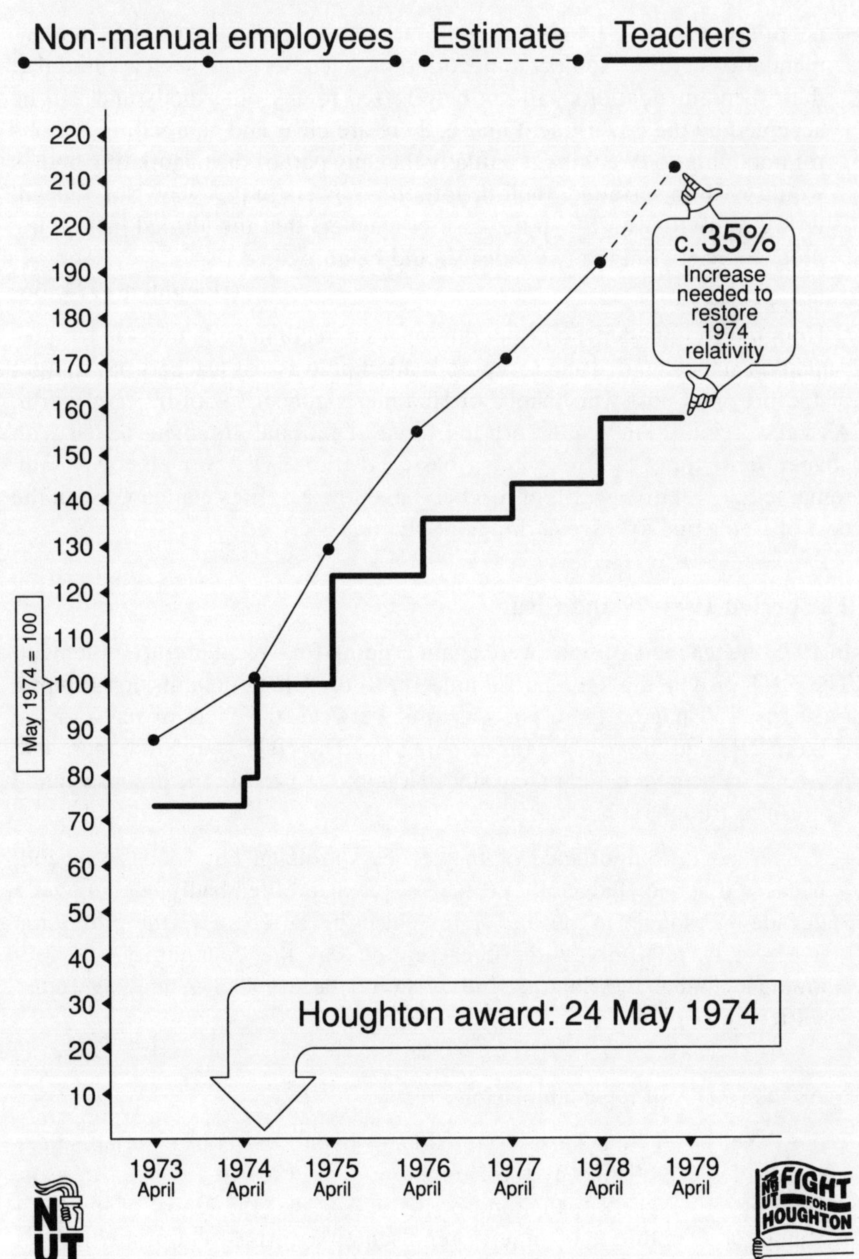

Figure 2.1 The NUT's case on pay erosion 1974–79

(Clegg 1980: 34–5). The exercise was fraught with difficulties and the Commission had to abandon the study by consultants as unsafe (Clegg 1980: 23). In the end, 'after deciding to set aside the results of the comparability study we had to look elsewhere for suitable comparator data. Like the Houghton Committee, we compared the salaries of graduate entrants to teaching with those of graduates going into other occupations' (Clegg 1980: 24). Despite this and the final awards teachers' pay remained below the relative levels recommended by Houghton.

Before we examine the situation since 1980 one further point needs to be made and that is the issue of differentials. The main source of these were the divide between classroom teacher scales and those of heads and deputies; the qualification levels; and gender. A major study of this last point noted that 'the male/female earnings differential of 22 per cent in the teaching profession arises partly from the greater concentration of women in the lower-paying primary sector, but mainly from differences in distribution by scale, men being relatively concentrated on higher scales' (Turnbull and Williams 1976: 968). The concentration of women in the primary sector is itself a reflection of choice by women and qualification constraints; and the relative position on lower scales is again associated with qualifications, and family related questions such as length of service and readiness to apply for and accept promotion (Turnbull and Williams 1974 and 1975).

The period 1980–94

By 1983 the salaries of teachers were given by the DES as ranging from £5,178 to £12,744 for classroom teachers and from £9,108 to £21,828 for heads (DES 1983: 15 and 18; see also Table 2.3). In January 1984 Keith Joseph made a major speech to the North of England Education Conference entitled 'Catastrophe or watershed?'. The answer, he believed, 'depends crucially not only on pay but also on the efficient use of resources' (Joseph 1984: 137). At the same time as the government sought higher standards in education it was announced that two-thirds of all teachers were earning less than the average weekly wage of £160 (*Times Educational Supplement* 20 January 1984: 1), and that more teacher jobs were being lost as a result of central government's cutbacks in local government funding.

In these circumstances the employers' offer of a 3 per cent pay rise in line with government pay policy was firmly rejected by the unions which asked for 7.5 per cent. There were already many signs of discontent among teachers with several LEAs experiencing industrial action over a range of issues. By April 1984 pay talks were deadlocked and when the employers refused to go to arbitration there followed a series of strikes in May and June. This was enough to force the employers to agree to arbitration, and in September the award of 5.1 per cent was made. Its inadequacy immediately prompted the unions to submit their 1985 claim with the threat of strike action.

The management panel case to the arbitration body was based on a set of

Table 2.3 Teachers' pay in 1983

Table 2.3a Qualified teachers (excluding head teachers and deputy head teachers) in schools, other than special schools and unqualified teachers to whom section 7(2) applies

Incremental			*Scales*		
point	*1*	2	*3*	*4*	*Senior teacher*
0	5,178	5,949	7,359	8,754	9,435
1	5,418	6,174	7,617	9,132	9,789
2	5,598	6,405	7,878	9,435	10,143
3	5,778	6,636	8,142	9,789	10,497
4	5,949	6,879	8,454	10,143	10,851
5	6,174	7,119	8,754	10,497	11,352
6	6,405	7,359	9,132	10,851	11,763
7	6,636	7,617	9,435	11,352	12,333
8	6,879	7,878	9,789	11,763	12,744
9	7,119	8,142	10,143	—	—
10	7,359	8,454	10,497	—	—
11	7,617	8,754	—	—	—
12	7,878	9,132	—	—	—
13	8,142	—	—	—	—

Source: DES

Table 2.3b Qualified deputy head teachers: schools, other than special schools

Incremental	*Group*											
point	*Below 4*	*4*	*5*	*6*	*7*	*8*	*9*	*10*	*11*	*12*	*13*	*14*
0	6,477	7,659	8,568	9,774	10,326	10,851	11,454	12,216	12,843	13,569	13,983	14,622
1	6,735	7,917	8,868	10,077	10,629	11,151	11,760	12,528	13,149	13,875	14,298	14,934
2	6,990	8,172	9,177	10,374	10,938	11,454	12,066	12,843	13,455	14,193	14,610	15,249
3	7,239	8,433	9,474	10,677	11,241	11,760	12,372	13,149	13,761	14,502	14,919	15,564
4	7,497	8,691	9,774	10,956	11,535	12,066	12,708	13,455	14,073	14,811	15,234	15,879
5	7,749	8,946	10,077	—	—	—	—	—	—	—	—	—
6	8,004	9,201	10,374	—	—	—	—	—	—	—	—	—
7	8,256	9,459	10,677	—	—	—	—	—	—	—	—	—
8	8,511	9,720	—	—	—	—	—	—	—	—	—	—
9	8,769	9,972	—	—	—	—	—	—	—	—	—	—
10	9,024	—	—	—	—	—	—	—	—	—	—	—
11	9,279	—	—	—	—	—	—	—	—	—	—	—

Source: DES

Table 2.3c Qualified head teachers: schools, other than special schools

Incremental	*Group*													
point	*1*	*2*	*3*	*4*	*5*	*6*	*7*	*8*	*9*	*10*	*11*	*12*	*13*	*14*
0	9,108	9,504	9,948	10,572	11,457	12,264	13,023	13,953	15,027	16,008	17.277	18,495	19,488	20,610
1	9,369	9,756	10,203	10,875	11,763	12,576	13,355	14,259	15,342	16,317	17.592	18,900	19,896	21,018
2	9,624	10,017	10,461	11,178	12,069	12,876	13,638	14,574	15,651	16,635	17.916	19,299	20,298	21,420
3	9,885	10,275	10,719	11,478	12,172	13,188	14,044	14,880	15,966	16,944	18.237	19,701	20,700	21,828
4	10,187	10,546	10,974	11,981	12,672	13,197	14,391	15,189	16,281	17,262	18.561	—	—	—

Source: DES

unconvincing arguments: lack of funds (affordability); that with high levels of unemployment they were not experiencing recruitment and retention problems (labour market); and that their final offer of 4.5 per cent was in line with settlements elsewhere in local government (comparability) (Management Panel 1984: 6 – see Table 2.4). The teacher panel's response was based on the restoration of the Houghton award through comparability (Teachers Panel 1984: 5 – see Table 2.5); and increased responsibilities of the job. The 1984 award restored nothing and left both Burnham and pay levels in a shambles. The resultant 1985–86 strike has been discussed above.

The first report of the IAC noted that the 1987 pay settlement imposed by the Secretary of State had given an average rise of 15.3 per cent to teachers and 18.4 per cent to heads (IAC 1988: 10), and it recommended a 1988 pay rise of 4.25 per cent across the board for all teachers. It also set the pattern for the following years of a national settlement with increasing scope for local flexibility and changes to the pay structure. This settlement did little to offset

Table 2.4 Teachers' pay settlements 1972–83

Date	*% increase*	*Primary and secondary: remarks*
1 April 1972	9.6	Arbitration award
1 April 1973	6.6	Negotiated settlement
1 April 1974	8.0	Negotiated settlement
24 May 1974	27.0	Houghton award: estimated to be worth 29% in the long term
1 April 1975	22.3	Arbitration award: included consolidation of threshold payments in payment since June 1974
1 April 1976	8.3	£6.00 p.w. pay policy
1 April 1977	3.8	£2.50/5%/£4.00 p.w. pay policy
1 April 1978	9.9	10% pay policy
1 April 1979	9.3	Plus £6.00 p.m. 'on account' and reference to the Standing Commission on Pay Comparability
1 January 1980	7.5	Subject to minimum increase of £288 a year £6.00 p.m. 'on account' deducted by 30 April 1980. Interim increase pending Standing Commission Report
1 January 1980	8.95	First half of Standing Commission Report based on uncorrected findings (full increases of 17–25%). Increase expressed as % of 1.4.79 salaries and is half of overall increase
1 April 1980	12	Arbitration award: increase as a % of full value of uncorrected Standing Commission findings (see also 1.9.80).
1 September 1980	8.95	Second part of Standing Commission findings. Increase expressed as % of 1.4.79 salaries.
	2.5 to 4%	Arbitration award: increase on full value of uncorrected Standing Commission findings.
1 April 1981	7.5	Negotiated settlement
1 April 1982	6.0	Arbitration award
1 April 1983	4.98	Negotiated settlement

Source: 1984 Management Panel submission to the arbitral body

Table 2.5 Movements in teachers' earnings compared with movements in average salaries

Date	*Salaries index (men and women)* *Index*	*£*	*Teachers' average salary (£)*	*Teachers' salaries as % of average salaries*
April 1974	157.0	2,259	2,440	108.0
May 1974[a]	157.0	2,259	3,098	137.2
April 1975	202.9	2,919	3,789	129.8
April 1976	244.5	3,518	4,287	121.9
April 1977	267.3	3,846	4,493	116.8
April 1978	300.0	4,317	5,007	116.0
April 1979	336.2	4,837	5,526	114.2
April 1980	420.7	6,053	6,743	111.4
April 1981	487.4	7,013	8,132	116.0
April 1982	533.0	7,669	8,801	114.8
April 1983	581.9	8,373	9,240	110.4
April 1984	627.0[b] (est.)	9,022 (est.)	9,656[c]	107.0

Source: 1984 Teacher Panel submission to the arbitral body

Notes:

[a] The Houghton Committee stated that 'Our proposed scales etc. are appropriate as at 24 May 1974. They may also be regarded as broadly appropriate at April 1974.'

[b] The estimate of the salaries index for April 1984 is derived by increasing the April 1983 figure by 7.75% (The increase in average earnings over this 12-month period)

[c] The 1984 estimate for teachers' is derived by increasing the April 1984 figure by 4.5%

the high level of teacher vacancies and falling morale and status of the profession (*Times Educational Supplement*, 22 September 1988: 9). The 1989 IAC report awarded 6 per cent to classroom teachers and 7.5 per cent for heads. As the TES editorial said 'the teachers' pay award is a bit better than most people expected, but the more closely you read the report of the IAC, the more inadequate it looks' (*Times Educational Supplement*, 24 February 1989: 20). This settlement further eroded teachers' pay and seemed to store up trouble ahead. Of course 1988 was dominated by the ERA, but teachers and their unions took the opportunity to argue that the government's reforms could only work with a well paid, well qualified and well motivated teaching force.

In 1990 the IAC recommended differential pay rises for different points on the scales, made major changes to incentive allowances, and imposed a pay spine for heads and deputies (Table 2.6). The last IAC report in 1991 proposed a 9.5 per cent award for all classroom teachers and 12.75 per cent for heads (Table 2.7). In 1992 the STRB replaced the IAC and its first award was for 7.5 per cent across the board. In 1993 the STRB recommended 1 per cent plus 0.5 per cent for assimilation onto the new pay spine thus keeping within government guidelines (STRB 1993: viii). In 1994 the STRB awarded 2.9 per cent across the board (STRB 1994: viii and Figure 2.2) and left the question of funding the cost to others. In both 1993 and 1994 the STRB made it clear that the award would do nothing to improve morale and would further erode the teachers' pay position, but that government economic policy was the overriding consideration in the final pay rise.

Table 2.6 Teachers' pay increase in 1990
Table 2.6a Pay increases for all teachers except heads and deputies

Incremental point	*Annual salary from 1.4.89 (£)*	*Recommended salary from 1.4.90 (£)*
1	8,394	9,000
2	8,730	9,500
3	9,060	10,000
4	9,390	10,500
5	10,167	11,000
6	11,046	11,750
7	11,712	12,500
8	12,372	13,250
9	13,092	14,000
10	13,923	15,000
11	14,694	16,000

Table 2.6b Pay spine for heads and deputies

Point	*Salary (£)*	*Point*	*Salary (£)*
1	18,300	26	26,400
2	18,600	27	26,800
3	18,900	28	27,200
4	19,200	29	27,600
5	19,500	30	28,100
6	19,800	31	28,600
7	20,100	32	29,100
8	20,400	33	29,600
9	20,700	34	30,100
10	21,000	35	30,600
11	21,300	36	31,100
12	21,600	37	31,600
13	21,900	38	32,300
14	22,200	39	33,000
15	22,500	40	33,700
16	22,800	41	34,400
17	23,100	42	35,100
18	23,400	43	35,800
19	23,700	44	36,500
20	24,000	45	37,200
21	24,400	46	37,900
22	24,800	47	38,600
23	25,200	48	39,300
24	25,600	49	40,000
25	26,000		

Source: IAC 1990

Table 2.6c Numbers and distribution of incentive allowances

	September 1989	*September 1990 (government plans)*	*September 1990 (committee recommendations)*
Primary			
A	37,000	37,000	40,000
B	19,200	19,200	20,000
C	3,000	4,000	4,000
Total	59,200	60,200	64,000
Secondary			
A	29,000	29,000	31,000
B	33,700	25,400	32,000
C	17,200	25,000	25,000
D	26,000	24,000	26,000
E	9,500	11,000	11,000
Total	115,400	114,400	125,000
Total primary and secondary	174,600	174,600	189,000

Table 2.6d Incentive allowance rates

Rate	*Annual amount from 1.4.89 (£)*	*Recommended from 1.4.90 (£)*
A	858	925
B	1,284	1,500
C	2,568	3,000
D	3,426	4,000
E	4,710	5,500

Source: IAC 1990

This is supported by a more detailed analysis of the NES data for the period 1986 to 1993. Table 2.8 provides average gross salary figures and the changes between 1986 and 1993 showed that secondary teachers (increase for men 91 per cent and women 94 per cent) had done better than those in the primary sector (increase for men 89 per cent and women 86 per cent). This pattern in favour of the secondary sector is further supported when the analysis is based on medians. In Table 2.9 the secondary teachers' median salary rose by 94 per cent for men and 97 per cent for women, while for primary teachers it was 90 per cent for men and 86 per cent for women. The relative spread of earnings has remained fairly constant. The ratio of the highest to lowest decile in earnings was between 1.6 and 1.8 for all categories of staff and has not changed significantly as between 1986 and 1993. This indicates that the internal relativities have remained largely untouched.

In 1994 a pay bill freeze looks set to stay for at least another two years, with pay rises only allowed through 'productivity' improvements. This is set

Table 2.7 Teachers' pay in 1990

Table 2.7a All schools: numbers of teachers by main scale point and distribution of incentive allowances by main scale point

Main scale point	*Total nos*	*Full-time regular teachers*					*Total FTEs*	*Part-time regular teachers (FTE)*					*PT reg nos*
		Incentive allowances						*Incentive allowances*					
		A	*B*	*C*	*D*	*E*		*A*	*B*	*C*	*D*	*E*	
1	935	10	16	3	2	—	52	—	1	—	—	—	102
2	982	11	17	—	—	—	89	1	5	—	—	—	220
3	1,267	44	36	2	—	1	145	1	7	—	—	—	300
4	6,553	176	140	4	3	1	309	6	9	—	—	—	650
5	8,442	545	298	17	2	8	512	12	25	1	—	—	1,087
6	9,309	1,247	652	39	7	10	962	22	39	1	—	1	2,061
7	9,500	1,519	1,018	80	19	16	1,652	43	89	4	—	—	3,481
8	16,315	3,311	2,517	288	71	17	2,387	82	117	7	2	—	5,001
9	18,069	3,511	3,300	563	136	16	2,838	89	170	13	3	2	5,807
10	21,572	4,642	4,370	840	284	31	3,825	131	240	15	4	1	7,614
11	159,729	21,983	45,521	14,346	20,049	6,298	4,927	198	456	59	39	13	9,683
Total	252,673	36,999	57,885	16,182	20,573	6,398	17,698	585	1,158	100	48	17	36,006
%	—	14.64	22.91	6.40	8.14	2.53		3.31	6.54	0.57	0.27	0.10	

Notes: Basic paybill £4,020.436m; incentive allowances £290.046m; average salary £15,943

Table 2.7b Primary schools: numbers of teachers by main scale point and distribution of incentive allowances by main scale point

Main scale point	*Total nos*	*Full-time regular teachers* *Incentive allowances* *A*	*B*	*C*	*D*	*E*	*Total FTEs*	*Part-time regular teachers (FTE)* *Incentive allowances* *A*	*B*	*C*	*D*	*E*	*PR reg nos*
1	586	4	2	2	—	—	31	—	—	—	—	—	62
2	537	3	—	—	—	—	50	—	—	—	—	—	112
3	669	23	4	—	—	1	86	—	3	—	—	—	189
4	3,869	87	13	—	—	1	182	5	—	—	—	—	395
5	5,069	305	61	3	1	3	307	7	—	1	—	—	674
6	5,293	703	153	2	3	9	586	16	2	—	—	—	1,313
7	5,403	861	290	6	4	13	973	28	11	1	—	—	2,118
8	8,487	1,823	738	28	7	11	1,330	56	21	—	2	—	2,876
9	9,134	1,860	1,042	62	10	11	1,467	55	30	7	1	1	3,095
10	10,691	2,689	1,419	104	15	12	1,866	83	29	2	1	—	3,795
11	54,649	11,668	12,915	1,383	229	77	1,857	100	59	7	2	3	3,715
Total	104,387	20,026	16,637	1,590	269	138	8,735	350	155	18	6	4	18,344
%	—	19.18	15.94	1.52	0.26	0.13	—	4.01	1.77	0.21	0.07	0.05	—

Notes: Basic paybill £1,640.387m; incentive allowances £50.777m; average salary £14,950

Table 2.7c Secondary schools: numbers of teachers by main scale point and distribution of incentive allowances by main scale point

Main scale point	Total nos	Full-time regular teachers Incentive allowance A	B	C	D	E	Total FTEs	Part-time regular teachers (FTE) Incentive allowances A	B	C	D	E	PT reg nos
1	331	5	3	1	2	—	18	—	—	—	—	—	34
2	423	8	1	—	—	—	33	1	—	—	—	—	98
3	551	21	4	2	—	—	49	1	—	—	—	—	96
4	2,557	87	31	—	3	—	110	1	2	—	—	—	225
5	3,157	234	71	9	1	5	163	4	5	—	—	—	339
6	3,662	539	216	24	2	1	316	5	2	1	—	—	634
7	3,612	644	359	56	13	3	554	12	8	1	—	—	1,111
8	6,887	1,467	1,065	193	57	6	878	22	10	3	—	—	1,771
9	7,709	1,615	1,385	384	114	5	1,162	32	23	3	2	1	2,291
10	9,309	1,904	1,865	589	230	16	1,621	43	29	9	3	1	3,140
11	93,821	9,997	26,300	10,941	18,771	5,870	2,553	88	118	36	30	6	5,000
Total	132,019	16,521	31,300	12,199	19,193	5,906	7,457	209	197	53	35	8	14,739
%	—	12.51	23.71	9.24	14.54	4.47	—	2.80	2.64	0.71	0.47	0.11	—

Notes: Basic paybill £2,110.175m; incentive allowances £208.999m; average salary £16,628

Table 2.7d Special schools: numbers of teachers by main scale point and distribution of incentive allowances by main scale point

Main scale point	Total nos	Full-time regular teachers Incentive allowances A	B	C	D	E	Total FTEs	Part-time regular teachers (FTE) Incentive allowances A	B	C	D	E	PT reg nos
1	9	—	9	—	—	—	1	—	1	—	—	—	3
2	15	—	15	—	—	—	4	—	4	—	—	—	5
3	26	—	26	—	—	—	4	—	4	—	—	—	6
4	98	—	94	4	—	—	6	—	6	—	—	—	11
5	167	—	162	5	—	—	19	—	19	—	—	—	34
6	283	—	270	12	1	—	31	—	30	—	—	1	57
7	354	—	336	17	1	—	65	—	64	1	—	—	125
8	736	—	671	62	3	—	78	—	74	4	—	—	150
9	897	—	782	106	9	—	104	—	102	2	—	—	197
10	1,076	—	939	123	13	1	158	—	155	2	—	—	294
11	6,997	—	4,959	1,643	297	98	247	—	233	13	2	—	449
Total	10,658	—	8,263	1,972	324	99	717	—	692	22	2	1	1,331
%	—	0.00	77.53	18.50	3.04	0.93	—	0.00	96.51	3.07	0.28	0.14	—

Notes: Basic paybill £171.848m; incentive allowances £21.251m; average salary £16,980

Table 2.7e Distribution of heads and deputies by new school group

School Group	*Primary*		*Secondary*		*Special*		*S56/other*		*Total*	
	Head	*Deputy*	*Head*	*Deputy*	*Head*	*Deputy*	*Head*	*Deputy*	*Head*	*Deputy*
1	5,053	2,918	12	14	—	—	125	18	5,190	2,950
2/1(s)	8,891	8,818	140	147	314	306	227	154	9,572	9,425
3/2(s)	2,243	2,240	347	404	570	544	98	82	3,258	3,270
4/3(s)	49	81	604	1,229	161	251	41	78	855	1,639
5/4(s)	1	4	1,627	3,901	7	23	18	66	1,653	3,994
6	2	—	510	1,406	—	—	3	14	515	1,420
Total	16,239	14,061	3,240	7,101	1,052	1,124	512	412	21,043	22,698
Average salary (£)	21,237	18,873	29,857	26,633	23,773	19,993	22,441	20,421	20,446	20,488

Notes: Paybill head teachers, £478.139m; Paybill deputies, £464.054m

Table 2.7f Summary of average salaries (excluding on-costs)

	Primary	*Secondary*	*Special*	*All schools*
Heads	21,237	29,857	23,773	22,721
Deputies	18,873	23,633	19,993	20,446
Main scale teachers (including incentive allowances)	14,950	16,628	16,980	15,943

Source IAC (1991)

Notes: Based on returns from 83 LEAs; main scale teacher figures include FTE of part-time teachers; all figures exclude London area allowances and inner London area supplements.

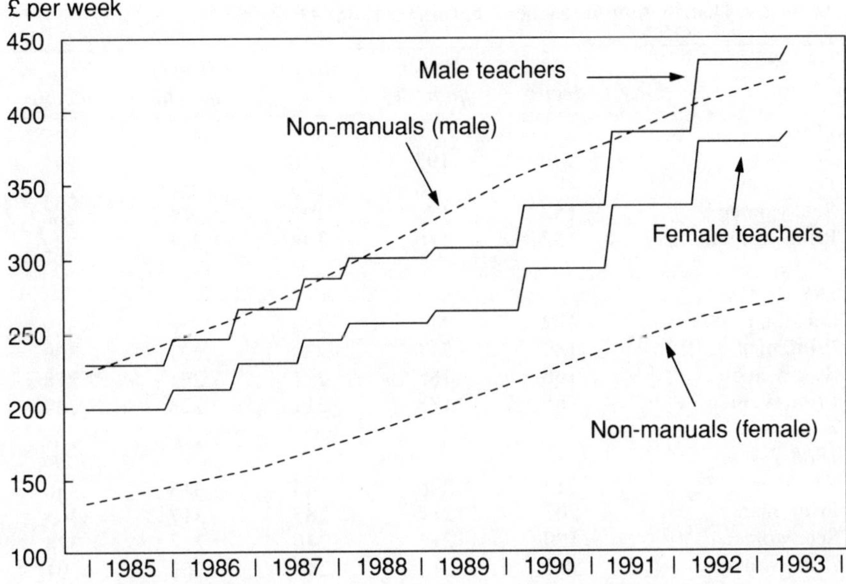

Figure 2.2 Average earnings of teachers (maintained schools in England and Wales) and all non-manual workers, by gender, 1985–93

Table 2.8 Average gross weekly earnings of teachers, 1986–93 (£)

Year		*Secondary*	*Primary*
1986	Men	233	227
1986	Women	202	198
1987	Men	250	242
1987	Women	218	209
1988	Men	287	283
1988	Women	250	240
1989	Men	309	299
1989	Women	271	258
1990	Men	338	327
1990	Women	301	285
1991	Men	381	373
1991	Women	338	320
1992	Men	435	414
1992	Women	382	362
1993	Men	444	430
1993	Women	391	369

Source: New Earnings Survey

Table 2.9 Distribution of teachers' earnings, 1986–93

	Lowest decile	*Lower quartile*	*Median*	*Higher quartile*	*Highest decile*
1986					
Sec. men	170	197	228	257	297
Prim. men	178	198	225	251	277
Sec. women	152	171	197	226	260
Prim. women	152	176	198	215	242
1987					
Sec. men	182	211	242	278	319
Prim. men	189	211	239	271	300
Sec. women	166	188	211	241	278
Prim. women	165	188	211	228	259
1988					
Sec. men	213	246	275	315	358
Prim. men	207	247	285	317	345
Sec. women	190	213	246	274	324
Prim. women	182	213	246	262	301
1989					
Sec. men	235	267	299	344	382
Prim. men	223	267	300	340	369
Sec. women	202	236	267	296	345
Prim. women	189	227	265	289	317
1990					
Sec. men	262	298	331	373	417
Prim. men	255	299	330	366	400
Sec. women	224	267	302	331	373
Prim. women	210	253	286	314	354
1991					
Sec. men	302	336	377	409	461
Prim. men	261	332	376	417	452
Sec. women	244	306	337	374	408
Prim. women	227	278	330	358	397
1992					
Sec. men	339	383	430	470	539
Prim. men	288	362	412	472	509
Sec. women	270	343	385	430	470
Prim. women	258	316	362	401	455
1993					
Sec. men	342	388	443	482	557
Prim. men	300	368	427	492	533
Sec. women	289	362	389	443	485
Prim. women	262	327	369	405	460

Source: New Earnings Survey

alongside the slow introduction of performance-related pay, low levels of recruitment, an uncertain future for Review Bodies, and loss of pay relative to the private sector (IDS 1994: 1). The two key issues for school teachers are workload and performance-related pay (IDS 1994: 92). These points are supported by a recent survey of developments in public sector industrial relations which takes a damning view of government policy in this area. 'In imposing pay norms and specific criteria, the government has been wrong-footed by trying to reconcile the irreconcilable. To move away from national-level collective bargaining, as they have done through the use of a range of alternative mechanisms, requires a degree of independence from central government to which ministers have paid avid lip-service, but in practice have diluted by recent actions' (Bailey 1994: 119). Bailey later highlights the tensions between review bodies setting national wage levels and local employment units trying to be flexible in response to budgets. The most important point however, given the IDS evidence from the New Earnings Survey of relative falls in teacher pay, is that 'the predominant concern of public sector union leaders, past and present, has been the pay of their members relative to the private sector as a whole, or sections within it' (Bailey 1994: 127). Or as Jack Dash, the unofficial dockers' leader, put it more bluntly the purpose of trade union activity with regard to employers is to 'separate them from their cash' (Dash 1969: 174).

This analysis of teachers' pay has shown that since 1987 and the abolition of collective bargaining the system has been dominated by government's economic and political concerns rather than the needs of the education service and/or the advice of the experts – even those experts appointed by government onto the IAC and STRB. Others have affirmed our general concern over the lack of any government strategy that 'in the context of the 1988 Education Act, pay determination requirements remain unclear' (Bailey and Trinder 1989: 16), and that the major determinant of teacher pay has been and still is based on notions such as the 'going rate' and 'fair rate' (Beeton 1989: 10).

In these circumstances we would expect increasingly low levels of national pay settlements as government seeks to reduce *de facto* the power and importance of the STRB and national pay rates as it further cuts funding and substitutes them for market-driven school pay policies based on performance and business needs. 'Governing bodies of all schools are beginning to realise the enormity and complexity of the issues surrounding local management of salaries' (AGIT-LDBS 1991: 1), and 'governing bodies, too, need to produce a pay policy' (Unwin and Weeks 1991: 28).

What we have tried to show is that such policies in the past have led to disaster – either protracted strike action with all that entails in lost education, disrupted school effort and alienated teaching staff, or to low morale and teachers withdrawing effort and leaving the profession and young students not opting for teaching as a profession. The immediate future is bleak. Government now dominates national pay determination with no interest in long-term supply issues and no concern for the views of the teachers, their unions and their employers. Local pay determination is fraught with dangers for the profession and the education of the children. The heart of the problem remains the fact that government is devolving 'responsibility for decisions to schools themselves' (*Choice and Diversity*, DFE 1992a: 55), but not power. In the case of pay, the most important cost for all schools, power to decide pay levels will reside with central government through funding limits, and the extent to which teachers can be saved from the 'rough justice' of such national schemes when wedded to arbitrary and inconsistent local decisions will largely depend on the role of the unions in any localised bargaining system.

3 Teachers and their organisations

INTRODUCTION

Teachers make up one of the largest single occupational groups in the economy, but they are divided between six trade unions organising teachers in state schools in England and Wales; the National Union of Teachers (NUT), the National Association of Schoolmasters and Union of Women Teachers (NASUWT), the Association of Teachers and Lecturers (ATL – formerly the Assistant Masters and Mistresses Association, AMMA), the National Association of Head Teachers (NAHT), the Secondary Heads Association (SHA) and the Professional Association of Teachers (PAT). The Educational Institute of Scotland (EIS) is the main union for teachers in Scotland's different state education sector.

There is increasing evidence among teachers that there is overwhelming support for the principle of a single organisation to represent teachers, and the continuing existence of such a number of unions has long been a source of frustration among teachers and of puzzlement among observers. Teacher trade unionism has a long and complex history, and we argue here that the current structure of teacher unionism is rooted in the early struggles of the teacher organisations to gain some control over the conditions of their members' working lives as the state education system took shape. Different strands of trade unionism emerged as the workforce changed shape. The characteristics of the three main classroom unions, NUT, NASUWT and ATL, are rooted in distinct, but not necessarily separate, trade union traditions.

Teacher unions have played a major role in shaping the education system as a whole. Teachers organised themselves into strong associations to address their concerns about their conditions of service and about their professional activities – aspects of teaching that are in fact inextricably bound together. The dominant strand of teacher trade unionism for over some hundred and twenty years has been embodied within the NUT, exemplified by this union's traditional concern with collective bargaining as the main method to determine the rights of teachers and with the enforcement of a single national pay scale – the rate for the job – as a central organising principle.

This chapter explores the three main trade union traditions, how they came to be adopted, and their continuing relevance. First, we examine the structure and composition of the teacher workforce, looking at the development of the state education system, at the growth of the teaching occupation, and at the school as a place of work. We outline the importance of the labour market for teachers, briefly considering the stability of the workforce, and we consider the nature of teaching as a job. We then discuss the different forms of trade unionism, drawing from the main literature on trade unions. This provides us with a starting point for a look at teacher organisations, where we put forward a taxonomy of teacher unions that draws out the main differences between them. This sets the context for an analysis of the growth of the teacher organisations, and for an examination of their structures and their internal organisation.

THE TEACHER WORKFORCE AND WORKPLACES

The workforce

This section explores the main differences within the profession as discussed in relation to pay in the previous chapter, and then makes brief comments on the labour market and workplace features necessary to understand the development of teacher trade unionism. In 1992 there were 442,000 teachers employed by LEAs in England and Wales (STRB 1993: 63). Nearly 400,000 teachers have full-time teaching posts in about 25,000 English and Welsh nursery, primary and secondary schools. About two-thirds of the full-time teachers are women, a proportion that has been more or less constant throughout the post-war period, while other characteristics of the teacher workforce have shown marked change. Four-fifths of the 179,000 full-time primary school teachers, and nearly half of the 206,000 full-time secondary teachers, are women.

Primary school teachers outnumbered secondary by at least two to one until the post-war period, as shown in Table 3.1. The expanding primary sector was overtaken by the even more rapidly expanding secondary sector in the 1970s, with the secondary sector continuing to embrace a growing proportion of teachers during the contraction of the 1980s. The primary sector employs about the same number of teachers now as it did in 1930, whereas the number of secondary teachers has increased tenfold in the same period. There are now more teachers in the secondary sector than there are in the primary.

During the post-war period the ratio of men to women secondary teachers has remained fairly constant at about 45 per cent, while in the primary sector, which has grown much less rapidly, the proportion of women has grown from three-quarters to four-fifths, as shown in Tables 3.2 and 3.3. In both sectors the proportion of graduates has increased significantly. Three-fifths of secondary teachers are graduates, compared with one in four primary teachers.

Table 3.1 Full-time teachers in England and Wales (thousands, selected years)

Year	*All*	*Primary*		*Secondary*	
		N	*%*	*N*	*%*
1900	119	119	99	—	—
1910	173	163	94	10	6
1920	186	168	90	18	10
1930	194	172	88	23	12
1937	196	170	87	26	13
1946	196	128	65	68	35
1950	208	130	63	77	37
1960	269	133	49	137	51
1970	326	162	50	161	50
1980	442	198	45	244	55
1986	403	171	43	231	57
1991	385	179	47	206	53

Source: DES

Table 3.2 Full-time men, women and graduate primary teachers in England and Wales (thousands, selected years)

Year	*All*		*Women*			*Men*		
	N	*Grads %*	*N*	*%*	*Grads %*	*N*	*%*	*Grads %*
1950	130	3	95	73	2	36	27	6
1960	133	—	101	76	—	32	24	—
1970	162	5	121	75	4	41	25	7
1980	198	15	152	77	13	46	23	20
1986	171	26	134	79	24	37	21	33
1991	179	—	144	81	—	35	19	—

Source: DES

Table 3.3 Full-time men, women and graduate secondary teachers in England and Wales (thousands, selected years)

Year	*All*		*Women*			*Men*		
	N	*Grads %*	*N*	*%*	*Grads %*	*N*	*%*	*Grads %*
1950	77	38	35	45	36	42	55	41
1960	137	—	62	45	—	75	55	—
1970	161	36	67	41	31	94	59	40
1980	244	50	110	45	45	135	55	54
1986	231	61	108	47	57	124	53	64
1991	206	—	99	48	—	107	—	—

Source: DES

Tables 3.4–3.10 look at women and men teachers separately and in more detail. The proportion of teachers who are graduates has trebled and, while the gap between women and men has narrowed, nearly two-thirds of men now hold graduate level qualifications compared with two-fifths of women. Meanwhile the proportion of teachers who are head teachers has also changed. Fully one-third of male primary teachers are head teachers, compared with only one in fourteen women.

In 1950 three-quarters of women teachers and nearly half of men worked in primary schools. By 1986 the balance had shifted considerably. The number of male primary teachers was nearly the same, but this represented only a quarter of all male teachers. The number of women primary teachers increased by about 50 per cent, but the number of women secondary teachers trebled over the period. However, the number of male secondary teachers also trebled.

Table 3.4 Women teachers in England and Wales, selected years

Year	*Total thousands*	*Graduates % of total*	*Heads % of total*
1950	130	11	12
1960	163	13	9
1970	190	13	6
1980	262	27	4
1986	242	39	5

Source: DES

Table 3.5 Women primary teachers in England and Wales, selected years

Year	*Total thousands*	*% of all women teachers*	*Graduates % of total*	*Heads % of total*
1950	95	73	2	12
1960	101	62	—	12
1970	121	74	4	8
1980	152	58	13	7
1986	135	56	24	7

Source: DES

Table 3.6 Women secondary teachers in England and Wales, selected years

Year	*Total thousands*	*% of all women teachers*	*Graduates % of total*	*Heads % of total*
1950	35	27	36	10
1960	62	38	—	3
1970	67	35	31	2
1980	110	42	45	1
1986	108	44	57	1

Source: DES

Table 3.7 Men teachers in England and Wales, selected years

Year	*Total thousands*	*Graduates % of total*	*Heads % of total*
1950	77	25	16
1960	107	32	14
1970	136	30	13
1980	180	46	10
1986	160	57	10

Source: DES

Table 3.8 Men primary teachers in England and Wales, selected years

Year	*Total thousands*	*% of all men teachers*	*Graduates % of total*	*Heads % of total*
1950	36	46	6	15
1960	32	30	—	31
1970	41	30	7	32
1980	46	25	20	29
1986	37	23	33	32

Source: DES

Table 3.9 Men secondary teachers in England and Wales, selected years

Year	*Total thousands*	*% of all men teachers*	*Graduates % of total*	*Heads % of total*
1950	42	54	41	18
1960	74	70	—	7
1970	94	69	40	5
1980	134	75	54	3
1986	124	77	64	3

Source: DES

Table 3.10 Head teachers in England and Wales, selected years

Year	*All*			*Primary*			*Secondary*		
	N thousands	*Men %*	*Women %*	*N thousands*	*Men %*	*Women %*	*N thousands*	*Men %*	*Women %*
1950	27.9	46	54	16.8	32	68	11.1	67	33
1960	29.3	52	48	22.2	44	56	7.1	74	26
1970	29.0	60	40	23.4	56	44	5.5	78	22
1980	28.7	61	39	23.6	56	44	5.1	84	16
1986	26.8	59	41	21.8	54	46	4.9	83	17

Source: DES

The main divisions within the teacher workforce are those between primary and secondary, women and men, qualified and unqualified, and classroom teacher and head. They are important factors in our examination of industrial relations today – the composition of the workforce has a significant bearing on both the nature of trade unionism and on the conduct of industrial relations. These are discussed in more detail later in this chapter, but for now the following main points can be summarised.

First, the state sector has become more evenly balanced between the primary and secondary sectors. The concerns of secondary school teachers have acquired more and more importance during the post-war years. Differential pay between the two sectors has been a major concern, particularly of the NUT, and, although a common pay structure has existed since 1919, average earnings have remained higher in the secondary sector (see chapter 2).

Secondly, the primary sector is mostly female, while the secondary sector is evenly divided between women and men. However, women are less likely to be promoted than men, with men taking most head teacher positions and receiving higher average earnings in both sectors.

Third is the trend towards an all-graduate occupation. The issue of qualifications is important for the organisations of skilled and professional workers as they strive to protect their members under adverse labour market conditions. Most teachers, and many commentators, draw a distinction between the practices of professional associations and other trade unions. We consider this point in more detail below.

Arguments about differential pay between the primary and secondary sectors, about separate bargaining arrangements for heads and deputies, about teacher accreditation and training, and about equal opportunities are central industrial relations issues. These concerns of teachers have been a major factor in determining the types of unions that they have built, a theme that we return to later in this chapter when we discuss the development of the trade unions. As Turner (1962) and Hughes (1967) have argued, the structure and composition of the workforce has a powerful influence over the development of trade unionism.

The labour market

Levels of both supply and demand for teachers are determined through a combination of political decisions, mostly to do with the level of funding, and through analysis of demographic trends. Levels of spending on both teacher training and on teacher salaries have an impact on the number of entrants to teaching. Political decisions about spending levels and about the ratio of pupils to teachers have an impact on the flows of labour into and out of the teaching profession.

The number of primary school students rose from just under 4 million in 1950 to just over 5 million in 1972, and then fell steadily to just over 3.5 million in 1985. A rise to about 4.2 million is projected for the year 2000. In the secondary sector, the number of students rose from 1.7 million in 1950 to 4.1 million in 1979, falling to just under 3 million in 1991, with a projected rise to 3.3 million in 2000. As the DES noted 'during the 1960s a period of acute teacher shortage at a time of a rapidly growing pupil population was followed by a vastly increased supply of teachers, which culminated in the 1970s in teacher unemployment' (DES 1990: 1). The pattern of growth in the post-war period till the early 1960s contributed to the relative stability of industrial relations, with difficulties then emerging in the allocation of teacher labour, and eventually to industrial action.

The allocation of teachers between subject areas has been constantly debated throughout the life of the comprehensive state system, with shortages of some subject teachers occurring at the same time as the over-supply of others. For example, the 1988 Secondary School Staffing survey showed that 71 per cent of tuition in Computer Studies was by teachers without a post-A level qualification in the subject, compared with 19 per cent of Physics and 8 per cent of French. On average, 28 per cent of tuition was by teachers without a post-A level qualification in the subject. Making the large adjustments necessary to correct these imbalances raises important industrial relations issues to do with pay, training, workload and job security. Similar problems can occur between the primary and secondary sectors when rates of expansion or contraction are different. There are also regional variations, with shortages occurring throughout the 1980s in London and the rest of southeast England.

Not all those who train to be teachers actually become teachers. About a third of those qualifying in the early 1980s did not become teachers in the two years after qualifying (Education, Science and Arts Committee 1990: 19). The flow of teachers out of teaching in state schools has increased steadily throughout the 1980s, from 7.5 per cent in 1982 to 10.3 per cent in 1991 (STRB 1993: 74). About 6 per cent of teachers change jobs in the state education sector each year (IAC 1991: 71). These relatively low rates of wastage and turnover create a favourable recruitment climate for the trade unions, and are conducive to stable workplace industrial relations.

New recruits from the external labour market into teaching include new entrants, mature entrants, and re-entrants. During the 1980s the proportion of re-entrants has increased from 32 per cent of all entrants in 1980 to 58 per cent in 1988, falling back to 52 per cent in 1991 (STRB 1993: 80). Retention of membership during time out of teaching has become an important part of maintaining union numbers and in focusing on changes in union policy and bargaining priorities.

The workplaces

Table 3.11 shows that between 1950 and 1972 the number of schools was fairly constant at about 23,000 primary schools and 5,000 secondary. While the number of primary schools remained constant, the number of pupils increased by 30 per cent and the pupil : teacher ratio declined from 30 : 1 (it had been 48 : 1 in 1900) to 26 : 1. In the secondary sector, the number of schools increased by 10 per cent while the number of pupils doubled and the pupil : teacher ratio dropped from over 20 : 1 to 18 : 1. Schools were getting bigger, with the number of pupils rising rapidly while the number of teachers rose even faster. Subsequently during the 1970s the primary sector contracted, followed predictably by contraction in the secondary sector in the 1980s. An upturn of primary school pupil numbers in the late 1980s is set to continue into the next century.

Table 3.11 State sector pupils and schools, selected years

	Primary			Secondary		
	Schools thousands	*Pupils millions*	*Pupils/ school*	*Schools thousands*	*Pupils millions*	*Pupils/ school*
1950	23.1	3.96	171	4.77	1.70	356
1955	23.7	4.60	194	5.14	1.91	372
1965	22.9	4.27	187	5.86	2.82	481
1970	23.1	4.91	213	5.39	3.05	566
1976	23.4	4.77	204	4.92	3.93	789
1981	23.0	4.07	177	4.89	4.08	834
1986	21.3	3.57	167	4.52	3.60	796
1988	21.1	3.62	172	4.38	3.28	748
1989	21.0	4.17	199	4.27	3.14	735

Source: DES

The average number of teachers in each primary school has increased during the post-war period from about five to about eight, while in secondary schools the increase has been threefold, from about 16 to over 50. Industrial relations are affected by workplace size. Both the Labour Force Surveys (*Employment Gazette*, January 1993) and the Workplace Industrial Relations Surveys (Daniel and Millward 1983; Millward and Stevens 1986; Millward *et al.* 1992) showed that, *ceteris paribus*, union density increases with the number of employees in the workplace, suggesting that secondary schools are likely to be more organised than primary. Small workplaces present organisational difficulties for unions, and it could be argued that there is a 'critical mass' of potential members that must be present in a workplace before a high level of membership density can be developed. In their analysis of the 1991 Labour Force Survey Beatson and Butcher comment that 'union density was considerably higher in workplaces with 25 or more employees' (1993: 673). Nevertheless, as we show later in this chapter, schools are highly unionised even though they tend to fall within the category of 'small' when measured by the number of employees. The significance of the relatively small size of primary schools as employment units will be more important when school managers seek to introduce HRM practices into schools, and when conflict may be difficult to resolve at the level of the school once formal industrial relations procedures have been removed.

The notion of 'critical mass' also applies to union representation and organisation. Larger workplaces are more likely to have a union representative among the employees; in 1984 half of establishments employing fewer than twenty-five non-manual workers had a union representative, compared with three-quarters of establishments employing 25–100 (Millward and Stevens 1986: 79). Brown *et al.* concluded from their earlier survey that there may be 'a critical size for steward continuity, with workplaces of under 500 manual employees having a significant tendency to have less continuity of service' (Brown *et al.* 1978: 142). They found that the degree of organisation, durability and other indicators of well developed and stable union organisation all showed a positive correlation with size of workplace. This has not been the case for schools, but current pressures to create school-level employers in the form of heads and governors may make it harder for unions to organise and represent their members. On the other hand the tradition of trade union membership allied with emerging issues such as redundancy and performance-related pay may help to strengthen the trade union position.

There is one further difference between schools in the state sector – between the LEA maintained schools and the voluntary schools. Over a fifth of pupils in the maintained sector attend some 3,000 voluntary controlled and 5,000 voluntary aided schools (Harris 1990: 12–13). Two-thirds of these are Church of England, with the remaining third being mainly Roman Catholic. Tensions between teachers in the church schools and in the non-denominational schools affected the developing teacher organisations in the early days of the school system (Tropp 1957: 153). The creation of grant-maintained status has introduced a further division within the state sector, which may renew the basis for such tensions. The tendency of the reform process to break down the uniform national system could have a disintegrating impact on the trade unions. On the other hand, the recession-driven process of closure of some schools and expansion of others may lead to higher concentrations of teachers. What happens will partly depend on the nature and history of the teacher trade unions.

TEACHER TRADE UNIONISM

Types of union

One common way of defining trade unions is to divide them into the categories of craft, industrial and general:

> Craft unions are those which organise workers practising a particular skill, or practising any one of a group of related skills. Industrial unions are those which organise all workers in a given industry, whatever the job they perform. General unions are those which organise all workers regardless of skill or industry, or at least workers of various grades in a number of industries.
>
> (Clegg 1972: 41)

However, as Clegg noted, no contemporary union organises on the basis of skill alone, no union organises all workers in any industry, and the category of general is so loose as to be of little analytical value. The school teacher unions organise those who practise the skill of teaching, but so do the college and university teacher unions. More importantly, teaching is not organised in the same way as is the activity associated with the practice of craft skills. The teacher unions do not seek to organise all workers in the education industry (whatever that may be), and they are clearly not general unions.

In a later attempt at categorisation, Clegg distinguishes between public sector unions, private industry unions with relatively simple structures, and conglomerate unions. This puts the teacher unions in the same category as the National Union of Public Employees, the National Union of Mineworkers, and the Post Office Engineering Union (Clegg 1979: 167), to name only a few unlikely organisations sharing some similarities in that their structures and their spheres of recruitment are relatively straightforward. The differences between them are many, and Clegg takes the view that the only way to understand union structures is to examine each union individually. A more reliable taxonomy of trade unions focuses on trade union behaviour rather than on structures, examining objectives and the methods used to pursue them. Union structures are rooted in the actions of trade unionists, and differences between unions reflect their adoption of the objectives and methods appropriate to their particular circumstances.

The Webbs defined a trade union as 'a continuous association of wage earners for the purpose of maintaining or improving the conditions of their employment' (Webb and Webb 1894: 1). They argued in a later work (1897) that there were three main ways the unions could pursue this broad objective. The first was through the Method of Mutual Insurance, where Friendly and Out of Work benefits enabled the union to prevent members from accepting employment on terms and conditions injurious to the trade. Employers would be forced to conform to the union rate and conditions by the refusal of the workers in the trade to take employment with them.

The second Method was that of Collective Bargaining, where conditions of employment were determined by agreement between representatives of the employees and the employers. The Webbs pointed out the main drawback of this Method: its 'perpetual liability to end in a strike or a lock-out' (1897: 221). Thirdly, the Method of Legal Enactment refers to trade union action to secure the enshrinement of conditions of employment in legislation. While conditions of employment may fluctuate under the Method of Collective Bargaining, in accordance with prevailing labour market conditions, under Legal Enactment they are established on a more permanent basis.

Within these three Methods, the Webbs identified two Devices. The Device of the Common Rule encapsulates the trade union objective of establishing rules covering the conditions of employment of whole groups of employees, to counteract the inherent weakness of the individual employee when bargaining with the employer. The Device of Restriction of

Numbers refers to those unions which preserve conditions of employment by controlling the supply of labour. The Webbs then go on to discuss the assumptions underpinning trade union action. The Doctrine of Vested Interests expresses a concern with maintaining customary conditions and rates of pay, and is closely associated with the Device of Restriction of Numbers. The Doctrine of Supply and Demand asserts that during times of good trade the highest possible rates of pay should be sought. However, the corollary of this is that workers in a weaker position must accept the bare minimum. The Doctrine of the Living Wage argues that employers should pay neither what is customary nor the minimum they can get away with, but according to need.

The Webbs based their analysis on a study of the manual worker trade unions; indeed for them the term 'trade union' applied only to manual worker organisations. However, they did give some attention to non-manual workers, writing on 'the Professional Associations of Brainworkers' in 1917. They argued that the activities of the professional associations were rooted in three motives or impulses. The advancement of knowledge and the practice of the profession is driven by the Creative Impulse. The Fellowship Impulse embraces the desire for friendship and solidarity among like-minded people, and its corollary, the desire to exclude those who do not share the same outlook and aspirations. Professional self-government is rooted in this impulse. Finally, the Possessive Impulse stems from 'the desire to secure for the members of the group all the remuneration and status which the community can be induced to accord' (Webb and Webb 1917: 36). We return to these themes later in this chapter, when looking in more detail at the development of the unions.

At this point we can pick up the particular methods used by professional workers to regulate the terms of their employment, first mentioned in chapter 2. Under the Possessive Impulse groups of professionals attempt 'to protect themselves by a statutory register of legally qualified practitioners; to ring themselves round with degrees, diplomas and certificates; and to insist . . . that all persons not possessing these particular hall-marks are incapable of performing the service required by the community' (Webb and Webb 1917: 37). As a method of protection, the statutory register is the main difference between the professional associations and the trade unions.

Although the Webbs prefer to restrict their use of the term 'trade union' to the organisations of manual workers, they are clear that the professional associations use trade union methods, particularly the methods of mutual insurance and legal enactment, practising the device of restriction of numbers and guided by the doctrine of vested interests. The method of collective bargaining is not appropriate for those professionals whose earnings are based on fee-paying individuals. However, when large numbers of practitioners are in salaried employment then 'we begin to see them taking to collective bargaining, insisting on a standard rate or common minimum of remuneration, resorting to concerted refusal to accept employment, publicly boycotting "unfair" employers, and even – in the case of the teachers and doctors – employing the weapon of the strike' (1917: 41).

A teachers' register? – the search for professional unity

It is the employee status of school teachers that gives the main clue as to their failure to establish a statutory register of legally authorised practitioners. However, this failure was not for want of trying. Since the early nineteenth century the practitioners of the professions have sought to achieve the self-regulation of their professions. The Law Society was established in 1825, the Royal Institute of British Architects in 1832, and the General Medical Council was set up in 1858 by Act of Parliament. The latter consisted entirely of medical practitioners, kept a register of those qualified to practise, laid down the qualifications for admission to the register, and had the power to remove from the register. The College of Preceptors was established in 1846 by the proprietors of some private schools with the objective of establishing teaching as a self-regulated profession (Gosden 1972: 18), adopting the General Medical Council as the model for a Scholastic Council.

The National Union of Elementary Teachers (NUET, the forerunner of the NUT) supported the principle of registration, in line with their objectives of raising the social position of elementary teachers and driving unqualified teachers out of the profession. The union joined the Scholastic Registration Association, which was formed by the College in 1863 and survived until 1873 (Tropp 1957: 100).

The principle of registration was accepted by all of the teacher organisations, but the secondary associations would not agree to a single register for all teachers for fear of being swamped by the much larger numbers of elementary teachers through the NUT (Baron 1954: 135). This basic division of interests blocked the unification of the profession within a Scholastic Council, with the secondary teachers being the main opponents of unification. When a Teachers' Registration Council was formed in 1902, it established a single register with separate columns for elementary and secondary school teachers. The NUT objected to the separation of elementary and secondary teachers into different lists and to their small minority representation on the Council. The council and the register were abolished in 1906.

The second teachers' register was established in 1912 and survived until 1949. The Teachers' Registration Council controlled only admission to the register, rather than to the profession. The creation of the Burnham Committee in 1919 provided an alternative forum for teachers' organisations to exert influence over the education system through collective bargaining. The 1944 Education Act gave the Minister of Education the power to grant qualified teacher status, and the Council was abolished in 1949.

Teacher organisations had campaigned throughout this period for a self-regulating profession as a means of securing an advantageous position through control over the supply of labour. This was not achieved, and collective bargaining was established as the main method of regulating teachers' pay and conditions. The Webbs point out that the strike is a corollary of this method and, as we have seen in chapter 2, teachers have not been shy of using this weapon from time to time. But teachers' activities are central concerns of the state, and loss of public support can have adverse political consequences. Other trade unionists have to face up to this problem too, 'but it is more acute for a group which cultivates a professional image while at the same time it acts as an industrial trade union' (Adam 1982: 199).

Consequently the regulation of teaching by a statutory body remains an issue that surfaces from time to time. Moves by Education Ministers to relax entry qualifications, particularly in periods of teacher shortages, have usually met with renewed calls from the teacher unions for a General Teaching Council. This response has been made at other times of threat to the effectiveness of teacher organisations. During the 1960s the clamour for teacher unity grew louder in the face of both incomes policy and TUC involvement in making decisions about public expenditure. Attempts to create a single teacher union failed yet again, but eventually in 1969 Secretary of State Edward Short, an NUT member and union-sponsored MP who supported the demands for professional status, overcame the opposition of his officials and set up a working party with representatives from the unions along Burnham lines (Coates 1972b: 56). The resulting report recommended the establishment of a Teaching Council of forty members, with fifteen appointed by the Secretary of State, ten from the NUT, three from the National Association of Schoolmasters (NAS), one each from the Incorporated Association of Head Masters (IAHM) and the Association of Head Mistresses (AHM), and two each from the Association of Assistant Mistresses (AAM), the Assistant Masters Association (AMA), the Association of Teachers in Technical Institutions (ATTI), the NAHT and the ATCDE (Association of Teachers in Colleges and Departments of Education). The NUT and ATTI rejected the report, unable to accept the provision for veto by the Secretary of State of any recommendation made by the proposed Council.

Teachers have failed to develop professional unity under the aegis of a General Teaching Council. Some teachers may look on with envy at the self-controlling register of other professionals, but it seems unlikely that teachers themselves will ever achieve such control. First, many of the members of the self-regulating professions are not employees, and school teachers' functions are closely linked to their status as employees. The duties of teachers, and their conditions of employment, are becoming increasingly codified and enforced through state rules and managerial control, rather than through professional discipline, an important development that we explore in detail in chapter 4. Secondly, educational activity is so closely linked with the ideological perspectives of social progress and public order, that the state is unlikely to give up its control of educational standards and teacher training. Indeed these aspects of control have been tightened up recently with the introduction of the national curriculum and with the abolition of the Advisory Committee on the Supply and Education of Teachers. Thirdly, even if self-regulation were to be achieved this would not necessarily enhance their bargaining power in respect of issues over which the regulatory body has no powers, such as salaries. Finally, as the professions in the National Health Service are finding out, the regulation of conditions at the workplace, including issues like health and safety, the interpretation of national conditions, and the allocation of workloads are not simply enforceable through self-regulation, even though professional codes may exist.

A general teachers' union? – the search for trade union unity

The teacher organisations sit within the Webbs' definition of a trade union, employing the methods and devices of trade unions as they strive for greater regulation over their members' jobs. Coates (1972b: 60) supports our argument in chapter 2 that the sustained national militancy of the 1960s increased the influence of the teacher unions more than either professional unity or organisational unity. As teachers were unable to achieve self-regulation to defend and advance their interests, they turned to political lobbying and to collective bargaining, forms of activity usually associated with trade unionists rather than professionals. The differences between the trade unions, in their structure, government and policies, reflect the different methods adopted in the light of the circumstances facing each individual union (Turner 1962).

We can now turn to an exploration of the differences between the teacher unions. Carlson's analysis is rooted in a framework similar to that of the Webbs, as he outlines a taxonomy of teacher unions in the USA. He argues that unionism takes three main forms (which are not totally separable) – craft, company and industrial unionism – each of which has influenced teachers. Craft unionism rests on methods of union organisation to enforce rules about admission to craft jobs and about the practice of craft work. Control over jobs and work by the craft practitioners was ensured by shop steward activity to enforce the rules of the craft. Carlson draws parallels between the protection of skill by craft unions and the protection of professional rights by teacher unions.

> When teachers argue that they should be treated more as professionals, they imply that they, as individual practitioners and as an occupational group, should be granted more job-control rights, including greater control over the organization of classroom activities, curriculum selection, teacher evaluation, teacher licensing, teacher preparation through apprenticeship with 'master' teachers, occupational-ethics performance standards, and so forth.
>
> (Carlson 1987: 297)

The method of legal enactment, the device of restriction of numbers, and the doctrine of vested interests have been deployed by teacher unions in successive attempts to secure these rights.

Company unionism, as described by Carlson, developed during the three decades of massive expansion of American capitalism at the start of the twentieth century, and was rooted in the notion that employer and employee have a common interest in the success of the enterprise. Within this unitarist frame of reference the task of the trade union is to assist management to improve productivity and product quality. In return for having the interests of workers looked after by the heads of the corporate families, unions would 'abandon the use of militant strike tactics and radical politics' (Carlson 1987: 298).

This was manifested in the role of the main USA teacher organisation, the National Education Association (NEA), in the government of the public school system. The NEA was represented on the various bodies that regulated the system, but the representatives were mainly senior administrators rather than classroom teachers. The interests of the education family were to be served by the educational administrators, state planners and policy-makers as they pursued the broader goals of the education system. 'When teachers complained that their concerns were ignored by their bureaucratic superiors, that their grievances were not seriously listened to, or that their salaries were too low, they were accused of being unprofessional, and of placing their own self-interest before the interests of children' (Carlson 1987: 299). As the Webbs pointed out, when a professional association is dominated by the 'superior grades' rather than by the rank and file, then the organisation is more concerned with the establishment of a hierarchical profession with an associated hierarchy of qualifications rather than with the establishment of a uniform profession with equal access to higher status positions through promotion by seniority (Webb and Webb 1917: 45).

The failure of company unionism to meet teachers' needs in the USA resulted in them turning to the third form of trade unionism. Industrial unionism emerged in America in the 1920s and 1930s as the new mass production industries employed rapidly increasing numbers of semi-skilled assembly line workers. The bitter struggles of the 1930s, during which these unions developed the tactic of the sit-down strike, led to a government-sponsored settlement to bring about industrial peace. Employers and unions each agreed to recognise certain rights of the other. It was agreed that workers had the right to organise, and to be represented by their unions in collective bargaining. In return, union leaders agreed to abandon the sit-down strike and to limit the scope of bargaining to pay and conditions.

The state played a key role in supporting this settlement, enshrining labour rights in the 1935 Wagner Act. Its apparent success in maintaining peace provided a model for regulating labour relations in the state sector, with President Kennedy extending bargaining rights to federal employees in the 1960s. Most teachers in America were unionised by the end of the 1960s (Cole 1969; Kerchner and Mitchell 1988). Thus teacher organisations became organised on industrial union lines and committed to collective bargaining as the main method of regulating the employment contract, bringing them ever closer to the broader working-class organisations under the umbrella of the main union confederation the AFL-CIO.

Although there are many differences between the American and British labour movements, Carlson's model can be used to illuminate the development of British teacher unionism, picking out the main ideological strands linking these developments together. Referring also to the analysis provided by the Webbs, we can suggest a broad taxonomy of teacher trade unionism. The elitism of 'craft unionism' is clearly applicable to teachers in this country, as teachers have created exclusive organisations to represent their interests. The professionalism of teachers and the defence of teacher autonomy have been central concerns of the teacher organisations. We argue below that this form of trade unionism is most applicable to the NASUWT.

'Company unionism' also has a well established presence, with teacher organisations represented on the plethora of advisory bodies that are locked into the education sub-government. One of the main services provided by the teacher unions is in developing classroom practice. The notion that the education employers ought to provide teachers with remuneration commensurate with their professional status, without teachers having to go through the vulgar process of asking for more money, remains powerful. The PAT, which explicitly rejects all forms of industrial action, is the clearest practitioner of this form of organisation, with ATL being the main voice of so-called 'moderation' among the three main unions.

'Industrial unionism' has a long tradition in the UK based in the state-sponsored settlement of the industrial relations crisis immediately after the first world war through the Whitley Committee. Among the teacher unions the NUT is the most committed to the defence of all teachers through collective bargaining, to the principle of the rate for the job, and to the broader objectives of the wider trade union movement.

These three forms of teacher trade unionism represent different ideological approaches as outlined in the previous chapter. However, it would be an error to apply these categories rigidly. While the ATL is clearly the union for teachers who are against collective action, the differences between the NUT and the NASUWT are more complex. Many of the present divisions between the national unions can be traced back to their origins in different segments of the teacher workforce, continuing to hold back the development of national unity on a basis that seems no longer relevant. The divisions may not now have the same material basis, but they do represent some continuity of ideology and politics, reflecting differences of approach both within and between all contemporary British trade unions – between collaborationist company unionism, sectional and separatist craft unionism, and broad-based industrial unionism.

THE GROWTH OF TEACHER UNIONS

Recruitment boundaries

There are six organisations seeking to recruit and organise teachers. The NAHT recruits heads, deputies and teachers paid on deputy head salaries in the UK. SHA recruits heads and deputies in the secondary sector only, ATL recruits classroom teachers only, and the NASUWT, the NUT and PAT recruit all grades of school teacher. The NUT recruits from 'those in the service of education in England and Wales, the Channel Islands and the Isle of Man'. The NASUWT recruits into 'full membership' from 'persons who are recognised as qualified teachers and persons whose contract of employment requires them to teach, lecture or instruct', and has members in Scotland, Northern Ireland, the Isle of Man, the Channel Islands, Germany (in schools for children of armed service personnel) and Gibraltar, as well as a few members in further and higher education. ATL (formerly AMMA) admits into 'Ordinary Membership' any 'teacher in a school or college in the United Kingdom of Great Britain and Northern Ireland who is not the Head of the School or the Principal of the College'. Thus each union has a different recruitment boundary. (The EIS in Scotland is the dominant union for all teachers in Scottish schools.)

As well as recruiting serving teachers from a variety of sectors and geographical areas, the unions also have categories of membership for students intending to become teachers, for members who have left teaching, and for members who have retired from teaching. Competitive recruitment means that a range of incentives are offered to potential members. These include free student membership, so that many students may join more than one union and wait until taking up their first appointment before deciding which union to join. Teachers may move between unions during their career, changing to the union that happens to hold the majority membership in the school. Competition for members can result in inflated levels of membership being claimed, as each union strives to assert itself as the authentic and representative voice of the teacher.

Union density

Union density and levels of membership can only be estimated, as the membership figures quoted by the unions often include student, retired and 'left the profession' members. Furthermore, as the unions have different boundaries it is difficult to identify the exact level of union membership for each union within a given sector of the teaching workforce in the UK. Nevertheless, trends can be examined and some particular points can be made about teacher unionism. First and foremost, it is clear that the level of union density has been consistently high. Beatrice Webb states that about 90 per cent of those eligible were in NUT membership in 1915 (Webb 1915: 2). In

1950 81 per cent of serving teachers were in one union or another, and in 1967 the density was 75 per cent (Coates 1972b: 4). The Labour Force Survey gave a density of 77 per cent among full-time employees in schools in 1991 (Beatson and Butcher 1993: 678), but this included non-teachers.

These density levels can be compared with those for the whole economy: 30 per cent in 1917, and 44 per cent in 1950 and 1967; and for white-collar employees: 12 per cent in 1911, and 33 per cent in 1948 and 1967 (Bain and Price 1980). By 1991 aggregate density had fallen to 33 per cent (Beatson and Butcher 1993: 676). In the public service sector as a whole, union density has been consistently high throughout the post-war period at about 60 per cent through the 1950s and 1960s and heading towards 80 per cent in the 1970s and 1980s (Waddington 1992: 296). Teachers were very highly organised by the early years of this century, and have remained among the largest and most unionised occupational groups ever since. Table 3.12 shows the pattern of growth of the main unions.

Origins and growth of the NUT

The NUT was initially founded as the National Union of Elementary Teachers (NUET) in 1870, as local teacher associations were drawn together into a national association by the controversy surrounding the Education Act 1870 (Tropp 1957: 109). By 1915 the NUT's membership had risen to 91,400, of whom 60 per cent were women. However, the union was dominated 'by the small minority of men who were college-trained and head teachers. The special interests respectively of class teachers, of women teachers, and of non-collegiate teachers seemed to be neglected' (Webb 1915: 9). Webb gives details of a number of sectional organisations that co-existed with the NUT, some of them having members who may or may not be in the union, some of them wholly within it. The National Federation of Class Teachers was established in 1892 to challenge head teacher domination and to assert the independence of classroom teachers. It ran slates for national executive elections, and by 1914 it claimed 25,000 members and had gained fourteen seats on the NUT's national executive committee. The head teachers followed suit, forming the National Association of Head Teachers in 1897. By 1915 they had reached a membership of 6,000, three-quarters of them also being NUT members.

The interests of certificated teachers without college qualifications were pressed through the National Association of Non-Collegiate Certificated Teachers, which claimed 40,000 members (within and without the NUT). The National Union of Uncertificated Teachers and the TUC-affiliated National Union of School Teachers organised among the 40,000 uncertificated teachers (36,000 of them women) who were at that time excluded from membership of the NUT. The union's early support for the establishment of a teachers' register had the objective of driving uncertificated teachers out of the profession.

Table 3.12 Union membership, selected years

Year	*NUT*		*NAS(UWT)*		*AMMA(ATL)*	
	In-service	*Total*	*In-service*	*Total*	*AMA*	*AAM*
1870	—	400	—	—	—	—
1880	—	11,892	—	—	—	—
1890	—	16,100	—	—	72	448
1900	—	43,621	—	—	1,593	636
1910	—	69,073	—	—	3,259	1,229
1920	—	115,440	—	—	6,752	5,157
1930	—	138,695	7,014	—	9,034	7,210
1940	—	150,871	8,629	—	—	—
1950	—	184,099	13,163	—	16,644	12,114
1960	—	225,181	22,651	—	26,000	17,233
1970	218,742	331,301	56,899	—	—	—
1971	176,900	310,223	67,964	—	—	—
1972	179,867	301,845	69,367	—	—	—
1973	189,925	209,168	76,141	—	—	—
1974	200,252	231,085	59,402	58,942	43,286	35,861
1975	221,359	243,534	82,713	59,400	40,075	37,612
1976	235,273	256,653	86,098	85,535	40,750	38,527
1977	245,104	267,032	102,031	127,056	40,840	38,015
1978	258,107	275,296	111,566	140,701	87,407	
1979	252,479	273,483	122,058	152,222	89,768	
1980	240,399	258,811	123,896	156,167	89,858	
1981	228,514	249,133	119,545	155,984	89,786	
1982	225,615	245,728	120,241	156,920	86,641	
1983	214,439	234,896	119,668	156,172	88,143	
1984	220,042	259,366	126,453	164,295	96,730	
1985	213,514	253,672	127,612	169,839	113,453	
1986	189,786	229,601	123,945	166,583	123,601	
1987	182,378	224,538	120,544	163,051	129,392	
1988	176,417	216,614	117,610	159,256	131,500	
1989	171,990	213,482	118,230	163,646	135,930	
1990	169,007	218,194	119,810	166,331	138,571	
1991	164,618	214,675	121,142	179,937	141,171	
1992	162,192	213,656	127,635	190,637	152,795	

Sources: Various sources, including the Certification Officer, union records and the TUC. Total membership includes non-serving teachers, retired and student members. Figures for ATL and predecessor unions' serving teacher membership are not available

Some women teachers were active in the women's movement at the turn of the century, and were involved in campaigns around demands for universal adult suffrage and for equal pay. A number of women's organisations were established within the NUT, and among these Webb lists the National Federation of Women Teachers, the Association of London Married Women Teachers, and the Women Teachers' Franchise Union. As well as campaigning around wider political issues these organisations also fought for increased representation for women within the union and for improved terms and conditions for women teachers.

These divisions, between senior teachers and classroom teachers, between qualified and unqualified, and between women and men, were openly expressed within the NUT in the early days. The holding together of the national union under such circumstances reflects an impressive determination to secure improved conditions through a united policy. The achievement of many of the early demands, and the developing shape of the public education system in England and Wales, made those differences more difficult to contain. Along with the other separate interests between the primary and secondary sectors they have had a profound impact on the teaching profession and on the teacher unions to the present day.

The important point about the NUT is that its practices and its structures developed on the basis of a broad membership base, bringing together qualified and unqualified, women and men. Rather than going the way of the professional organisation dominated by the 'superior grades', wedded to the doctrine of vested interests and relying on the device of restriction of numbers, the NUT reflected the demands of the mass of elementary school teachers. It adopted the method of collective bargaining as the main method of gaining control over teachers' working lives, seeking a single pay scale in line with the device of the common rule. Early NUT activity was driven by the possessive impulse, in that it sought high remuneration and status for all teachers. However, this was on an inclusive rather than an exclusive basis and, while the NUT did support campaigns to establish a statutory register of legally authorised practitioners, such campaigning was never an overriding priority. The method of mutual insurance was also applied very early on, with the creation of sustentation funds to support dismissed teachers, the maintenance of a 'blacklist' of bad employers, and the circulation of a list of ex-members expelled for breaking boycotts of listed employers (Horn and Horn 1979: 5–6).

Turner (1962) draws attention to the significance of union structures and the location of recruitment boundaries. He distinguishes between 'closed' unions that have tightly drawn recruitment boundaries, excluding most workers from membership, and 'open' unions that admit most workers in to membership. Closed unions, having a relatively small number of members with common interests, are likely to pursue a narrow range of objectives. Open unions, with a larger and more diverse membership composition, are likely to pursue a wider range of objectives. The structure and composition of the teacher workforce has an important impact on the structure of teacher trade unionism and on the concerns of the teacher unions. The teacher unions are occupationally closed, but the teaching occupation is not homogeneous. As the unions developed they reflected the differences between the various sections and groups within the occupation.

Thus the NUT at the turn of the century may be seen as a coalition of a large number of local and national teacher associations. In 1915, when it recruited only qualified teachers in elementary schools, Webb regarded it as having the characteristics of an 'amalgamated' union (1915: 3). The union opened up further when its 1919 conference decided to admit uncertificated teachers into membership and, reflecting its membership base among women teachers and the impact of feminist organisation, to adopt the principle of equal pay. The latter step was too late for the Women Teachers' Franchise Union and the London Unit of the National Federation of Women Teachers, which had broken away over the issue of equal pay to form the National Union of Women Teachers in 1909. It was too much for the National Association of Men Teachers, which became the National Association of Schoolmasters and mobilised against the principle of equal pay, finally splitting from the NUT in 1922. It was pay, above all other issues, that furnished the profile of teacher unionism and became the dominant theme in the industrial relations of the school sector.

Union growth may occur by amalgamation, by increased membership within the membership boundary, or by increased membership by extending the boundary (Hughes 1967: 6). The NUT was initially formed by amalgamation of local teacher associations, and it achieved further growth by a combination of extensions to the recruitment boundary and increased recruitment from the growing teacher workforce (see Table 3.1). This is significant, in that a union's relative size, and its ability to impose punitive sanctions on employers, may be taken as the main indicator of its strength, and of its consequent ability to win recognition by the employers. Bain rejects this explanation, arguing that 'government action and the favourable climate which it produced were . . . the main factors bringing about the recognition of white collar unions in the public sector of the economy' with the report of the Whitley Committee in 1917–18 being seen as playing a crucial role in generating the favourable climate (Bain 1970: 181).

However, we have already seen that teachers were highly unionised before Burnham, and it was this factor that helped to convince the government of the need to set up such collective bargaining machinery. Furthermore, the NUT was willing and able to mobilise sanctions against employers; it had already established a tradition of preparedness to take strike and other forms of trade union action (Webb and Webb 1920: 506; Seifert 1987). Both the nature of the early struggles, and the occupational diversity that became united under the umbrella of the NUT, contributed to its development as a general union for teachers. This was reinforced by the close cultural and social links between school teachers and the working-class parents of their pupils, often expressed through trade union and socialist activity. There are striking parallels here with the much later unionisation of teachers in the USA (Cole 1969).

Although the NUT had many of the characteristics of the open general union, it was only concerned with elementary school teachers for the first part of its history. It opened its boundary to secondary teachers, establishing a secondary schools committee in 1909, when some local authorities were setting up municipal secondary schools. By then there were already well established organisations of endowed secondary school teachers, who were quite different from the teachers in the public elementary schools.

Origins and growth of the Joint Four

The Association of Assistant Mistresses (AAM) was formed in 1884 by assistant mistresses in endowed secondary schools (AMA 1961; Hastings 1978), followed by the Assistant Masters Association (AMA) in 1891. Head teachers were represented by the Association of Head Mistresses (AHM) and the Incorporated Association of Head Masters (IAHM), formed in 1874 and 1891 respectively (Chapman 1990).

These four associations grew steadily with the expansion of public secondary education after the Education Act of 1902. They co-operated closely, forming a Federal Council of Secondary School Associations in 1906, later known simply as the Joint Four. The Joint Four shared the same premises and co-ordinated their activities through the Central Joint Committee, head masters taking the chair alternately with head mistresses, and the secretary being selected from the assistant masters and mistresses. The common views of the secondary associations were channelled through the Joint Four at both national and local levels, although they acted independently in salary negotiations. Recognised union status was gained at a very early stage, as the heads' associations had one seat each, and the assistants' had two each on Burnham from its inception.

Local Joint Fours came into being from 1919 (Price and Glenday 1974: 129); there were over 120 of them in 1959, by which time they had created 'an effective organisation of grammar school teachers and heads, and . . . their overriding purpose has been to give expression to grammar school interests' (*Education*, 3 April 1959). Already they were expanding their membership in secondary modern and comprehensive schools, the growth of which 'would be certain to lead to changes in the character of the Joint Four' (*Education*, 3 April 1959). By 1971 the AMA was recruiting from among women primary school teachers. At that time the mistresses and head mistresses associations provided the only women teachers on the Burnham Committee.

Each of the Joint Four organisations operated from a narrow base in the relatively small secondary sector. They had a common interest in protecting and enhancing the status of the secondary school teacher, at the expense of the much larger number of elementary school teachers. Consequently they would never agree to a statutory register that accorded equal status to all teachers, although they did agree that all teachers should be registered. These organisations have applied the main methods of trade unionism, but they were primarily guided by the device of restriction of numbers and the doctrine of vested interests. Webb quoted an AAM president, addressing some concerns among members, who argued that if 'Trade Unionism can mean the banding together of individuals recognising their common interest in order to obtain conditions of labour as shall react favourably upon the work itself, then we may plead guilty to the charge of such a union' (Webb 1915: 16). She enumerated the bodies upon which the AMA had applied pressure regarding salaries and job security, and she noted that this association had established an emergency fund to support members unjustly dismissed or acting in accordance with a boycott of a particular employer (1915: 17). The AMA, for example, put Haverfordwest Grammar School on its 'blacklist' from 1934 until 1947 over the dismissal of five teachers (Gosden 1972: 173).

None of the Joint Four organisations has initiated strike action, but the AMA considered it in 1954. They were frustrated by their lack of influence over the primary sector-dominated NUT in the Teachers' Panel as reconstructed in 1945. They shied away from using the strike weapon to support their rejection of the Burnham 1953 recommendations, and they remained within Burnham, fearing that withdrawal would marginalise them in educational politics and split the Joint Four (Gosden 1972: 77). The federal structure held together for nearly a century, ending with mergers. This stability was assisted by the Joint Four's common orientation towards lobbying through both formal and informal networks, rather than towards collective bargaining to achieve their goals.

Origins and growth of the NAS

The post-war period saw the consolidation of state sector education and the growth of comprehensive schools. Secondary teachers trebled in number between 1937 and 1950, increasing from 12 per cent of the teacher workforce to 37 per cent. Meanwhile, the primary sector contracted by 40,000 over the same period. This dramatic shift demanded a response from the unions among the teachers in the fertile recruitment ground of the secondary sector, and membership competition started in earnest. Recruitment boundaries became blurred, as all of the classroom teacher unions strove to assert their influence on the process of reorganisation.

As noted above, the NAS had split from the NUT in 1922. Its membership increased slowly, by 6,000 between 1930 and 1950, while the NUT's membership increased by 45,000 and the AAM and AMA's combined membership increased by 12,500 (see Table 3.12). If the NAS was to survive to challenge the NUT it would have to broaden its appeal. During the 1950s the NUT published a number of pamphlets attacking the NAS's policies, seeking to refute the NAS's claims to represent the best interest of men teachers and to have the best record for militancy. One pamphlet published in 1950 lists a number of the NUT's 'famous strikes', and claims that £250,000 had been spent on them. Another counters the NAS's assertion that the NUT 'surrendered to feminism and became an adjunct of the feminist movement' by arguing that 'NUT policy is professionally and educationally sound, and is not advocated to please a feminist majority'. Another argues for equal pay, noting that both the TUC and the Royal Commission on Equal Pay attached little importance to 'family needs' arguments in wage bargaining. The NUT's membership secretary in 1959 estimated that between them the NAS and the NUT had 'spent about £1¼m on fighting each other since 1921' (*Education*, 3 April 1959). In 1960 the NUT still outnumbered the combined membership of the other unions by three to one, although all of the others were growing more rapidly. The NUT claimed to have 80 per cent of primary teachers and 54 per cent of secondary teachers in membership and, put another way, 78 per cent of women school teachers and 54 per cent of men. Fifty-five per cent of NUT members were primary school teachers, and 33 per cent secondary, and two-thirds of the membership were women (Roy 1968: 158–61).

The NAS built a base among male classroom teachers in the secondary sector, taking militant positions on a narrow range of terms and conditions issues related to the interests of the full-time career teacher. It championed local action over local issues, and it mounted a vigorous criticism of Burnham's repeated failure to deal with some key issues. While criticising Burnham, the NAS also demanded representation on it (Latta 1969). A series of applications for membership of Burnham were rejected, and various deputations were ignored. By 1961 the association had the support of 235 (mostly Conservative) MPs, but this was still not enough. Coates (1972b: 62) argued that the only reason for refusing NAS access to Burnham was the government's desire to appease the NUT. This desire collapsed as the NAS began a series of strikes throughout 1961, and the NAS had two representatives at the Burnham Committee meeting in March 1962. The impact of recognition on the NAS was immediate. Membership increased by 40 per cent during the year, and the union was on the way to playing a significant part in school industrial relations.

After the implementation of equal pay the NAS's main aim was to gain increases to the main scale with additional long-service increments. It also argued strongly for the reform of Burnham, to weaken the institutional domination of the Teachers' Panel by the NUT. During the 1960s further steady growth was maintained under the same policies of both local militancy over craft/professional issues and national criticism of Burnham's (and the NUT's) failure to address the needs of the career teacher. The union began to participate in wider trade union movement activity, joining first the National Federation of Professional Workers and then, in 1968, following NALGO and the civil service unions into the TUC two years before the NUT. General Secretary Terry Casey, still remembered reverentially by leading activists, argued in the union journal that TUC affiliation would not imperil their political neutrality, and that 'the Conservative Shadow Minister of Labour is on record as stating that they believe that white-collar unions should affiliate to the TUC and help ensure that the TUC concentrates on its proper functions' (quoted in Latta 1969: 33).

In focusing on the narrow range of interests of the male career teacher the NAS was motivated by the fellowship impulse, bringing together the male teachers in the growing secondary sector who believed that the prospect of equal pay represented a threat to their interests. When the association seceded from the NUT it adopted the method of collective bargaining and the device of the common rule, but only over a narrow range of issues centred around the interests of this small group of like-minded men. By the time it gained real influence as a national union it already had existed for forty years as an elitist organisation, excluding nearly two-thirds of the teacher workforce from membership at the start of the post-war period. The structures and practices developed and consolidated during this long wait for power have had a lasting influence over the thirty years that followed.

Recent and current issues in union growth

By the 1970s the single-sex unions were looking increasingly anachronistic, and the NAS's dream of becoming the union for all men teachers was obviously unattainable. The reasons for maintaining a men-only union had vanished, for all practical purposes, over fifteen years earlier. Equal pay had been implemented in seven steps between 1955 and 1961 (Gosden 1972: 127), and the NUWT was dissolved in 1960. In 1968, when its application to join the TUC was challenged on the grounds of its opposition to equal pay, the NAS successfully argued that this was 'not strictly so' (Latta 1969: 32). Already in 1964 the NAS had supported the formation of the Union of Women Teachers (UWT); one view is that it was formed by NAS members' wives who would otherwise have had to join the NUT or the AAM, both of which were hostile to their husbands' NAS. While this explanation of the UWT's existence is not entirely convincing, the UWT remained small, reaching only 2,000 members by 1969 and relying on the NAS's legal and professional services (Latta 1969: 31). The close relationship between these unions was expressed through the formation of a 'Joint Two' in 1970, with national and some local joint NAS/UWT campaigns. This arrangement enabled the NAS to declare some 6,000 women members in its TUC affiliation in the early 1970s, even though the UWT was itself refused affiliation in 1974 (*TUC Annual Report 1975*). In that year the UWT leadership broke with the NAS (see membership figures in Table 3.12), principally over the issue of merger; a section of the UWT then broke away to form the Association of Career Teachers. The Sex Discrimination Act 1975 made exclusion from membership on grounds of gender unlawful, hastening the merger of the two unions in 1976 into the National Association of Schoolmasters/Union of Women Teachers (NAS/UWT) which then became the National Association of Schoolmasters and Union of Women Teachers (NASUWT). The end of the NAS as a men-only union was followed by an increase of some 40,000 declared members (see Table 3.12).

The Sex Discrimination Act was followed by further mergers of the Joint Four members. The AAM and the AMA merged into AMMA (now renamed ATL), and the Secondary Heads Association, SHA, was formed through the merger of the Head Masters Association and the Association of Head

Mistresses. The main union for primary heads is the National Association of Head Teachers, which started as the National Federation of Head Teachers' Associations in 1897 as a pressure group within the NUT (Tropp 1957: 156). Its core membership is thus among primary heads, with some members holding joint membership with the NUT.

One new union emerged in 1970, the Professional Association of Teachers (PAT). This was established by teachers opposed to the use of industrial action, its inaugural meeting resolving that 'it shall be a cardinal rule of the association that members shall not go on strike under any pretext' (Bryant and Leicester 1991: 61). It recruits from all teachers in schools, colleges and universities in the UK, and claimed 13,000 members in 1979, rising to 40,000 in 1985. The Conservative government granted recognition to PAT in 1981 by handing it a seat on Burnham. Recognition by LEAs is not universal, and its role in industrial relations is very limited.

Thus by the end of the 1970s the present pattern of teacher trade unionism was well established, rooted in a hundred years of activity by teachers to build their defence organisations. The nature of each union reflects its origin in a particular sector of the teacher workforce. The NUT retains the characteristics of the open general union, with its membership base in the primary sector, and with strong elements of socialist and feminist activity present within it. Its traditional orientation towards mainstream labour movement concerns and its attachment to collective bargaining continue to set it apart from the other unions. The NASUWT, continuing its role in pursuing the narrow concerns of the career-oriented secondary school teacher, is more like a closed craft union. ATL, with its roots in the independent sector and in the grammar schools, has adopted a form of trade unionism that rests on an assumed identity of interest between employer and employee. This union sees its role in providing an authentic voice for teachers to assist management in running a successful organisation.

This account of the growth and development of the teacher trade unions is generally a story of success. Density of trade union membership is high in the teaching profession by any measure and the main unions remain organisationally stable and industrially influential. They have done a good job, all in all, of carrying out the prime function of any union 'to protect and improve its own members' conditions' (Turner 1962: 12). The major weakness among the school teachers continues to be the divisions in terms of organisational rivalry and the underlying tensions within the profession which underscore that rivalry.

As Turner noted 'individual unions appear to have evolved separately, according to no common principle, and accepting no general pattern of membership-allocation or of internal organization . . . inter-union disputes are still not infrequent' (1962: 12). His main argument, based on a detailed historical study of cotton unions, is the link between the type of members a union recruits, the methods adopted by the union in terms of growth strategy and bargaining, and the ways in which the union conducts its own affairs and develops policy. He used colourful terms to express the possible different types of union organisation which might emerge from the various combinations of union type. Thus there are 'exclusive democracies' which tend to keep a tight control over entry which is limited to strict definitions of the occupation. In such a union full-time officials are an extension of the active membership and activists play a major part in union affairs. All the teacher unions approximate to this model, given their general uniformity of occupational membership groups, the importance of the lay activists, and that most officials are drawn from ex-union activists and therefore members of the profession.

Union growth among teachers was born out of the twin forces of state employment (of being a state employee) and the collective identity of the profession in a national education system. It thrived from greater state intervention, the adversity steeped in the managerial authority vested in heads and LEA officers, and in the struggles for higher status, equal pay and a common rate for the job. In the early 1970s it took strength from successful trade union organisation in defence of conditions of service and from pay increases founded in industrial action. These forms of success, however, opened the way for division as the profession changed in composition and the application of trade union principles split the teaching force. As the NUT fought harder to maintain a national bargained rate so it created two oppositional forces: the NASUWT's push for differentials to weaken national rate bargaining appealed to the growing numbers of secondary school 'career' teachers; and the AMMA's retreat from collective bargaining suited those in all sectors worried by industrial action and TUC affiliation. Growth then became a battle for existing members based on stronger and stronger claims to represent the special interests of certain categories of staff – some formalised in sector and/or qualification and others through ideological issues – and the decline of the NUT was matched by membership gains first for the NASUWT and later for ATL. This rivalry was based upon and fuelled by differences in policy and policy-making between the main classroom organisations.

THE GOVERNMENT AND POLICIES OF THE TEACHER UNIONS

Decision-making within trade unions is a complex issue. There are basic similarities between most unions in that an annual or biennial conference of elected delegates is regarded as the sovereign body, while a smaller elected national executive committee oversees the operation of the union between conferences. A permanent administration of paid officials carries out a range of duties connected with both the management of the union and the implementation of its policies. In some unions all paid officials are appointed by members of the national executive or by other paid officials. In others a number of them may be elected by the membership. Nearly all unions have units of both administration and government at local levels, in the form of branch and regional structures.

While there are formal structures which make clear decisions recorded in minute books, and while some decisions about election procedures and about industrial action are even subject to legal requirements, many decisions are made in ways that are less formal and are outside of the constraints of formal governmental structures. Union government in practice 'depends on the relationships between three groups: its full-time officials, that proportion of its members that take an active part in the union's management and the usually more passive majority of the rank-and-file' (Turner 1962: 289). These relationships are complex, and are shaped by the nature and structure of the workforce within the recruitment boundary, as well as by the ideology and aspirations of members and activists.

We have shown that the teacher unions have their origins within different sectors of the education workforce. As each union was formed it was shaped by the particular needs and aspirations of those building it, leading to the adoption of particular forms and methods of trade unionism. This section looks at the internal structures and at the democratic practices of each of the main unions in turn.

The NUT – the general union for teachers

The NUT is open to all grades of teacher, and its internal structures and processes of government are relatively open and democratic. The 488 local associations are the basic administrative units of the union. The boundaries of most local associations owe much to their origins as organisations of teachers founded in the nineteenth century. Where there are two or more local associations within an LEA area, reflecting the boundaries of smaller LEAs from the past, then those associations are grouped together into a division. The main union structures are shown in Figure 3.1.

Thus some local associations are administrative units only, while others also provide a focus for the purpose of organising negotiations with the LEA. Local and divisional secretaries who are involved in collective bargaining with LEA officers carry considerable responsibility and authority within the union. Successive local government reorganisations have reduced the number of LEAs, and consequently have concentrated the authority rooted in collective bargaining within a smaller number of union officers. The reforms of the 1980s have reversed this process.

Each local association is entitled to send a minimum of two delegates (up to a maximum of twelve, depending on the number of members of the local association) to the union's annual conference, which makes for a large and noisy body of delegates. Divisions are also entitled to two delegates. The conference is the sovereign ruling body of the union, although the leadership does not always implement conference decisions immediately. For example, the 1989 conference decided to set up a political fund and, while the necessary

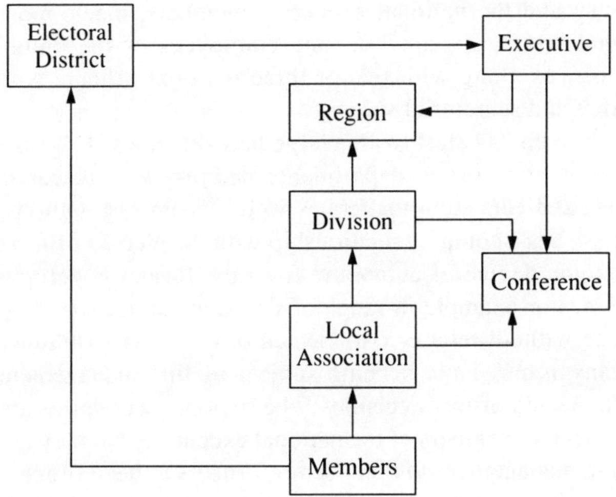

Figure 3.1 The structure of the NUT

rules have been drawn up, no date has been set by the national executive for the legally required ballot of the membership.

The local associations are grouped into twenty-seven electoral districts for the purposes of electing the members of the national executive, which is responsible for ensuring the operation of the union between conferences. Once elected, members of the executive serve for a two year term of office. The executive has a number of committees, the main one being the policy and resources committee which deals with the management of the union's finances, parliamentary relations, relations with political parties, media relations, staffing, premises, and relations with the TUC. This committee has sub-committees dealing with campaigns, industrial action, legal and professional services, and international relations, peace and disarmament, and there are working groups on specific issues as they arise, such as the EC and the single market, and the House of Commons Select Committee on teacher shortages. Other committees include: organisation and administration; membership and communications; professional unity; salaries, superannuation, conditions of service, health and safety; and education and equal opportunities. The union's code of professional conduct is upheld by the professional conduct committee, which may adjudicate on cases referred to it concerning 'actions which are alleged to be injurious to the interests of the profession or professional honour of any member'.

A regional tier of organisation is being developed, introducing elected regional councils into the areas covered by the full-time regional secretaries. Membership of the ten regional councils includes both representatives from the divisions and members of the national executive from within the region, meeting normally once each school term. The regional executive, consisting of the regional secretary and the national executive members, meets more frequently. The regional secretaries are full-time employees of the union, based in the regional offices along with two or three regional officers with casework, administrative and secretarial support.

In 1990 the union employed 244 staff, with a large bureaucracy of full-time officers based in London head office departments dealing with research, publicity, legal services, and education matters as well as with negotiations. This hierarchy of officials has a complex relationship with the elected officers of the union, and has some degree of autonomy from the formal governing committees of the union. For example, a range of decisions about spending priorities might be made without reference to elected officers. As with other large open unions, many issues have become subject to line management decisions rather than to elected officer decisions. The regional secretaries are in regular contact with elected members of the national executive, but they are accountable through line management to other senior officers at head office.

Elected officers at national level come from within the general NUT membership, but they do not reflect the composition of the membership. Members of the National Executive Committee tend to be senior teachers from secondary schools, and women on that committee were outnumbered by men by two to one in 1991. Women members outnumber men by three to one, but three-fifths of the full-time officers are men (Labour Research Department 1991: 8). At school level nearly two-thirds of school representatives are women, although in secondary schools two-thirds are men. The Keele survey of the three main unions found that 45 per cent of all primary school representatives were in the NUT, reflecting the union's membership base in smaller primary schools. This creates problems for union organisation and for membership participation. Members in smaller workplaces are less likely to have a union representative, are less likely to be involved in union meetings and, if they are geographically isolated as well, are less likely to have contact with the trade union. We discuss workplace union organisation more thoroughly in chapter 6.

The activist layer of the NUT is thus more likely to come from the better organised secondary sector, where there are greater opportunities for creating a base of support. Furthermore, much activity within NUT is centred around factions. Socialist and feminist traditions of activity within the union continue to have an important impact on the NUT's policies. Policy stances are the result of lengthy internal debate, and are subject to continual revision and renewal as the balance of internal political forces shifts between left and right. The presence of an organised left wing has ensured that broad policy remains generally in line with the mainstream of the labour movement, while the currently ascendent right wing leadership has brought about some internal restructuring to centralise decision-making.

Thus the NUT's similarity to unions with open structures in other parts of the economy extends into the realms of both practice and policy. While it did participate in early moves to establish a Teachers' Register to restrict entry to the profession, and while it still has the object of securing 'an acceptable form of self-government of the profession', it has remained committed to free collective bargaining as the main way to protect and advance the members' interests (Baron 1954). It has taken official industrial action since 1896 (Seifert, 1987: 16–18), and has a long tradition of left wing activity within it (Tropp 1957: 215–16; Seifert 1984).

It has also an established tradition of seeking to exert political influence. Teachers' associations have lobbied the government's Department of Education since the 1850s, and the NUT has enjoyed consultation through both formal and informal avenues on public education policy since 1911. As well as applying pressure to the administration, the NUT has also sought to influence Parliament itself. In 1877 the NUET conference decided to seek direct representation by teacher MPs, and the first two teachers were elected to Parliament in 1895 (Tropp 1957: 141–2). The union managed to protect its non-partisan non-party stance by sponsoring candidates from all of the main parties, and the first two elected were Conservative and Liberal. The union's graphic account of its campaign against a pay cut imposed in 1931 by the government against the wishes of both sides of Burnham gives an indication of its ability to use the method of legal enactment to mount sustained pressure on MPs individually and collectively (NUT 1931).

During the 1950s and 1960s incomes policy and other aspects of government economic policy were having an impact on teachers' pay and on the development of the education service. The NUT had by this time become deeply involved in education policy-making, being consulted by government on the widest range of education issues. However, the government was increasingly turning to consultation with the TUC over economic issues. The teacher organisations had remained outside of the TUC, being hostile to the perceived political alignment of that organisation – most of the TUC's affiliates were also affiliated to the Labour Party. The 'pay pause', announced by Selwyn Lloyd in 1961, resulted in the government's refusal to implement the settlement negotiated in Burnham. This spurred the NUT and the Joint Four, along with several other white-collar organisations, to launch the founding of the Conference of Professional and Public Service Organisations (COPPSO) in 1962.

COPPSO sought representation on the National Economic Development Council, similar to that granted to the TUC. The (Conservative!) government insisted on consultation with the TUC only, which resulted in COPPSO's collapse as first NALGO and then others withdrew and affiliated to the TUC (Spoor 1967: 551–8). The NUT affiliated in 1970, recognising this as the only option if it was to achieve anything by influencing government through the method of legal enactment. The government had succeeded in driving the NUT into a closer formal working relationship with the wider trade union movement.

In that year the NUT organised 65 per cent of the teaching workforce. By 1988, after ten years of continuous decline, this had fallen to 40 per cent.

Along with the restructuring of the education service proposed under the then Education Reform Bill, this prompted a restructuring of the union's staffing. Headquarters staffing was 'streamlined' and additional staff were provided in the regions. Part of the streamlining process included a reduction in the frequency of the national journal, *The Teacher*, to eight issues per year. School representatives also receive regular editions of *NUT News*, which is in a format suitable for display on notice boards.

By the end of 1992 the NUT claimed 213,656 members paying a subscription income to the union of £9,801,000 and with total gross assets of £9,186,000 (Annual Report of the Certification Officer 1993: 44–5). This made it the tenth largest union in the UK. This does not appear to be the profile of a union in crisis. None the less, the NUT is going through a period of introspection, falling membership and uncertain policy direction. It has responded to the 1988 reforms with important developments in regional structures and it still has a politically lively set of activists, but it has become fearful of further loss of members to the NASUWT and ATL. This fear corresponds with Turner's views of the demise of some of the cotton unions that in adversity they represented the organisation rather than either the membership or the wider industry. The NUT is flirting now, as it has in the past, with a teachers' register and with new definitions of professional unionism. Its future, however, must lie with its past as the union that best represents the interests of all teachers through a national rate for the job as the basis upon which all teachers must be paid in any planned national educational system.

The NASUWT – the craft-professional union

> We in NASUWT must restate our belief in the central importance of the craft of teaching . . . . All else is peripheral to the whole business of what goes on in schools.
>
> (NASUWT president, *Career Teacher*, spring 1989)

Structurally the NASUWT has some similarities to the NUT (see Figure 3.2), reflecting its origins as a splinter group growing at the NUT's expense. It has 387 local associations grouped into federations for the purposes of negotiating with LEAs, and it is divided into thirty-three districts for the purpose of electing national executive members. There are thirteen regional officials, mostly involved in individual casework and as advisors to federation secretaries and executive members during collective bargaining at the level of the LEA. Among many members and activists of both the NUT and the NASUWT, their often close co-operation within these apparently similar structures point logically to merger between the two. But these unions' origins and different traditions continue to militate against such unity, in spite of the need for it in the face of the government's assault and contrary to the policies of both organisations as determined by their annual conferences.

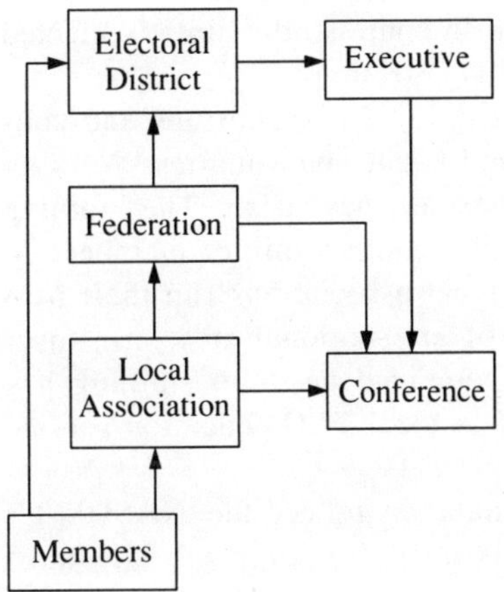

Figure 3.2 The structure of the NASUWT

Local associations send delegates to the annual conference on the same basis as the NUT – at least two delegates per local association, with an extra delegate for each hundred members after the first hundred, and without any upper limit. Federations send two delegates also. While the NUT's annual conference is often riven with factional activity as it debates the 'soft-political' issues of the day, the NASUWT's agenda consists solely of 'bread and butter' issues of concern to career professionals. This orientation is enshrined in the rule book; one of the union's objects is 'in particular to ensure that the salary scales encourage the recruitment to and retention in the teaching profession of career men and women teachers'.

Members of the national executive play a major role both nationally and locally, as with the NUT, taking part in local negotiations and providing a strong link between the membership and the leadership. A strong tradition of disciplined militancy has been weakened by compliance with the provisions of the 1980s legislation on ballots for industrial action. Prior to this the executive would issue instructions, which would be followed by most members. This discipline included the use of expulsions for strike breaking. However, the issue of industrial action illustrates only one aspect of the union's highly centralised organisation.

Much of the executive's authority is delegated to a small committee known as the officers group, which consists of the president, immediate past president, senior and junior vice-presidents, and treasurer. The treasurer and the junior vice-president are elected annually by secret ballot of the full membership. After a year of office the junior vice-president then has a year as senior vice-president followed by a year as president. With a maximum of only two changes of personnel per year (only one if the ex-president then becomes the treasurer) this group of five can acquire a concentration of authority and power approaching oligarchy. In contrast, the directly elected members of the executive are subject to annual election.

There are five committees of the executive: salaries, pensions and conditions; education; recruitment; training; and equal opportunities. Working parties are established on particular issues as they arise. The training committee organises courses for local activists, and committee members do much of the tutoring. Some of the larger local associations run their own training programmes but, in the absence of any regional structure, most provision is controlled centrally. As the perceived need for training has increased under LMS the union has turned to local TUC education service providers to develop and run courses.

Birmingham head office staffing continues to reflect the NASUWT's narrow range of concerns; the senior officials are all former members, almost all men, and almost all former secondary school teachers. Here the parallel with craft unions is striking in that the senior officials share the background of their core membership, being teaching practitioners rather than trade union professionals. Only a small number of staff are assigned to research, trade union education, and publicity functions, and only the most senior officials play any significant political role.

The thirteen regional officials are mainly caseworkers, although they also advise local officers and executive members during negotiations with LEAs. More recently the union has appointed a number of assistant regional officials and other field officers to assist with the extra case-load resulting from LMS, and several new offices have been opened to serve the regions. The regional officials are under line management control from head office, and there is no regional tier of union organisation. Regional meetings do occur in some areas, but these have no formal role in the union's government.

This union's centralised operation has been assisted by the application of computer technology. Membership lists and subscriptions are controlled from the centre, and are used to support a highly efficient system of distribution to local representatives. This database allows selective mailings to be made through the in-house printing and mailshot organisation. Members in schools, school representatives and local association secretaries can be targeted for briefings and other union publicity materials, with a rapid response to national developments being possible. The *Career Teacher* is a newspaper format journal appearing once or twice a term. It also appeared in magazine format once a term, now renamed as *Teaching Today*. Both are mailed direct to members. Local officers with the appropriate hardware can gain on-line access to the central membership register, a powerful tool for generating local mailing lists and for monitoring recruitment campaigns.

While the NUT's membership has declined since 1978, the NASUWT's has increased steadily, dipping slightly for three consecutive years in the late 1980s. Women have joined in increasing numbers, and now outnumber men by a small margin of 2,000. However, women were represented by under 20 per cent on the national executive and by less than 25 per cent among regional and national officers in 1990 (Labour Research Department 1991: 9). The Keele survey found that over half of NASUWT primary school representatives were women, but in secondary schools nearly 85 per cent of school representatives were men. The union has the smallest number of primary school representatives, and the highest number of secondary, reflecting its membership base.

The NASUWT continues to act in line with its roots in the separatist and elitist NAS, with policy-making controlled at the centre by a tight group of full-time officials and elected officers. Union activity is focused around a narrow range of conditions of service issues, to the exclusion of broader labour movement concerns. Membership participation in union activity is based in the larger secondary schools, and is centred on conditions of service rather than on internal union debates. The union has no political factions visibly active in it, although many of the leading activists are also active in the Labour Party. Paradoxically, the lack of a dissenting tradition within the union gives it the ability to act decisively on occasions. The NAS was the first teacher union to affiliate to the TUC, in 1968, and the NASUWT was first to set up a political fund, in 1989. Reporting the results of a survey of a sample of teachers just before the 1992 general election, the NASUWT announced that only 17 per cent would vote Conservative, compared with 48 per cent Labour.

At the centre of NASUWT policy is the notion of 'collegiality'. The concept is difficult to pin down, but is associated with rhetoric that asserts the centrality of the classroom teacher in the education service, calls for a non-hierarchical salary structure, and seeks the participation of all teachers in the management of schools. This is used to justify calls for the establishment of clear pay differentials based on job descriptions. It is through this 'big idea' that the NASUWT seeks to revitalise its narrow focus on craft-professional issues; as the 1990 junior vice- president put it, 'the collegiate approach . . . would focus finance on teaching in the classroom, the central activity in education' (*Career Teacher*, spring 1990). The very vagueness of the concept gives the centralised leadership the freedom to interpret and re-interpret policy as and when necessary.

The NASUWT remains the second largest teacher union between the NUT and ATL. In December 1992 it reported that it had 190,637 members paying £5,754,000 in subscriptions and with total gross assets of £11,058,000 (Annual Report of the Certification Officer 1993: 44–5). This makes it the twelfth largest trade union in the UK and it appears to be flourishing. Membership numbers are relatively stable after many years of strong growth and this reflects both the static nature of the teacher workforce and the intense rivalry with both the NUT and ATL. The union remains strong in action but weak in coherent principles. Thus both its support for the STRB and its belief in pay differences located at school level in 'collegiality' are at best vague responses to its line on the central role of the career teacher. This policy problem added to a lack of opportunity for decisive local action has taken some of the attractiveness away from the union. It has in general moved closer to the NUT in policy terms, but has responded quite distinctly to the advent of LMS.

The NASUWT has decided to rely more than ever on lay activists to deal with LMS related issues in the schools, and has not responded robustly in organisational terms to the new order. The future for the union, as for the NUT, is unclear – it must soon decide whether it upholds its own traditions of fighting through industrial action for the narrow craft interests of its main constituents or to abandon these in favour of some school-based corporatism. Failure to be decisive may witness a period of decline as members defect to its rivals.

ATL – the non-TUC alternative

In 1978 the four single-sex secondary teacher associations merged into two organisations, AMMA for classroom teachers and SHA for heads and deputies in secondary schools. AMMA changed its title to ATL in 1993. ATL is the only teacher organisation to exclude heads and deputies from membership, maintaining a continuing link back to its origins as organisations of assistant masters and assistant mistresses. There are 109 branches, most with boundaries that are coterminous with the LEAs. The union's structure is shown in Figure 3.3.

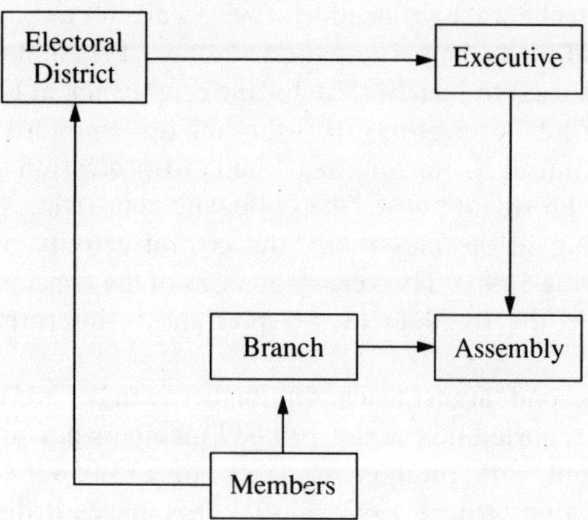

Figure 3.3 The structure of the ATL

ATL's annual conference is known as the Assembly, and its size is restricted to a maximum of 600 including members of the executive committee, which is limited to a maximum of 100 plus the officers. Each branch is entitled to a minimum of two Assembly representatives, with additional representatives proportionate to the number of branch members. Electoral districts are established for the election of the executive. Committees of the national executive include finance; conditions of employment; legislation and parliamentary; education; defence, which decides on assistance to individual members 'in professional difficulty', monitors legal assistance to members, and monitors 'trends affecting the personal and/or professional security of members'; international; policy promotion; and member services. Members of the executive are required to stand for re-election after two years.

Like the NASUWT, ATL's staffing is concentrated at the centre, with some forty officials and support staff at head office in London. There are a number of locally based field officers and casework officials, many operating on a retainer plus fees basis, serving branches and members. There are no regional structures. The centralised membership system can supply branch officers with listings for local mail-shots, and is also used for direct mailings to members. *Report*, the union's journal for members, is produced once or twice each term, and *Update* is sent at more frequent intervals to schools in a notice board display format. Substantial resources are devoted to producing publicity materials, leaflets and booklets that are well researched and attractively presented.

Unlike the NASUWT and the NUT this union does not have a strong orientation towards collective bargaining. It declares itself to be 'an independent, registered trade union and professional association' and, while it is not against the use of industrial action in principle, it allows individual members the right to exempt themselves from industrial action should the Association ever sanction it. Neither ATL nor its predecessors have ever organised the kind of activity repeatedly referred to by the Webbs as the corollary of collective bargaining, the strike. The creation of the pay review body has suited ATL well, sitting comfortably with its managerial-professional orientation.

Membership is concentrated heavily in secondary schools, taking up nearly two-thirds of the 78,500 members in primary and secondary schools in the UK in 1990. Membership in the independent sector is still relatively strong and influential at over 14,500 in 1990, equivalent to over half of the then membership in primary schools. Growth in the primary sector has thus been relatively slow, but it may have speeded up recently; in 1992 AMMA was claiming 37,000 members there (about a quarter of total membership). Women make up 70 per cent of the membership, and they outnumber men among the senior union staff. However, the majority of branch secretaries are men based in secondary schools, and over two-thirds of secondary school representatives are men. Nine out of ten primary school representatives are women. The Keele survey found that ATL has about the same number of secondary school representatives as the NUT, suggesting that even though the union originated in the secondary sector it is not the best organised there.

ATL continues to operate in a way that is aligned with the 'company union' model. It argues for a 'common sense' approach, with management playing its true role of providing leadership and direction, and with the employers showing proper regard for dedicated professionals, while the union provides management with a well regulated flow of information about the needs of both pupils and their professional teachers. As there is no commitment to the principles of collective bargaining, which is seen as adversarial and therefore as counter to the desired identity of interest and purpose between employers and employees, there are no mechanisms within the union for membership participation in the determination of collective bargaining policies. Branches and branch officers have never operated as centres of resistance through industrial action, although they have organised pressure on LEAs. There is no tradition of branch-based organised internal pressure on the union leadership, leaving the leadership free to pursue its objectives without interference from the members. ATL is structured around and oriented towards the organised flow of information rather than around the mobilisation of resistance to the employers.

Accordingly ATL places stronger emphasis on the method of legal enactment than do the two TUC affiliates. It accords a higher priority to the establishment of a General Teaching Council 'analogous to the General Medical Council'. However, during merger talks with PAT in 1991, which would have formed a 'bigger, moderately-based union', AMMA would not agree to adopt PAT's no-strike rule. Nor would they agree to continue PAT's recruitment of head teachers, and the talks failed (AMMA *Update*, No. 54, December 1991).

The ATL is a strange creature in trade union terms. It does not ban but does not take part in industrial action if at all possible. It will link up with other unions on some issues but remains outside the TUC. It has virtually no regional or local organisation, and shows little interest in collective bargaining. Yet with 152,795 members it is listed as the sixteenth largest union in the UK with membership contributions of £5,933,000 and total gross assets of £3,624,000 (*Annual Report of the Certification Officer 1993*: 44–5). It has grown through taking members from the other unions and this has been on the basis of its opposition to industrial action, the more TUC and left leanings of some of the leaders of the other unions, and from its high public profile as an organisation deeply concerned with professional matters. Its future depends on two developments: its ability to recruit in the further education sector at the expense of NATFHE; and its response, both in policy and in practical help, to the issues thrown up by LMS. Our view is that the ATL is least well placed of the big three unions to deal with LMS.

PAT – the no-action union

PAT was established in 1970, growing rapidly in the mid-1980s during the 1984/5 strikes, and stabilising at a plateau of 41,000 (see Table 3.13). While PAT's membership was growing, so was the NASUWT, SHA, NAHT and AMMA. Only the NUT's was declining. Over 80 per cent of its members are

Table 3.13 PAT membership

Year	*Membership*
1984	27,902
1985	39,333
1986	41,536
1987	43,108
1988	42,053
1989	42,793
1990	41,795
1991	41,174
1992	41,264

Source: Certification Officer

women. This organisation recruits among all classes of teacher in England and Wales, Scotland and Northern Ireland.

PAT's orientation towards trade unionism is indicated by its rule number 4, which states that 'Members shall *not* go on strike in any circumstances.' This is described in the Members' Handbook as the association's 'Cardinal Rule' – the handbook gives additional clarification as follows:

> The Council of the Association has clarified the Cardinal Rule further by saying that:
> (a) The term strike action is to be interpreted to include all forms of industrial action;
> (b) The cardinal rule requires members to continue to carry out both contractual and non-contractual duties during any dispute;
> (c) Withdrawal of goodwill, working to rule and refusal to perform voluntary duties previously carried out are all strategies which come under the umbrella of the Cardinal Rule and are consequently incompatible with membership of the Association.
>
> (PAT 1994: 8–9)

This emphatic rejection of all forms of industrial action leaves PAT with none of the recognisable features of trade unionism, in spite of the organisation's claim to be an independent trade union. This is an extreme version of company unionism dressing up its pro-managerial stance with a concern to capture the moral high ground by putting 'Children First' (PAT's motto). It implies that taking industrial action is automatically against the interests of children, and therefore against the interests of teachers. For PAT, taking industrial action in defence of educational standards is a contradiction in terms. Rather than face the world as it is, PAT members are more concerned to face the world as they think it ought to be. In their idealised world those who have been fortunate enough to gain leadership positions as managers ought to listen to the teacher professionals through their mouthpiece; conflict only arises because of people who refuse to behave 'properly'.

According to the rules, the sovereign body of the association is either a general meeting or a meeting of delegates, as decided by the Council. There are no rules on the appointment of delegates in the rule book. The Council is elected for a three year period, with no electoral constituencies other than the two seats reserved for the independent sector and two for the further and higher education sector. There are committees covering professional services, education, and finance and general purposes; executive committees for Scotland and Northern Ireland; an advisory group for Wales; and committees for tertiary education and for the independent sector.

PAT has a small head office staff based in Derby. It is unable to provide the necessary support for members in local difficulties and deals with industrial relations issues on a member by member basis. The union has failed to gain strength from the developments of LMS although its voice was listened to with some respect by senior government figures when they planned the reforms of schools. Our prognosis for PAT is that it will struggle to survive the localisation of industrial relations issues and institutions and will tend to leak members to ATL.

NAHT

The National Association of Head Teachers recruits 'Head Teachers, Deputies, Principals and Vice-Principals of educational establishments recognised as such by NAHT national council and Teachers in such establishments who are paid on Deputy Head/Vice-Principal salaries'. It claims to represent over 80 per cent of all heads in England and Wales and to have 'thousands of deputy heads as well as many members in Northern Ireland, Scotland, Isle of Man, Channel Islands, British Forces Schools and overseas'. Membership is equally divided between women and men. Local organisation is in local associations, which are grouped together into branches where there are a number of them within an LEA area. Membership levels are shown in Table 3.14, and the structure is shown in Figure 3.4.

There are thirty-one districts for the election of the National Council, which is advised by committees for each of secondary, middle, primary and

Table 3.14 NAHT membership

Year	*Membership*
1984	24,119
1985	29,762
1986	31,749
1987	34,048
1988	34,855
1989	35,238
1990	39,891
1991	38,140
1992	38,086

Source: Certification Officer

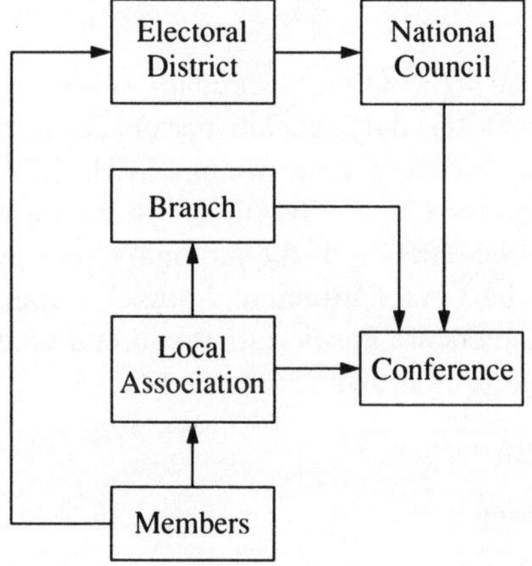

Figure 3.4 The structure of the NAHT

special schools. Members serve for a three year term of office, and the council has the power to delete policy which it deems to be out of date. Only six of the thirty-three council members listed in the handbook are women. Women are not only under-represented among head teachers; when they do get to be heads they are then under-represented in the heads' organisation. Some sixteen specialist full-time head office staff based in Haywards Heath are listed in the association's handbook, along with eleven regional officers. There is no regional tier of organisation.

As well as producing a termly journal and a bulletin for members the NAHT also supplies members with a range of reference publications. It also owns a company which provides management development courses, consultancy services and publications, available to both members and non-members.

The NAHT has a high profile in the education world since it does represent the majority of head teachers upon whom has fallen the main responsibility of making LMS work. The NAHT has some difficulty with its role as a union for managers and is unlike most other organisations of this type. All of its members have been promoted through the ranks of classroom teacher, and most belonged to other teacher unions before joining the NAHT. This means that many have strong views on what a union should be about and also that the managerial mantle is worn with some misgivings, especially under the present changes. As a result the NAHT makes pronouncements about school and educational matters in general, seeking to be the voice of reason and experienced leadership, but must also comment on the particular problems facing head-managers as employees. At the moment the union leadership seems to be holding both elements together, although there is little evidence that the majority of NAHT members support the union's policies on several important aspects of the 1988 reforms.

SHA

SHA recruits 'any Head or Deputy Head of a public secondary school or college' in the UK education system. It is the only teacher organisation to restrict itself to the state sector. Branches are coterminous with LEA boundaries, and SHA has the clearest regional tier of government in the form of Areas. These form constituencies for the election of the national Council, and the Area Committees provide a link between national and branch levels. There is no delegate conference, all members are entitled to attend and vote at the annual general meeting. The structure is shown in Figure 3.5.

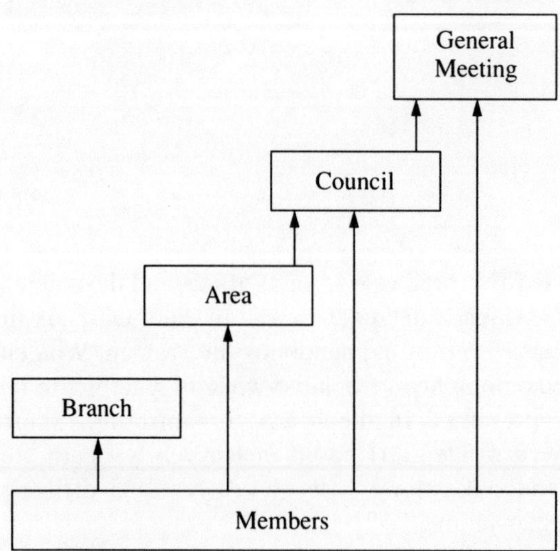

Figure 3.5 The structure of the SHA

The national council is elected from the Areas, and is supplemented by members elected from the national membership. Area representatives serve for a maximum of three years, national representatives for nine. The main committees are as follows: education; salaries and conditions of service; public and parliamentary; professional; and management support. Other standing committees, reporting to either the council or one of its main committees, include: deputy head teachers; grant maintained; publications; international; LMS; legal services; appraisal; equal opportunities; and special educational needs.

Unlike the NAHT, SHA has grown steadily over the last decade as deputies in secondary schools have turned to a heads' association in preference to the main classroom unions (see Table 3.15). This reflects the increasing movement of the head's role towards that of manager and resource allocator rather than teaching colleague. SHA has set up MAPS (Managerial and Professional Services), a wholly owned private company running a management development programme and providing a management consultancy service. Along with government departments and business sponsors SHA is setting up the National Educational Assessment Centre at Oxford Brookes University. This organisation is intended to develop head teacher management skills and to assist governors with head teacher recruitment. Members receive the Association's 'Managing' series of books, as well as the termly journal *Updates* and the bulletin *Headlines*.

Table 3.15 SHA membership

Year	*Membership*
1984	5,682
1985	6,704
1986	7,087
1987	6,702
1988	7,099
1989	7,452
1990	7,604
1991	7,776
1992	8,027

Source: Certification Officer

Alongside its developing orientation as an organisation of managers, SHA retains a formal commitment to trade unionism. It advises members faced with industrial action by teaching or non-teaching staff to 'accept it, adjusting their managerial role accordingly, if necessary preventing part of the school from functioning should the proper labour not be available'. Moreover, they 'should take no action which will have the effect of mitigating the action of the other association' (SHA 1993: 28–9). SHA has a clear and prominently published equal opportunities policy, ensuring women and ethnic minority representation on committees and including the establishment of targets. Women make up 30 per cent of the membership.

Its small head office staff in Leicester find it increasingly difficult to cope with the demands of presenting a case to the STRB, handling and co-ordinating local issues and being the main voice of secondary school heads and deputies. As a result the union relies heavily on its regional organisation and especially lay activists. In this sense SHA is the nearest of all the unions to Turner's model of an 'exclusive democracy', and shows both the strengths and weaknesses of that type of union.

CONCLUSIONS

We have seen that, from their earliest years as state employees, teachers sought to protect their interests and to influence government policy through well organised and professionally independent unions and associations. Overall they have been successful and until the early 1970s the NUT led the way both in its influence on government and its domination of the pay determination system. In this the NUT represented two central features of the profession which were first the need for a common rate for the job irrespective of gender, school or qualification, and second the belief that state school education should be available to all free and within a national system properly funded.

In the 1970s both of these pillars were being undermined by government policies including incomes policy and the development of the myth that the nation could not afford such an education system as comprehensive schools suggested. The result was years of industrial action which allowed ATL and to a lesser extent PAT to recruit teachers alienated by such overt use of trade union tactics. This period also saw the development of ideas on pay to supplant the national rate with local and performance rates which helped develop both the separateness of the heads and deputies and the collegiality of the NASUWT's new found craft protectionism. This latter increasingly appealed to secondary school teachers convinced, wrongly in our view, that their status and pay was being held down by the links with the primary sector. The position now is that the NUT, NASUWT and ATL are in a bitter rivalry over members and the policy high ground, and the main beneficiaries of such division remain the government and ultimately the employers.

The teacher workforce is a major preoccupation of the government for two main reasons. First is the state's interest in the outcome of school education, and second is its cost. Both the nature of the work that teachers do, and the size and composition of the teacher workforce, are issues that the government has an interest in seeking to control. From the teachers' point of view this need to control teacher labour represents a threat to their job security, to their status, and to their autonomy.

The purpose of school education cannot be reduced to the pursuit of knowledge in the abstract; schools are located within society at large, and they both shape it and are shaped by it. While we do not suggest that schools have the *function* of preparing pupils to be willing workers within a capitalist system, serious consequences would follow if schools produced large numbers of young people who did not share the values associated with capitalism, who did not possess the skills required by employers, and who did not conform to the discipline expected of paid employees. A coincidence of interests has to be taken for granted: that industry needs certain types of workers in certain quantities, and that school leavers need jobs that industry can only provide in certain proportions. The school education system (including the private sector) might be said to be working correctly when it produces entrants to each segment of the labour markets in the correct quantities. Whatever else happens in schools, school leavers must emerge from them equipped with skills, with knowledge, and with attitudes that are appropriate to their status as potential employees. School teachers must prepare their pupils to accept the discipline of work, and to accept that a few of them will achieve high status in well paid and satisfying jobs, while most of them will work harder for much less in unsatisfying routine jobs. When schools fail to deliver the right sort of young people it is usually the teachers that take the blame. As Tropp notes, by the 1840s teachers already 'were made responsible for the universal degeneration of every generation of children compared to the one preceding' (Tropp 1957: 148).

The question as to whether teachers can be trusted to ensure the desired outcomes has been explicitly voiced during the 1980s. The introduction of the national curriculum and the requirements on regular testing place tighter constraints on the autonomy of teachers and on their freedom to innovate. Alongside this, the introduction of the appraisal procedures now required by law enables links to be established between teachers' performance in the classroom and their terms and conditions of employment. Failure by any teacher to provide the right sort of teaching could lead to a blight on career prospects, to withholding of pay rises, to disciplinary action, or to selection for redundancy. These are mainstream industrial relations issues, and we consider them in more detail in chapters 4 and 5.

As well as a concern for educational outcomes, the government also has a view on the cost. The debate on cost is usually linked to outcomes through the notion of 'value for money', to achieve the desired outcomes at the least cost. Since some 70 per cent of education spending is on teachers' salaries, cuts in the salary bill must be the most significant way of cutting costs. Teachers' pay has been the main focus of union organisation throughout the history of the teacher unions, with the NUT arguing for a single pay scale, the secondary teacher organisations opposing levelling down to the level of primary teachers, and the head teachers currently in favour of a separate scale for heads.

We have considered pay determination in detail in chapter 2, and we look at the implications of locally determined pay through workplace bargaining in chapter 5. However, we can establish here that the union response to the breaking up of the national pay scale is not likely to be uniform. ATL has faith in the capacity of appraisal systems to deliver 'fairness' in the form of the best rewards to the best teachers, while the NUT faces the problems of serving the many and varied pay problems of members scattered in small primary schools. NASUWT appears to relish the prospect of its well-organised secondary school members doing well out of local pay determination.

A second way of holding down costs is to employ fewer teachers and make those remaining work harder, spending more time in front of more pupils in the classroom. The length of the working day, and the division of working time between teaching, preparing lessons, and doing other duties has become increasingly important as school managers have sought to tighten their control over teachers. There is a clear drift towards the codification of teachers' duties, where none previously existed. Hours of work are now specified (since 1987 teachers must work at the direction of the head teacher for 1,265 hours per year on 195 days per year), and teachers no longer have supervisory responsibilities at meal times. If teachers' labour can be intensified, that is if they can be made to work more hours in the classroom rather than out of it, then fewer teachers are necessary.

Additions to the workload of the classroom teacher, both by the imposition of the national curriculum and testing prescriptions and by reducing the number of teachers in order to meet budget requirements, represent major challenges for the unions. The direction of teachers to perform specific tasks cuts across their autonomy in the classroom, and the reduction of non-contact time cuts off any escape from the stresses of classroom teaching. The traditional responses to pressures of this nature may be either individual, through increased levels of absenteeism, or collective through trade union organisation. By late 1994, organised activity against over-work appeared to have been patchy, although the 1993 national boycott of the pupil testing requirements by all three classroom unions did represent a concerted mobilisation aimed at changing the government's regulations.

Another way to achieve reduced costs is by substituting expensive qualified teachers with cheaper unqualified ones. This issue was one of the earliest concerns of the NUT, and the establishment of an all-graduate profession was a key goal. It has surfaced again, with the introduction of the licensed teacher scheme. In primary schools the increased use of classroom assistants provides opportunities to run larger classes with fewer teachers. The dilution of teacher skills, through the introduction of less skilled labour into the classroom to alter the skill profile of the school, adds another twist to the attack on the autonomy of the classroom teacher.

The potential threats of removal of autonomy, of intensification of work, of dilution, and of de-skilling have been faced by employees throughout the history of capitalism (Braverman 1974), and have shaped both their defence organisations and the responses of those organisations. In the following chapters we draw out the changes taking place in the school system, in the environment within which the teacher unions operate. We will see that the unions face a number of challenges, including measures to exclude them from decision-making, the substitution of pay review for collective bargaining, falling relative pay levels, and human resource management techniques in the workplace. We will also see that the ending of the national system of collective bargaining is accompanied by the disintegration of national terms and conditions of employment. In this chapter we have traced the origins of the teacher trade unions in different sectors of the teacher workforce, tracing the development of the complex structure of trade unionism among school teachers in England and Wales in the 1990s. The unions have no recent tradition of workplace bargaining, and the workplace representatives have little experience of negotiating.

However, the fact that the teacher workforce is highly unionised is important for the future of industrial relations in schools (Seifert 1992a). The recent reforms introduce a range of substantive issues that can only be settled at the level of the school. This raises the question of control over school-level industrial relations; in particular whether either management or trade unions have the ability to gain control over workplace-related issues. The development of workplace union organisation is affected by a range of external and internal factors (McCarthy 1966; Brown *et al.* 1978), including the education reforms in general and the introduction of LMS in particular. The activity of workplace representatives, and the nature of their relationship with management, are also likely to be affected by these changes (Batstone *et al.* 1977; Terry 1983). Furthermore, the formal arrangements for industrial relations activity, the joint consultative committees and joint negotiating committees at LEA level, may need to be replaced by arrangements at school level (Marchington 1987; Millward *et al.* 1992).

These issues are taken up in more detail in chapters 5 and 6, where we examine the unions' responses to the reform programme. In particular we need to have regard to the impact of the abolition of national bargaining and of the continuing inter-union competition. Adjusting to life without Burnham may prove difficult for all of the unions – indeed the government may have assumed that ending national bargaining would leave the unions without a role.

4 Employers, managers and the management of human resources

INTRODUCTION

This chapter seeks to illustrate the nature of the crisis facing school managers and employers. With the decline both in the LEA personnel function and in the application of LEA-wide collective agreements there is an institutional gap and a knowledge gap. This will affect the implementation and interpretation of national agreements and LEA procedures, having major implications for school practice, especially with regard to the settlement of disputes. Familiar issues will become more difficult to resolve and this will lead to new power relationships within the school as between senior managers and staff (Johnson 1984a). For example, if the school appoints a new teacher and allegations are made of unfair practice and/or if a teacher disagrees with their appraisal and/or if teachers and managers disagree over the disciplining of pupils and/or if there are conflicts over the allocation of teacher workload and/or if there are problems with the competence of colleagues then how will such matters be resolved? Traditionally some of these would have been dealt with through union and LEA officers in liaison with school staff, but this may no longer be possible (Stenning *et al.* 1984).

With the withering away of traditional industrial relations institutions there emerge new ways of daily managing schools. This might include a more managerial approach rooted in the development of HRM practices, or it might require the emergence of school level bargaining mechanisms, or it might lead to a dangerous vacuum in decision-making and expertise. This chapter provides a brief comment on the nature of state employment, and then discusses current employer and management rights and concerns. The rest of the chapter deals with the introduction of HRM into schools with particular reference to employee resourcing, appraisal and performance-related pay (PRP), and employee relations. Many of these themes are then re-examined in light of our and other research in chapters 5 and 6.

The central point is that the breakdown in LEA-wide personnel and industrial relations functions means that some of them must be devolved to schools, and that this requires school managers to take decisions previously outside their competence. This opens the door to both poor-quality decision-making and, more importantly, to the creation of a management–staff split in schools with all that implies for the continuation of team management and whole-school development. In this way the teacher remains an employee of the LEA (the local state agency) but increasingly becomes like an employee in the private sector because of the implementation of market forces and HRM practices. We have seen in chapter 3 the importance for teacher trade unionism of the employee status of teachers, and we can now examine the special aspects of being a state employee.

Aspects of being a state employee

Being a state employee, whether directly employed as with the civil servants or indirectly through some public corporation such as mines, railways and the health service, has had a special place in British political economy. What is it about state employment that conjures up such a variety and strength of opinion?

The miners, for example, fought long and hard to have their employment wrested away from private coal owners. As early as 1892 the miners were able to win TUC policy that 'the enterprise [mining] should also be, like the Post Office, a State department' (Page Arnot 1979: 105). For them several important themes merged with nationalisation and many were listed in the 1946 Miners' Charter – modernisation and increased productivity figured high on the agenda as part of the belief that in a socialist Britain all workers ought to fight for economic recovery. Most of the points in the charter, however, reflected deep seated labour issues – acceptable levels of redundancy pay, proper youth training, lifelong training for job improvement, new safety regulations, decent compensation for illness and injury, wages to keep up with other occupations, seven hour day, respectable pensions, adequate medical examination and treatment, and wider improvements in the mining towns and villages and in welfare provision (Page Arnot 1955: 269–71).

So, for miners, working for the state implied significant improvements in working conditions as well as greater say through the NUM over management decisions. A similar position was taken by other workers, especially the railwaymen (Bagwell 1963). This combination of socialist aspiration which involved both a worker voice in the management and direction of the industry for the common good and better conditions of service was decisive. The experience of the private mines and railways was both of poor investment and poor working conditions. This situation was generalised to a broader vision of a socialism with public employment – Wal Hannington among others saw nationalisation as the means beyond all others to solve the misery of the distressed areas when he noted that 'the fact that natural resources, side by side with human resources, lie idle year after year is a sure indication that there is something basically wrong' (Hannington 1937: 251).

Such a summary discussion shows that state employment is not an obvious or trivial aspect of the employment relation. If the workers in major industries felt that nationalisation offered special benefits to themselves and the nation then what was the feeling within the public services? In the case of doctors many were reluctant to be 'nationalised' under the NHS in 1948. Michael Foot in his biography of Bevan believed that the main cause for their concern was 'a non-political conservatism, a revulsion against all change' (Foot 1973: 103). This, in Foot's view, was more important than the real conservatism of the BMA leadership or the fear that state employment would undermine clinical freedom. Whatever the issues, and Foot's account appears as accurate as any, by the late 1980s the doctors and the BMA were fighting equally strongly to stay state employees and resist the drift back to a private medical profession.

Teachers are in a different position. The profession itself grew up within the state structure erected through the 1870 Act (Gosden 1972). Most never knew private education, although many suffered from repressive local school boards. But it was the 1918 Act that brought schools and teachers into the full ambit of national state employment. Here was guaranteed central government finance for secondary expansion, here was the raising of the leaving age to fourteen, and here were greater safeguards for the teachers themselves as state employees. The 1918 Act was only the formal mark of the struggle for rights and recognition of the teachers in these years. As Simon noted, 'the teachers' organisations bridged a gap to join hands with other branches of the education service in favour of reform, while also bringing support to those within the Labour Party intent on making advance towards "secondary education for all" the chief point of policy and of action to realise it' (Simon 1974: 18).

In this sense there was struggle, some of it imbued with the same concerns as the miners and later the doctors, to improve and safeguard working conditions and have some say over the direction of the service. The most symbolic episode to combine these features was perhaps the Burston school strike in 1914 (Edwards 1974). The issues were many and closely interwoven, but the central matter was that the local unelected school authorities decided to rid themselves of the local teacher, Mrs Higdon, because she taught the children about matters, such as land reform and agricultural workers' rights, which were not in keeping with the views of the local landowners and clergy. She was dismissed and after some delay the NUT provided her with national support. In the end the children attended an alternative school taught by Mrs Higdon and avoided the official school. This case, as with hundreds of others, again illustrates the main concerns in state employment – protection of employee rights, both individual and collective, and some mechanism to help determine management policy.

Thus the historical tradition that underpins the demand for state employment and the theoretical issues concerned with directing industry and service towards a democratically determined common good, rather than the vagaries of the free market, have created a strong desire and widespread support to work in and for public services. This may lie behind the professionalism of teachers which allows them to have a special relationship with their daily occupation. In recent years, particularly in the 1980s, this position has been consistently challenged with a new orthodoxy that state employment need not and in fact should not provide either the benefits assumed above in the protection of working conditions or some control over management of the service and/or industry. This view was most thoroughly developed in general by the Centre for Policy Studies and their position, endorsed by Mrs Thatcher and Sir Keith Joseph, was that nothing should stand in the way of commercial objectives.

The redefinition of this aspect of state employment has led some commentators to develop a notion that the state was a 'model employer' and is no longer. Fredman and Morris argued, for example, that the most important distinguishing feature of the state as employer is 'the power to govern, either by initiating legislation or by the exercise of executive powers' (Fredman and Morris 1989: 7). One example they give is the 1987 Teachers Pay and Conditions Act which abolished the collective bargaining machinery for teachers.

This view is largely based on the doctrine espoused by the Priestley Commission (1955) which sought to regularise the position of the ever growing numbers within state employment, and to lay out the liberal pluralist position that there was an explicit trade-off between private and public employment. The public sector would tend to pay less and provide fewer opportunities for individuals and/or individual units to earn extra than private sector employment. In exchange the public employee would enjoy greater job security, better pensions, a more regulated workplace, full collective bargaining rights, and some degree of control over decisions. Most of this was quantified through the civil service Pay Research Unit which embodied the essential pay principle of fair comparisons.

All of this is well known, but the question remains about the actual historical experience of state employment and the expectations of certain groups of workers about the benefits of state employment. It is largely wrong to talk about the state as a model employer. Whatever the Whitley reports recommended, and whatever good practice existed, was not the direct result of any institution of the state, nor of those in positions of power and authority within the state, to create a better form of employment for their employees. The function and practice of state employment was rooted in the nature of the state itself and in the specific struggles waged by various sections of the community to secure state employment and state control/ownership of given services and industries.

Conservative groups which throughout the nineteenth century created a more powerful and active central and local state did so in the interests of controlling and directing the forces unleashed by industrialisation and world competition. None was done in the interests of the employees, community or users as such. What was possible, and sometimes happened, was that these groups singly or together forced on the relevant state agency and government better employment conditions, more accountability to local communities and greater say for users. Once again the government of the day is seeking to concentrate more power in its hands in order to remove the power and influence of the LEAs, and once again this will be contested as individual schools fall foul of the ever tighter financial regulations and national curriculum. The battle ground will increasingly be in schools rather than at LEA level and the battles will be fought over central managerial issues of control over performance and rewards.

EMPLOYERS AND MANAGERS: DETERMINING SCHOOL PRACTICE

Most of the reforms with which school teachers and managers have to come to terms are top-down changes. While there was recognition that the dominant tradition was wearing thin and while familiar debates within the educational world continued to rage, none the less there was little evidence for any groundswell of opinion from teachers and/or parents for the changes that have been introduced. This section provides a brief summary of the policy direction of the senior civil servants at the DFE (previously the DES and sometimes referred to as such), and then examines the meaning of the new employers and managers in terms of their industrial relations and personnel duties and functions.

Senior civil servants at the DFE (DES)

The strongly held views that state employment should provide for better conditions of service and for more say over decisions came from both socialist ideas and practical struggles. The fact that more often than not state employment combined neither of these themes illustrates the reluctance of state elites and conservative philosophy to accept such aspirations. For the teachers, as was noted above, the start of state employment, as we understand it and as they expressed it, was really in 1918. From that time Burnham was supposed to provide the necessary, but clearly not sufficient, conditions to allow the teachers through their organisations to bargain for both better pay and more say.

The Burnham system provides a good example of how central government was able to play a major role in the employment of teachers even though local authorities were the legal employer. This illustrates Clay's central point about the tension when paymasters do not employ, and employers do not pay (Clay 1929). Over the years the balance of pay bill costs have been increasingly met by central government, and this is reflected in the tightening of central government controls over the LEAs as seen in the 1965 RTA and again with the 1987 TPCA and 1988 ERA.

This trend towards centralism and the deconstruction of any commitment to being a 'model employer' was further developed in the 1980s. The reassertion of long standing conservative views on the nature of state employment for teachers and others was possible given the weakness of the teacher organisations, the decline in professional status, the loss of community politics, and the removal of LEA and parent power. Lawrence has traced some of this through the policies and activities of senior figures within the DES.

He argued that in the late 1980s four factors dominated government and DES policy-making: expenditure cuts, falling rolls, the accumulation of critical HMI reports, and the drive towards centralism (Lawrence 1992: 106). The cuts in expenditure were seen as a positive way forward in the economic recovery and were helped by falling school population. For now we will comment on the last two points and how the undermining of teacher professional independence paved the way for the move to central controls over the curriculum.

This was foreshadowed when in 1982 Keith Joseph published HMI reports for the first time in line with the 'customer knowledge' thesis. It crudely states that for a free market to operate both customers and providers must have as much knowledge as possible about competing schools through indicators such as academic league tables and truancy rates. This coincided with the *Teaching Quality* (1983) white paper which gave HMIs more powers, and set the scene for propaganda about the efficacy of comprehensive education. 'Behind the thrashing about over curriculum control was old Black Paper mythology, constantly repeated in the party conference resolutions, that standards were falling. In fact this was clearly not the case' (Lawrence 1992: 110).

The 1988 ERA came from a predominantly conservative view of education rooted in the independent schools. The vast majority of education secretaries of state and permanent secretaries at the DES come from independent schools. It is quite clear that this background 'does suggest a certain remoteness from the public sector, a remoteness, aloofness, and distancing' (Lawrence 1992: 111). The importance of this is indicated by Lawton when he argued that 'teachers in state schools occupy a number of positions in direct conflict with current Conservative ideology, and, in particular, they appear to enjoy security of employment and are not susceptible to 'normal' market forces' (Lawton 1988: 155). Furthermore, 'it has been convenient for the DES and (some) members of HMI to support this policy, partly because it increases their own power of influence . . . they want a more uniform system with less autonomy for individual institutions' (Lawton 1988: 166).

The main aspects of the 1988 Act which added to further centralisation were: first the national curriculum; secondly the powers it gave to (returned to) the Secretary of State; and thirdly LMS, which 'provided the Secretary of State with more duties and the DES with more powers' (Lawrence 1992: 116).

The hallmark of policy with regard to the withering away of LEA powers, namely centralisation and attacks on teacher autonomy, come from a state elite in which the right-wing instincts of government ministers found a happy accord with the pernicious conservatism of the DES leadership. Lawrence concludes his damning study with the view that, 'the external agenda for the 1979–92 education programme revolved round the government's economic strategies, the policy of curbing local authority expenditure and the substantial increase in unemployment having the most direct influence on educational services' (Lawrence 1992: 144).

The employers

The employers have a duty to carry out the policies of government as mediated through the senior civil servants in the DFE. One important aspect of the current reforms is the extent to which they are top-down and have been enforced on employers often against their wishes. This in itself causes immense difficulties for all concerned, but such problems are further exacerbated through the less than transparent relationship in law and in practice as between duties and responsibilities for the employer, the school governors and the head teachers. The resulting crisis of both institutional forms and know-how practices has left employers floundering for a role in the educational sub-government.

The LEA remains the employer in general under the 1944 and 1988 Acts for those teachers in schools with delegated budgets, but not in opted out (grant-maintained) schools. The relationship between school managers – heads and deputies – governing body, LEAs, DFE officials and ministers has always been less than clear. For many years after the 1944 Act there was an assumed partnership arrangement by which LEAs had the greatest say in the management of schools in terms of strategic policy, and heads and deputies dominated operational management practice. The role of governors was variable but often supportive of school management without being obtrusive, and the DES and ministers tended to be hands off with regard to school affairs. This system was very variable as between schools and LEAs, and often obscured important power relationships and decision-making (Seifert 1989). In terms of industrial relations the 'LEAs engaged in local bargaining with union representatives . . . Local agreements covered such matters as redeployment, voluntary service, and cover for absent teachers' (Stenning *et al*. 1984: 128).

The first point is that managers, whether they are heads or LEA officials, are answerable to the employer. Managers, in this sense, are the agents and representatives of the employer and, as far as employees and their unions are concerned, decisions by managers reflect employer policy and have the authority of employer support. This means, in extreme cases, that teachers can be dismissed and schools closed by the employer acting through managers. This represents an important aspect of both state employment and collective bargaining: that managers are required to carry out the policy of the employer but that they may be subject to strong countervailing influences from their own profession, their own union, their own service culture, and their own expectations of being a head teacher and/or LEA official.

This is the aspect of school and LEA partnership that has enabled consensus among the education profession, widely defined, to play a major role in both the formulation and implementation of much government policy. It is this that the government of the late 1980s and early 1990s has sought to remove in order to reduce the influence of educationalists and public sector employees on decision-making. The test of the system has been in extreme cases when the normal power relationships have been exposed and broken down. The most famous example, perhaps, was at the William Tyndale school in 1975 (see chapter 2 for details). The main issue was who runs the school? Was it the head and/or the staff, the LEA, the governors, the HMIs, the parents, the teacher unions, the DES, or the ministers? One consequence of that battle was to aid the government in centralising their power over school management through media attacks on 'irresponsible and leftist' councils.

Other examples have included the Honeyford case when a head, supported by the conservative establishment, sought to publicly thwart LEA policy over multiracial education in 1984. Another was in 1985/6 in Poundswick school when the teachers and governing body expelled pupils for racist and sexist graffiti, and then the LEA restored the children to the school, resulting in industrial action (see chapter 2). Scores of cases of this type exposed the increasingly fragile nature of the so-called partnership, and each allowed the Secretary of State to make political capital from the allegedly over-powerful role of the LEA and teacher unions in these affairs. Each lent popular support for calls for tighter central controls. The logic of this led to the 1988 Act and the start of LMS. In industrial relations terms the reforms will make such cases more frequent and more serious since the potential clash between heads supported by governors and the residual LEA officers applying remnant legal duties will be harder to resolve. The potential damage was recently shown in the 1993/4 case of the head teacher in Hackney who decided not to take up subsidised tickets to *Romeo and Juliet*. The resulting furore in the press, the threat to take disciplinary action against her by the LEA and the support of the governors for the head suggests that it may be harder to fill the power vacuum left by the LEA than central policy-makers believed.

In short, then, the legal position of employers has been radically altered by the reforms, which have subsequently had a significant effect on contracts of employment. The legal aspects are still unresolved and the precarious relationships between employees, employers and the government remain set to disintegrate.

'Maintained' schools form the vast bulk of state schools in England and with the exception of the GM school the LEA has overall responsibility for these schools. All LEAs are required to have education committees and they must appoint a Chief Education Officer (CEO) to administer the service (EA 1944 schedule 1 and s. 88). In contrast the new GM schools are maintained by the Secretary of State, and City Technology Colleges are not defined as 'maintained' for the purposes of the legislation. The LEA still has a general duty under the 1944 Act to secure efficient education for primary and secondary pupils. In general the courts have taken the view that this is at best a target duty which leaves LEAs with wide discretion in practice. This also covers the supply and employment of teachers required to carry out the duty to provide 'sufficient schools'.

School staff will continue to be employed by the LEA, but in GM schools all staff will be transferred from LEA employ to that of governing body (ERA 1988 s. 75(6)). Such teachers as are transferred will retain all previous employment rights and their pay and conditions will continue to be governed by the STRB.

As Harris notes 'the employment of teachers is closely regulated – by general employment law and by specific legislation' (Harris 1990: 59). Lyons and Stenning (1986) are amongst many experts who constantly advise head teachers to keep abreast of the range of employment legislation covering individual rights. Our main concern is to note the legal aspects most relevant for industrial relations and to indicate the extent to which they will impinge upon school management. There are three areas briefly considered – collective law, school law and individual rights.

Some legal aspects of the employment relationship

The Burnham committees under the 1944 and 1965 Acts only negotiated on pay, and therefore conditions of service were left to a set of informal arrangements. In 1967 efforts were made to formalise some aspects of teacher duties such as school meal supervision, and this eventually led to collectively bargained agreements located in the Burgundy Book in 1978. The exact nature of these duties was challenged during the 1986 strikes in which teachers and their unions 'took advantage of the "grey areas" in the contract in planning their campaigns' (Fredman and Morris 1987: 217). The result was a series of court cases in which the courts upheld the employers' view of the teachers' contracts. For example, 'Scott J. relied heavily on the concept of the professional nature of teachers' jobs in holding that refusal to cover was a breach of contract' (ibid.: 220). Finally the government decided to impose a solution to many of these issues through the 1987 Teachers Pay and Conditions Act. As has been noted the Act requires teachers to be available for work on 195 days and 1,265 hours per year. The legal position is that the Secretary of State can impose conditions of service through an Order, and that other issues covered include cover for absent colleagues and additional hours of work. As Fredman and Morris conclude 'the most striking feature of the Order, however, is not what it contains, but what it omits. . . . Most importantly, the Order omits the guarantees as to class size and non-contact time viewed by the unions as central to any deal' (ibid.: 224).

The 1987 Teachers Pay and Conditions Act, as noted above, was born out of government reaction to teacher strikes rather than from a coherent strategy on teacher duties and work. It none the less 'provides the authoritative version of imposed contractual obligations' and sets out the powers of heads which include 'directing the professional activities of teachers' (Saran 1989: 91). The key issue here is the extent to which conditions of service are negotiated through unions or imposed with or without consultation by school level managers. After the 1987 Act most of the unions considered a failure to consult on many school matters such as job descriptions would be a breach of conditions of employment, but LEAs took the view that ultimately the head could impose new job descriptions. On some issues, such as cover for absent colleagues, several LEAs used current local agreements or custom and practice which tended to be better than the conditions in the Order. The determination of these issues for the day-to-day operation of schools is a matter of vital importance. Both the outcome in terms of prevailing arrangements and the procedures by which the outcome is achieved – imposition, consultation, negotiation – are of concern to all the parties involved in school industrial relations. In our survey of head teachers in 1993 54 per cent agreed that school managers can benefit from negotiations with teacher unions and only 8 per cent disagreed. We also found that only 5 per cent agreed that negotiations with unions would reduce their authority while 57 per cent disagreed. This suggests, therefore, that there is widespread belief in the benefits of taking the staff along with management decisions and that implies dealing through the unions.

Much of the legal regulations peculiar to the 1988 Act empower the Secretary of State to modify the duties of employers and rights of employees. These powers were extended in 1989 through the Education Order (Modification of Enactments Relating to Employment). On the whole all staff are covered by general legislation in this area of employment law and also by the nature of the contract of employment. Transfers to delegated budget schools and/or to GM schools do not alter employees' rights under common and statute law.

Schools, however, are covered by some special laws on issues such as staffing levels where there is a general duty on the LEA under the 1944 EA to provide sufficient personnel. The 1989 Teacher regulations provide that 'at any school . . . there shall be employed a staff of teachers suitable and sufficient in numbers for the purpose of securing the provision of education appropriate to the ages, abilities, aptitudes and needs of the pupils'; and in addition the regulations require that among the staff there is a head and that the teachers must be suitably qualified.

There have been some general problems over recruiting teachers qualified to teach the national curriculum. As a result the government has made provision for the use of 'licensed' teachers and those from the EC. The 1989 regulations apply to LMS schools and GM schools. They prescribe qualifications, health and physical capacity standards necessary for employment, and allow the Secretary of State to bar a person from teaching on medical grounds, misconduct, and educational grounds.

The general rule in regulation 13 is that 'no person shall be employed as a teacher at a school unless he [*sic*] is a qualified teacher in accordance with

Schedule 5'. There are however some exceptions to this, and a qualified teacher must have received notification from the Secretary of State to that effect. Certain teachers can be employed to teach at school even though they are not qualified, for example, temporary appointments to teach children who are visually impaired and student teachers. In 1989 the licensed teacher scheme required less than normal qualifications from applicants. The importance of qualification is twofold: first, it maintains the status, professionalism and pay of the teachers and has been defended with some vigour as with separate industrial action in Scotland and in England and Wales in the early 1960s. Secondly, at the moment the government is seeking to deskill some teaching activities and thereby reduce the pay bill, and this has led to some resistance from teachers and their organisations.

The appointment of staff until LMS was made under the Education (No. 2) Act 1986. The LEA had a duty to consult with the head and the governing body before appointing fulltime teachers. Vacant posts for heads had to be advertised nationally and suitable applicants interviewed. An appointment panel (with not less than three LEA and three governors) recommended and then an appointment was made. The CEO or his/her representative had the right to attend all proceedings. Since 1988 the balance of power in all appointments has shifted from the LEA downward to the governing body, but the procedures remain similar. For headships the governing body must now notify the LEA of the vacancy, advertise it and then interview (by at least three governors). The governing body recommends an appointment to the LEA, the employer. The LEA cannot veto appointments other than on grounds of qualification. For other teachers the governing body has 'virtually total control' (Harris 1990: 78).

In all cases governing bodies and LEAs must abide by all legislation covering individual worker rights including anti-discrimination legislation such as the 1975 Sex Discrimination Act, the 1976 Race Relations Act, and the 1970 Equal Pay Act. They must also abide by the various employment acts and head teachers must understand the importance of the legislation for the conduct of staff management.

For example, in schools without delegated budgets the LEA can dismiss as employer after consulting with head and governing body. Both disciplinary and grievance procedures operate at LEA level after negotiations with the trade unions, and guidelines on how these operate are available from the LEA, the teacher unions and ACAS. In LMS schools, covered under ERA 1988 schedule 3, nearly all power passes to the governing body. It establishes disciplinary rules and procedures, and the DFE advice is to follow good LEA practice. Power to dismiss now rests with the governing body although the LEA must be informed. 'For the purposes of unfair dismissal and by virtue of the Education (Modification of Enactments Relating to Employment) Order 1989, the employer is, following financial delegation, always the governing body' (Harris 1990: 85). Industrial tribunal awards made against the employer for unfair dismissal, for example, are made against the LEA.

Other examples of the relevance of the law to the performance of head teacher and governing body duties are taken up later, but the real issue remains the extent to which school management teams will be able to maintain managerial control over legal rights and procedures.

The contract of employment

Whatever the statutory peculiarities of teachers' employment under the 1988 ERA the individual contract of employment remains the fundamental element upon which the employment relationship is based. As Wedderburn noted 'few individual contracts of employment are arrived at by the bargaining that is implied in such a description' (Wedderburn 1986: 106) namely that of an ordinary contract based on a system whereby two or more people agree to regulate their legal relationship. Most rights of the parties are laid down through collective negotiations between employers and trade unions.

The heart of the employment relationship for teachers, as for other workers, rests in the contract of employment. Each teacher has an individual contract with the employer who must state in writing the main duties required of the employee along with other information such as job title, pay level on appointment and place of work. The rest of the contract can be found in other documents such as the original advertisement for the post, any further particulars and any extra notes from the interview and subsequent correspondence. In addition the actual actions of the employee at work determine much of the contract. As Lyons and Stenning noted 'while the head teacher is not normally empowered initially to formulate the substance of the employment contract, as the person responsible for the conduct of staff management within the school, the head teacher inevitably influences the way(s) in which contractual relationships develop, such as the introduction of rules applying to staff' (Lyons and Stenning 1986: 307).

Most important for our purposes, however, is the reference within the individual contract to collective agreements (Curson 1983). For example, the employee can be disciplined through the disciplinary procedure which has been agreed between the LEA and the teacher unions. In addition the pay and conditions of the teacher are determined through the collective act of the STRB after consultation with teacher unions and employers. In determining the extent and nature of the contract the law assumes that the contract itself is made between free and equal parties – the individual employee and the employer. This legal fiction does not correspond with the realities of the labour market and the greater power of the employer. The assumed equality and freedom suggest a view of the world dominated by individualistic notions of free choice and neo-classical economics about free markets. As Cohen (1988) has shown neither stand up to any scrutiny and both fail because they ignore the circumstances under which people agree to work. The fundamental weakness of the individual in both labour market and law provides the basis for collective organisation, action and agreements.

It is central to this question that the nature of an employee is contrasted with the self-employed. The importance in part resides in those rights in statute only attainable by employees such as unfair dismissal and redundancy payments. There is a real legal crisis in precise definitions of employee partly caused by the historical development of the law itself and more recently compounded by the dramatic increase in the diversity of work patterns within the labour market. As Wedderburn noted 'the law has been left behind. The legal status of many of the workers in so-called atypical employment is often uncertain' (Wedderburn 1986: 117). This has become more murky with the advent of new types of incorporated school, licensed teachers and the buying-in and telecommuting aspects of educational provision.

Special additional problems mount when the employee is temporary, casual, self-employed or a homeworker. This again becomes complicated when there are transfers of employment which are partly covered by TUPE and the EC acquired rights directive (Napier 1993). All of these suggest that the individual employee is barely protected from the power of the employer and that the defence of what most teachers perceive as their employment rights and their special expectations as state employees will come only through collective bargaining based on well organised unions.

The 1987 and 1988 legislation created a framework within which employers of school teachers, either LEAs or governing bodies, were more closely controlled in their employment policies by central government than at any previous time. This centralisation was based on the need to control the teacher pay bill and to reduce the influence of the profession on what was taught. Above all it was based on the view expressed so directly by John Major in his speech to the 1992 Conservative Party conference that 'if local authorities cannot do the job, then we will give the job to others'. The job being to attain 'high standards, sound learning, diversity and choice in all our schools'. With the removal of the LEA as the principal employer unit the government has created a new set of tensions and reinvented an old set of conflicts in which employers will find it ever more difficult to plan, to control the direction of educational policy, and ultimately to manage the schools.

School management

The changes in the nature and location of the employer alongside other changes in the role of governors have meant that there has been a shift in management power within schools. This shift both requires and allows school managers to intervene more directly in industrial relations issues such as pay, conditions of service and disciplinary and grievance cases. The involvement of heads in these areas, with or without governor assistance, will change the relationship between heads and other staff and will alter the very nature of the job of head teacher. In addition, the governors' powers over the head teachers' activities will also influence the ways in which management of staff is conducted.

School managers in the shape and form of heads and deputies and to a lesser extent some governors have been granted greater authority to run their schools than before. This gain has come at the expense of the LEA, but has been, to some extent, cancelled out by the increased powers of the DFE and the Secretary of State. The main mechanism for this new enhanced control has come from financial freedom embodied in the LMS formula, although it is still unclear how much real freedom of action will ultimately result from this new system. As Harris states:

> school governing bodies have had their role changed dramatically under the education legislation of the 1980s. Under the Acts of 1980, 1986 and 1988, LEAs' powers and responsibilities with regard to running of schools have been restricted. In many areas over which the LEA has traditionally, in the majority of schools, been autonomous, such as staff appointments, the school day, use of school premises, exclusion of pupils and, most significantly, expenditure, governing bodies have gained considerable sovereignty.
>
> (Harris 1990: 103)

Our interest here lies in the relationship between the governing bodies and the heads and deputies. Under the 1986 Act the instrument and articles of government of the school control the detail of the governing body itself and also set out its duties with regard to running the school. We cannot be concerned here with the general aspects of governor powers, but we should note that under the 1989 regulations decisions can be delegated to committees and individuals. In practice most of the important operational aspects of the school can be delegated to the head. It is too soon into the new order to be clear as to how the actual decisions will be made, but allowing for wide variation, the main impression is that most schools operate with the head in control, governors still largely supportive and not involved on a daily basis, and the LEA more involved than government had intended. The key to the way in which power and authority within schools is decided lies partly with the traditions of the school, the head and the rest of the staff, but much will depend on how LMS itself works through the school system.

The local financial management of schools represents, without any doubt, the most spectacular loss of LEA control over education in the post-war period. Essentially governing bodies will acquire control over their own budgets. The only limits are the total amount allocated on a formula basis and a small residual amount kept by the LEA for central services.

There has been a vast amount of literature and advice about LMS since its inception and we do not need to rehearse all of the arguments here. The debate tends to centre around either the principle underlying LMS associated with the rhetoric of market competition or the success and failures of practical implementation. One chief education officer expressed early reservations about the principle as well as anyone when she argued that:

> schools do not exist in total isolation and whilst flexibility in resource decision-making is, I know, welcomed by heads, the role of the LEA to look after the needs of all children it serves seems to me endangered if we perceive of each school as a private company competing rather than collaborating with its neighbours, not least when resources are limited.
>
> (Tuck 1988: 148)

The government view has been expressed in many places. The basic stated argument was recently summarised thus, 'the Secretary of State intends to extend the benefits of LMS. His aim is to build on the progress that has already been made towards pupil-led funding and delegated management, so as to increase schools' control over resources and thereby improve the standards of education which they provide' (*DFE Circular 7/91*, page 3). The key logical jump is between controlling resources, including human resources, and higher standards. This fits well with a general government position that the fundamental issue in the public services is not the level of resources but their management. Improve management and you simultaneously improve standards and reduce costs. According to this model, management will not be improved as a result of the enlightened self-interest of the teachers; it can only be forced to change through greater central controls and formula funded budgets (Smyth 1993).

This is in line with the HMI report to the DFE on LMS. It summarised the situation very clearly if a little too simply thus:

> following ERA the DES issued Circular 7/88 which required LEAs to draw up schemes for local management. Under LMS schemes the funds were allocated to all maintained schools according to a formula set by the LEA but within regulations specified by the DES. Of that formula 75 per cent had to be determined by the number of pupils in the school, with weighting for different ages (so-called 'age-weighted pupil units'). The remaining 25 per cent could take account of other factors, such as premises and special needs. The second element of LMS was the delegation of the control of this money to the governors in partnership with head teachers. It is for them to determine how that money is allocated to staffing, buildings, classroom resources and other items of expenditure, for the purposes of the school and subject to any conditions made by or under the LMS scheme. In essence delegation gives schools the power to deploy public money assigned to them as they choose, and to enable them to benefit from any economies they achieve.
>
> (HMI 1992: 7)

The report restated government policy on LMS, which is that it has two main objectives: first to increase the schools' control over resources, and second to improve standards (HMI 1992: 8). The DES has stated that 'effective schemes of local management will enable governing bodies and head teachers to plan their use of resources, including their most valuable resource, their staff, to maximum effect in accordance with their own needs and priorities' (*DES Circular 7/88*).

The Inspectorate's report noted several impacts of LMS on teaching staff: (1) the appointment of younger less experienced staff; (2) increases in the use of non-teaching staff; (3) more part-time teachers; (4) more staff participation in decisions; and (5) more time spent in meetings and the growth of administration by senior teachers and governors – 'many governors are finding the volume of work daunting. Much more time of senior managers is taken up with administration' (HMI 1992: 16).

The first three points above are largely due to the system 'since the average cost of teaching staff is at least 75 per cent of the total budget, there is an incentive to try to save money by employing fewer or cheaper staff' (HMI 1992: 23). This last point is of particular concern to both the teacher and non-teacher unions. The GMB thought that 'some governing bodies will cut the pay and conditions of support staff in order to make savings' (GMB 1991: 4). They also felt that there would be redundancies, lower health and safety standards, lack of consultation and worse industrial relations. Several teacher unions produced guides for governors in which, for example, the extent of discretion over pay is listed and in which union policy is clearly stated: 'decisions regarding governors' discretion is not a matter which should be left to the governing body to determine without formal consultation/negotiation with the recognised unions in the school' (NASUWT 1992a: 13).

Despite the best efforts of the government and government supporters the evidence so far indicates a cautious and unenthusiastic acceptance of delegated budgets, and of the resulting changes in the balance of power as between the heads, governing bodies, LEAs and central government (Sinclair *et al.* 1993a and 1993b; Bach and Winchester 1994). The clear winner is central government which has accrued more power and more control than ever, and the clear losers are the LEAs. Even the *Times* noted with dismay that the 1992 white paper 'is one of the most dramatic extensions of Whitehall power seen since the war' (29 February 1992). The remaining balance as between heads and governing bodies within any framework decided by the DFE and the little left to decide by the LEAs will vary from school to school and will add to the uncertainty of teaching standards, conditions of service and school performance.

Neither the new employers nor the new school managers with their extended local powers have come to terms with the new balance of power within schools. The LMS system creates a beggar-my-neighbour approach to school competition and this is fuelled by central government controls over the budget formula and publication of performance indicators. Such controls have been further extended by the new and more oppressive role of the HMIs. The pressures on school managers are immense, and it is our contention that in general they can only be resolved through downward pressures on unit labour costs. This can be achieved, within the school context, through work intensification, de-skilling and selective reward management. The extent to which these can be realised depends on resource levels, union resistance, staff acceptance, government policy, and the administrative practices of school management teams. One important aspect of this is the introduction at school level of human resource management techniques and considerations in order to control staff more precisely through appraisal and performance-related pay, to reprofile staff through selected staff education and appointment, and to increase managerial freedom by smothering trade union activity. The government has created the legislative and political framework for these initiatives, but are heads able and/or willing to take them up?

THE MANAGEMENT OF HUMAN RESOURCES

One general view of the emergence of HRM as an important part of the management of British enterprises in the 1990's suggests that it, in all its forms, simply represents a modern version of managing resources in a recession. In a recession with weakened trade unions and a government largely hostile to the interests of labour employers will be forced by financial stringency and market competition to push down unit labour costs. This will be more urgent in labour intensive industries. The special feature of the recession of the 1990s has been the efforts by government to introduce these aspects of market-based recession into the public services. This results in employers and managers behaving *as if* they were in the private sector and subject to the discipline of the market. The dominant slogan for managers in the private sector is 'more for less', that is productivity and/or efficiency gains at all costs. If this is the case, in crude terms, then an important issue for the management of recession in public services becomes the implementation of the necessary changes with the minimum of opposition. The main features of the changes based on this model include work intensification, de-skilling and lower unit labour costs through reductions in staffing levels and/or lower relative rates of total remuneration. One possible way to minimise opposition to these changes is to try to convince staff of the benefits and/or inevitability of the changes, and this is achieved through isolating staff as individuals and seeking to convince them of the correctness of this new model management.

HRM, then, can be seen to contain elements of these processes: work intensification through job analysis and performance management; de-skilling through job evaluation and new appointment systems; and reward controls through performance-related pay and fewer senior posts. In addition there is an important persuasion aspect to the package contained in team briefings, management away days, meet the management sessions, and quality circles. In this way the introduction of HRM or at least HRM techniques into schools represents one response to the crisis of management caused by underfunding and the 1988 reforms.

There are three strands of the debate on HRM which need to be disentangled before any attempt is made to discuss current school issues. The first is the distinction between the general concepts of personnel management, human resource management and industrial/employee/labour relations; the second is the practical impact of the move in law and practice from LEA personnel functions to shared LEA and school management functions over staffing issues; and the third is the separate but related concept of the introduction of human resource management into schools alongside LMS.

How best to define these concepts itself presents a problem. We could simply say that personnel management is whatever departments in large organisations entitled personnel do, or we could suggest that personnel management is whatever the contents pages of the major textbooks cover. We could use IPM definitions or try more academic ones. Whichever approach we adopt, however, we might be accused of bias and lack of serious intent. The definitional and conceptual issues, while not identical, nevertheless, matter. They are important for three reasons: first, because inaccurate and/or inappropriate language confuses and distorts the arguments; secondly, because in attempting to judge changes we need to know what precisely has changed; and thirdly, in attempting to analyse and explain the changes we need to be sure that they are substantive and significant rather than trivial and superficial.

So far academics have been unhappy about both the definitions and the concepts, and they have struggled to identify and agree precise and usable terms. So where to begin? ACAS (1990) have produced among other things, an *Employment Handbook*. Its contents cover many familiar employment matters of interest to teachers and others such as absenteeism, appraisal, collective bargaining, contracts of employment, disciplinary procedures, equal opportunities, flexible working practices, grievance procedures, health and safety, hours of work, job design and job evaluation, labour turnover, pay and grading, personnel records, recruitment and selection, redundancy, and training and development. These collectively are referred to as the topics of 'employee relations' to be of help for those organisations without specialist 'personnel expertise'. ACAS does not distinguish between 'personnel' and 'employee relations'. So what?

Yet most textbooks on personnel management divide the subject into main areas such as employee resourcing, reward management and employee relations. In this case the latter is subsumed under the generic term of personnel. These days authors such as Armstrong (1991) feel obliged to discuss the concept of personnel and contrast it with HRM.

Armstrong, like most other authorities, sidesteps the issue of what exactly personnel management is by referring to a list of concerns. These typically include some rather vague general target ideals such as 'obtaining, developing and motivating the human resources required by the organization', 'creating a climate of employee relations which develops feelings of mutuality and encourages cooperation' and 'making the best use of the skills and capacities of all those employed in the organization' (Armstrong 1991: 27). This overstated set of unitarist management aims treats neither the subject nor the practice as problematic. All that is left, perhaps, therefore is to *describe* the functions and activities and skills and then provide some anecdotal examples.

Armstrong claims that 'it is now generally agreed that human resource management does not replace personnel management, but it does look at the processes involved from a different perspective. Its basic philosophies may also differ significantly from traditional concepts of personnel management' (ibid.: 33). This is just not the case – whatever HRM is it is not different in perspective/philosophy from personnel management. They both share almost all aspects of management outlook on every issue. The differences, if such can be determined by empirical study rather than endless claims, are in emphasis only. In general terms leading protagonists such as Guest have argued that, 'HRM is a more central, senior-management driven strategic activity' (Guest 1991: 152) and takes the view that personnel management as a central company wide function may be replaced by more involvement of line managers in the HRM decisions within a national policy framework. In this way the personnel function of the LEA might be replaced by strategic decisions from the DFE and operational implementation by school managers. What is unclear is how this works in practice since there is little evidence of HRM being fully used (Storey and Sisson 1990 and 1993; Purcell and Ahlstrand 1994). A more critical assessment of HRM looked at the driving force behind its implementation and concluded that competition and crisis were major factors (Blyton and Turnbull 1992: 8). This leads us back to schools: the decline in LEA personnel services, the competition for pupils and the crisis in the management of schools will force school managers to reduce unit labour costs through the implementation of some HRM techniques.

Our survey of heads indicates that the vast majority intended to continue to seek advice on personnel and HRM issues from the LEA, and other survey and case study evidence presented later also shows that few school-based managers either wanted to or were able to carry out these functions.

Before a brief outline of personnel and HRM in schools it is worthwhile to pause for reflection. The overwhelming weakness of the management position here is, in general, its neglect of power relations based on economic forces, control relations based on employment forces, and conflict relations based in the nature of employee status and witnessed through organised and unorganised demonstrations of opposition. HRM and personnel experts cannot explain, and often do not even attempt to do so, the existence of conflict at the place of work and its relationship to the nature of the business.

In the case of school education the entire process of management, especially personnel/HRM type management, has been obscured by the equality of professional status of managed and management, and by the nature of the employer, the LEA at arm's length from the operational management unit – the school. In this sense, therefore, the management function and the personnel/HRM function, has been mainly located at LEA level and conducted mainly by and through LEA officers. In this situation the power, control and conflict relations while existing in schools have often been either hidden or distorted by the professional relationship and nature of the business, and as significant by its location at LEA level. The importance of such arrangements for 'good' education and peaceful schooling has been mistaken by the Conservative government's reform programme. Later in the book we will show how the LMS and national curriculum reforms have relocated control and conflict within the school rather than within the LEA. The consequences of this analysis not only make the entire personnel/HRM debate seem trite and narrow but will have profound implications for all aspects of future schooling. Ward Griffiths, deputy chief executive of Kent County Council, expressed his position on the future of personnel management in local authorities: 'I suggest that the increasing recognition that effective people management is the critical factor in organisations' success means a central and strategic role for personnel is essential' (Griffiths 1993: 42). He goes on to note that in labour intensive industries the key role for the personnel specialist is to support line managers in making the best use of resources through, for example, performance management, harmonisation and flexible conditions of service.

This suggests, as noted above, that school managers are going to be left with a great deal to do. With the withering away of national pay setting, with highly regulated market competition giving the DFE great powers over strategic matters, and with staff under pressure to perform 'better', the cocktail for conflict at school level is being shaken. When this is overlaid onto the fumbling new relationships between the LEA, the governing body and the senior school managers then the mixture may be explosive. The point is that as authority and power relations are explicitly located at school level then the need to prevent conflict through traditional institutional remedies such as grievance procedures, joint consultation with unions and formal disciplinary procedures becomes greater just as most managers are being persuaded that either conflict will not emerge or that it can be dealt with through HRM methods. This means a crisis of management dealt with by school-based managers. How will they cope?

Employee resourcing

Employee resourcing is the generic term for efforts by the management on behalf of the employer to staff the business with the people needed to run the business. It involves notions of strategic planning in as much as there is a strong implication that this entails both *knowing* and *getting* the required staff. This is clearly the basis for much government thinking and is high on the terms of reference of the STRB, as set out in Baroness Blatch's letter to Sir Graham Day, namely 'to enable maintained schools to recruit, retain and motivate sufficient teachers of the required quality' (STRB 1994: 45). It is also the way in which personnel managers attempt to analyse and control the internal labour market and is also the point of entry of the organisation into the external labour market. So the main areas of concern are to: (1) identify the future staffing needs of the school and decide whether they can be met from promotions and retentions or whether new staff will have to be employed; (2) devise policies and procedures for both assessing and developing staff with a view to motivation, retention and possible promotion; and (3) venture into the external labour market based on advertisements, recruitment and appointment.

HRM planning

This covers human resource planning and the first step, then, is to accurately assess the staffing needs now and into the future. This was until the 1988 reforms: a process based on turnover, slow changes in growth and/or decline of staff numbers, some changes in syllabus, and close school liaison with the LEA which would be the dominant partner in both resource allocation and planning. Under the LMS and national curriculum reforms the immediate future requires quite radical assessments of staff mix and numbers and makes it difficult to base current needs on current staff and to guess future needs. But who within the school will be able to do this? Our survey indicated that 70 per cent of heads would continue to seek advice on recruitment from the LEA and only 4 per cent from a designated member of staff.

HRM planning is part and parcel of business and budget plans, but of course school managers have no simple independence from the immediate past and over the level of resources. The requirements of strategic planning are hardly met at all by the LMS system. Managers can draw up the relevant forecasts and estimate pupil numbers, formula funding levels, and therefore future total staff numbers. They can also model the future through known retirement dates, shortage and surplus subject areas, and current grades. In this way near future promotions, retentions and turnover can be assessed. This can be done in primary schools more readily, perhaps, than in secondary schools. The small numbers of staff in any school, compared with the wider business world, make errors more costly, forecasting more risky and the use of models less relevant. This managerial flexibility is seen as a vital part of the new freedoms. However, this flexibility must operate within a national labour market in which any school is one of 26,500 maintained schools bidding for teachers while constrained by pay levels still mainly determined by government through the STRB.

This is not to deny the usefulness of recruitment and retention plans. A recruitment plan will look at the main sources of recruits, the post(s) to be filled, and methods of attracting good candidates. Similarly a retention plan will examine current pay levels and enhancements, job redesign, performance targets and training needs. But the notion of HRM planning goes way beyond this.

A major part of any HRM planning will involve the examination of the use of alternatives to full-time permanent staff. This type of plan tends to be based on a crude core–periphery model of labour markets and school skill mix needs. The general proposition is that schools will wish to reduce the non-teaching and marginal duties of teachers in order to employ cheaper less well qualified staff and release qualified expensive teachers to concentrate on teaching. This suggests a core staff of permanent well paid teachers and a peripheral staff of non-teachers and less well qualified teaching staff along with those on part-time and temporary contracts. Such a model seeks to make the school management flexible in terms of responding quickly and cheaply to changes in budgets and pupil numbers. The periphery staff, the argument runs, have fewer rights and are less well organised and so are easier to employ and dismiss. They may well be women from the local labour market, while the core will tend to come from a national labour market of better qualified teachers (Hakim 1990).

The logic of the model is that skill mix adjustments, flexible working conditions and flexible contracts enable the management both to increase efficiency through driving down unit labour costs and to raise productivity through more intensive use of more expensive staff. This possible operational model for schools suggests a free market competition for pupils and a unitarist management perspective accepted throughout the organisation. Neither these preconditions nor the efficacy of the core–periphery model exist in practice for schools. The market is highly regulated by the DFE, the flexibility is not as readily achieved nor as readily accepted as is assumed and, most important, this vision of a well managed school neglects the costs in management of running such a system. It is also odd that the advocates of these models want both more flexible conditions of service and more harmonised conditions of service. Best evidence indicates that flexibility within individual contracts is minimal (IRS 1994), and that flexible means flexible in terms of business need only.

Job analysis and description – work study for teachers

Part of the *knowing* of what type of staff are required is based on an analysis of the jobs being done and likely to be needed. Analysis may be too strong a term for what follows but the basic tools are first a description of the job and then the application of a variety of 'scientific management' techniques in order to be sure that the work is done (Taylor 1911). Later the purpose may be to suggest better ways of doing the job or alternative persons to do part of the job or its enhancement or its abolition in part or entirely. The simple purpose for managers is that the more they, *qua* managers, know of what is involved then the easier to control the person doing the job, and it also raises possibilities of cheapening the job through substitution – by mechanisation, automation and/or computerisation, and/or by less skilled and less expensive staff members. It is often the first stage in job evaluation and in its more traditional form as applied to manual and technical and clerical staff it is usually seen as work study.

Job analysis involves collecting, analysing and setting out certain information about the job/task/competence. This includes, *inter alia*, the overall purpose, nature and scope of the job in terms of tasks, operations, duties, accountability, performance criteria, competencies and responsibilities. This list is, of course, descriptive rather than analytical. The methods of discovering what the job holder does include interviews and observation as well as task analysis and critical incident techniques. These need not detain us here. The points to note are that time and money has to be expended to gather that data and that time and money must be invested to analyse the data. There are also issues, which for teachers might be acute, associated with the reliability and validity of the data collected, the rights of employees being so watched, and the subsequent use of the data to facilitate skills analysis. This latter might well lead to skill reductions and to the removal of the employee or some of their tasks. Once the close supervision and monitoring of teachers is undertaken by school managers then traditional team and/or collegial relationships among staff can dramatically alter as the subordination of the majority of staff becomes a clear part of management practice (Johnson 1984b).

The great advantage of the LEA officers carrying out the duties and functions of teacher control and dismissal was that repercussions could be restrained within the school as the LEA could be the outside agency to blame for muddle and/or lack of fairness. Once these activities are carried out by school managers no such escape route exists, and therefore the insistent question is who within the school will now be responsible for these actions and decisions?

Throughout the personnel management literature there is no mention that these processes have a purpose which might be in conflict with those of the workforce and that their main objective is to gain control over labour processes in order to reduce the control exercised by the individual staff member. In this way it represents an element of power relations in which power is being concentrated into the hands of fewer generalist managers and away from individual teachers in the classroom. Such processes may be wrapped up and presented as scientific, progressive management and even business imperatives. Whatever the gloss, the history of the introduction of such activities has been either conflict to prevent work study and distort it, or conflict after its implementation in terms of resistance to the new conditions (Gomberg 1948; McCarthy and Parker 1968).

For teachers this power conflict has usually been kept within the bounds of professional debate and school based teams, although sometimes staff meetings erupt into confrontations (Ball 1987). When conflict has emerged it is either whisked away rapidly to LEA and official union level in order to prevent interference at the point of production (Purcell and Sisson 1983) or it has become bogged down in bitter personal feuds and angry resentment sometimes leading to walk-outs by the staff. The usual solution to efforts by school managers to exercise greater supervisor controls over their colleagues has been a standoff in which professional autonomy of the individual is wedded to the collective protection of the teaching force against intrusions into their job territory. The teacher trade unions have played a major role in monitoring and channelling these conflicts into professional rather than industrial relations issues and processes. As a result the unions have come under attack from leftists accusing them of hiding the nature of the exploitation of the teachers and therefore dodging the class struggle content of education, and from rightists accusing the unions of preventing effective and efficient management and therefore of being instrumental in the waste of public money, in the erosion of public confidence in standards, and in blocking the benign influence of market forces. From the previous chapter it is obvious that the main classroom teachers are not equally in the dock on all charges, but their role has been substantial in the arguments over the applicability of traditional work study to teaching.

Recruitment and selection

Once jobs have been described, severally analysed and then placed into the strategic HRM plan linked with business plans and forecast budgets, then if, and only if, there are either vacancies or new posts required does the process of recruitment and selection begin with its aim the event of an appointment. Here we are into the *getting* part of employee resourcing. Again the time and money spent in this exercise should not be underestimated and certainly must be costed.

The 1988 ERA outlines the correct appointment procedures, and these are well stated in most LEA guidance handbooks. The main processes in this task are to define the requirements through job descriptions and specifications and deciding the terms and conditions of employment; then attract candidates through advertisements and other means; and finally to select candidates through shortlisting and interview.

In recent years more attention has been accorded to these activities especially for senior staff. One step has been to develop person specifications which might include one of numerous plans such as the seven-point plan which covers: physical make-up, attainments, general intelligence, special aptitudes, disposition, circumstances and interests. Once you are committed to this kind of system you must initiate ways of discovering whether or not the candidates possess them.

In the selection of candidates you compare your requirements with the attributes of those applying. Easy to say, obvious to try, but hard to do. Interview through selection boards requires some notion of planning the interview and asking the best type of questions. There are strong arguments for and against asking identical questions to every interviewee, but such dogma takes no account of the realities of the interview. One way out of the subjective and sometimes heady atmosphere of interviews is the use of psychometric tests. These are usually out of place for teachers. In general, selecting teachers is more straightforward in that all of the candidates are relatively similarly qualified. The real difficulty with school-based appointments is that most of those on the appointment panel have little experience of appointing anybody.

The relative importance of different selection methods has been traced for teachers by several authors (Banfield and Fearn 1987) and for managers in general by others (Robertson and Makin 1986). Reilly and Chao (1982), for example, took the view that only biodata and peer evaluation merited serious examination alongside standardised tests. Much of the research evidence in the selection and appointment of teachers has come from interviews with heads (Evetts 1991), but no substantial studies have been made in terms of 'successful' outcomes. The appointment of heads and deputies has received less attention although the costs of getting it wrong for the school and the pupils would appear very high. A more recent study (Bland 1994) has shown that in the appointment of heads and deputies there was widespread use of job descriptions, CV analysis and references, but little take-up of forced reference check, psychological tests, in-tray exercises and the delivery of a prepared presentation. This suggests that selection and appointment in schools lags behind the practice of other organisations, and that neither LMS nor HRM will change this in the near future.

In all cases the governing body is bound by anti-discrimination law such as the 1975 Sex Discrimination Act and the 1976 Race Relations Act. Once the proceedings start the CEO (or representative) has a duty to give advice and has the right to attend all proceedings. The LEA will provide model job descriptions, person specifications and other further particulars for the panel, and it will provide training in interview technique and advice on selection and interviewing.

In the case of other teachers the basic proceedings are the same, but important differences relate to the levels at which advice and decisions are made. The CEO has no duty to be present or advise. The governing body may delegate their right to appoint to one or more governor, or the head, or the head and governor(s). The governing body can appoint internally and/or appoint someone nominated by the LEA without advertisement. Only if these two methods either fail or are not necessary will an advertisement be required.

Many LEAs' guidance provides a series of reasons for knowing the job descriptions of the staff. For example, Cambridgeshire suggest that job descriptions help 'effective management of a school . . . it describes management expectations and requirements of staff . . . it helps a teacher fulfil his/her professional duties effectively' (Cambridgeshire County Council 1991: I 17). However for school teachers many of the main aspects of the job are described by statutory order, such as the number of days and hours worked and basic duties of the standard scale teacher. This also applies to the general professional duties of head teachers.

Appraisal

Once the school has acquired new staff and/or promoted staff then their performance becomes increasingly of interest to their employer. The main method used at present to determine the job activities of teachers is appraisal. ACAS suggests that appraisals 'regularly record an assessment of an employee's performance, potential and development needs. The appraisal is an opportunity to take an overall view of work content, loads and volume, to look back on what has been achieved during the reporting period and agree objectives for the next' (ACAS 1988: 3). This is rather wide ranging but provides a starting point. Appraisal is often broken down into a set of performance management activities such as performance review, potential review and reward review (Armstrong and Murlis 1988: 157–8).

There is a host of related practical issues in appraisal – who should be appraised and how often? Who should do the appraising? Should employees see their reports? ACAS consider that for the schemes to work there are a set of necessary conditions: senior management commitment, full consultation about methods with all concerned including the trade unions, regular monitor of schemes, training of appraisers, and keep schemes simple (ACAS 1988: 8). In addition the process itself is open to further choices: what should the form contain (job descriptions, comments, plans)? What method should be used – rating 1 to 6, compare achievement with agreed targets, critical incident measures, narrative reports or others?

Even bland management consultancy textbooks recognise potential 'problems' with appraisal. These might include subjectivity and inconsistency; the tendency to demotivate staff if the scheme is not properly implemented; a lack of commitment from managers; and the threat of a link with pay (Armstrong and Murlis 1988: 158–62). Such are the potential difficulties that it was no surprise when the 1990 survey of workplace industrial relations showed that formal grievances concerning appraisal schemes came fourth in the league table behind pay, conditions and discipline (Millward *et al.* 1992: 205).

ACAS refer to systematic bias in appraisal as the 'halo' or 'horns' effect (ACAS 1988: 19) by which it is argued appraisers over score or under score one particular criterion, or simply are prejudiced. The difficulty with this traditional management response to shortcomings in the system is that it fails to disentangle bad practice and bad schemes from deep seated problems with appraisal. In the first instance, all admit there is bad practice but suggest it can be overcome by either better training of appraisers and/or more support from management. This may well be the case but it begs the question as to why managers are not supporting a system which if in operation we must assume is the policy of the organisation.

In addition even if managers support the scheme it may fail, the management consultants argue, because it is a faulty version of a good scheme. Change the scheme and the method of application and you solve the problem. Again this is self-fulfilling and does not bother overmuch with evidence. The more interesting question is whether or not such schemes can ever work in terms of their objectives, and whether the stated objectives (as copied from ACAS) are the real objectives of the enterprise.

In the largest survey on appraisal in the UK it was claimed that 'the dissatisfaction registered by over 80% of companies with their appraisal schemes is testimony to the problems' (Fletcher 1993: 34). Calling on Deming, the father of total quality management, Fletcher concludes that 'appraisal does harm because managers cannot effectively differentiate between individual staff and organisational systems as the cause in performance variation and that the latter rather than the former are the major factor' (Fletcher 1993: 37).

In the case of schools there is now an enormous amount of literature on appraisal of school teachers (Buras-Stubbs 1994). The vast majority is of little use in as much as it either describes the mundane or trivialises the issues (Stenning and Stenning 1984). In most cases it is just an extension of managerial views of appraisal in the wider world from whence it came (Marland 1986). In addition, most commentators do not bother with any historical approach in which the origins of teacher appraisal can be traced to party political initiatives and control mechanisms. Again the failure to address issues of control and conflict rob the appraisal debate of any substance. There are exceptions to this. Reynolds linked teacher union opposition to appraisal in the late 1980s to the implications of government policy rather than to appraisal itself. He argued that '*Better Schools* in March 1985, for example, explicitly linked appraisal and pay, by arguing that the Government welcomes . . . the introduction of systematic performance appraisal, designed to bring about a better relationship between pay, responsibilities and performance. Press discussion of appraisal (see Wilby 1986) has been concerned with it almost exclusively as a mechanism for identifying – and then sacking – the "worst" few per cent of the teaching force' (Reynolds 1987: 129). In a later piece Heywood also traces both the historical and political tension between the teachers' views of appraisal as part of professional development and the government's view as a control mechanism linked with pay. As he concluded 'systems of merit pay, if linked to appraisal, will throttle the benefits of a professional developmental process of appraisal' (Heywood 1992: 149).

As we noted above, efforts to apply this analysis to schools have been at best poor. Riches and Morgan (1989) provide a section on appraisal and development in their book. It starts with a quasi-religious piece from Drucker called 'the spirit of performance' set in a fantasy world in which managers with integrity control people striving for excellence in an organisation aiming to achieve extraordinary results. The final chapter of the same book compounds the otherworldliness of the work. Fidler's chapter on staff appraisal begins 'Whereas in fact what is quite striking, when looking at the theory of appraisal and its practice in well-managed industry, commerce and other public services, is that appraisal is quite positive and developmental'

(Fidler 1989: 190). He does not stop to consider what 'well-managed' or 'quite positive' might mean. The editors of this book on HRM in education feel they can contribute to our understanding of the topic in a labour intensive industry without any reference to pay and rewards, and in an industry dominated by collective bargaining and powerful and well supported trade unions with no reference to either. This is important because management techniques do not simply work under some universal rule. They succeed or fail according to specific and immediate management objectives, not the same as organisational or employee objectives, and only so far as the organisational features and environment allow them to succeed. Such features include attitudes of staff, union activity, management concerns, and employer policies.

A central tension with the implementation of appraisal is what started out as a mechanism to improve professional development (Cooper and Goodier 1989) has been hijacked by government in order to enhance the powers of school managers over their staff and to satisfy political considerations of controlling poor performers within schools as defined by business rather than professional criteria. This development, traced in the late 1980s, provides the best explanation for the muddle in which many observers and unions now find themselves. In 1989, for example, AMMA advised members 'not to discuss or participate in schemes proposed by individual head teachers, governing bodies or managers' (AMMA 1989) because the union policy-makers believed the best guarantee of appraisal as part of professional development was the scheme based on the National Steering Group recommendations and implemented through the LEAs. By 1992 the government had moved to compulsory appraisal within all schools and had tightened the control element through the insistence that teachers have to be observed teaching on at least two occasions. The union position now concentrated on the practicalities of implementation and all six unions took the view that 'the whole appraisal process including training must take place within directed time. To ensure that this is possible it may require a re-ordering of priorities for some or all staff and a reduction in other directed time activities'(Report of six teacher organisations 1992: 5). The key point is that schools undertake the scheme but that the main purpose of the scheme is control. As the NASUWT noticed: 'given that the purposes of appraisal include the use of appraisal evidence in pay, promotion, discipline and dismissal, schemes of appraisal ought to have had national consistency. The government has passed the buck onto LEAs. For LEAs now to do the same will result in glaring inconsistencies in the application of criteria' (NASUWT 1992b: 8).

The fact that appraisal is now part of the occupational requirement of school teachers' employment means that along with other HRM activities school managers will have to implement and budget for this particular process. The main reasons heads gave for not introducing appraisal were that 'schools do not have the time, resources or expertise to staff such schemes'

(James and Newman 1985: 163). However it is carried out in practice, appraisal for now has been introduced through top-down government instructions aimed at supporting the power base of school managers in their function of controlling their fellow professionals. In this way endless accounts of good and less good examples of how to appraise colleagues fulfil no useful managerial and/or educational purpose. It is the existence of appraisal linked with threatening consequences for pay and promotion (or worse – discipline or redundancy selection) that matters in terms of resulting conflict between staff and their managers. In our survey of heads 88 per cent said they would seek advice from the LEA on appraisal and this was top of the list suggesting deep worries about its implementation for the future of school industrial relations.

HRM requires that the management of human resources is intimately connected with the corporate objectives of the organisation. Assuming that these are clear and conform with accepted notions of coherence then the business plan of any given school would drive the HRM policies and eventually their practices. The labour intensive nature of schools and the unusually high level of dependence of the service achievement upon the teachers themselves means that the school objectives can only be met through HRM objectives. In this sense we must also assume that both government and the employers wish to improve performance through improving the performance of the teachers in the school. This requires, *inter alia*, the use of both reward management and performance management strategies and practices. The next sections examine both of these issues.

Reward management

Traditional personnel management definitions of reward management accord with the view that it is 'the process of developing and implementing strategies, policies and systems which help the organization to achieve its objectives by obtaining and keeping the people it needs and by increasing their motivation and commitment' (Armstrong 1991: 495). This entails, apparently, rewarding individuals in line with their value to the organisation. Rewards are supposed to control and shape the work behaviour of employees in the direction which the management assume will best benefit the organisation. The most important element in reward management is pay, and yet as Torrington and Hall point out 'a strange thing about payment is that managers seem to shy away from actually using the word' and that 'reward suggests a special payment for a special act, rather than regular payment for ordinary acts' (Torrington and Hall 1987: 487). They go on to further undermine Armstrong's case by pointing out that only 'a small proportion of employees may be paid on the basis of an added-value assessment' (1987: 487), and that the most common and best pay principle is that of fairness. This of course includes the felt-fairness of employees so important to teachers' views on pay comparability.

In another work Armstrong and Murlis take a more aggressively HRM line. They argue that payment systems must be 'competitive' and linked explicitly to contribution and performance. They go further to suggest that 'the primary aim of reward management is to reinforce the drive to improve organisational performance. The achievement of excellence . . . depends on attracting the right calibre of people and then, having got them, providing them with both financial and non-financial incentives and rewards which will maintain and indeed increase their motivation' (Armstrong and Murlis 1988: 12).

In practice, payment systems either pay by time or by results. The former still dominates most of the pay package of most employees, including school teachers. The principle is that you are paid monthly for carrying out your contractual duties more or less in accordance with your employers' needs and managers' direction. The use of payment by results and/or payment by performance has increased in the UK but they are always fraught with measurement and motivation issues. A workplace industrial relations survey noted that 'another managerial device for monitoring and encouraging workers' effort is incentive payments' (Millward *et al.* 1992: 258). These incentive payments include traditional piecework, payment by results and merit pay through group bonuses and/or individual payments. In 1990 the survey sought to quantify the extent of the use of merit pay 'which depended on a subjective judgment by a supervisor or manager of the individual's performance' (ibid.). They found that in 1990 this was the most common form of incentive payment to non-manual professionals with just over a third of establishments having some kind of system of this type. This seems to overstate the spread of merit payment systems since in another study Casey *et al.* found that non-manual workers in service industries receiving incentive payments rose for men from 10 per cent in 1979 to 18 per cent by 1984, but then fell to 15 per cent in 1989. For women the equivalent figures were 6 per cent in 1979 rising to 13 per cent in 1984 and falling to 12 per cent by 1989 (Casey *et al.* 1992: 25).

These writers argue that the experiences of the late 1970s and early 1980s 'led to a discrediting of at least certain forms of incentive systems' (Casey *et al.* 1992: 25). In general, the trend to flexibility was more concerned with the employment relationship, that is, greater freedom to recruit and dismiss as well as hours of work, rather than with payment systems. In the many detailed case studies of existing schemes a strong pattern of discontent and failure emerges. One study of performance-related pay in the Inland Revenue picks up as well as any other some of the issues: firstly that the central justification for its introduction is as a motivator. Once that is agreed then the practice comes under scrutiny: as the study concludes, 'our second, and most important, finding is that the positive motivational effects of Performance Pay have been, at most, very modest among Revenue staff . . . the number who felt motivated to a powerful degree was always negligible. Even worse, there is clear evidence of some demotivation among staff' (Marsden and Richardson 1991: 1; see also Marsden and Richardson 1994). It is difficult to square this weight of research evidence with claims of educational writers such as Tomlinson: 'performance-related pay is part of a necessary change to school and college culture, if standards are to be raised significantly without a massive and possibly wasteful input of new resources' (Tomlinson 1992: 2). He is deeply confused about the terminology, muddling up merit pay and performance rewards and further failing to acknowledge the copious research evidence against the efficacy of the system he proposes (ACAS 1992). Indeed Tomlinson simply provides an educational veneer for performance-related pay as another mechanism to control teacher professionalism through enhancing the powers of school managers, and therefore his references to better teachers leading to better education for children are misdirected.

It is pay above all else that matters. Brown notes that 'amid this complexity, pay and hours of work stand out as by far the most conspicuous part of the reward package' and 'consequently, the satisfactory management of employment requires the satisfactory management of remuneration' (Brown 1989: 249).

Pay is the major part of any reward strategy and that pay is awarded either on the basis of performance/results/outputs or on a time rate which itself is composed of a mixture of market rates and fair comparability. School teachers have more or less enjoyed the comparability model which was built into the major pay inquiries (Houghton 1974 and Clegg 1980) and underscored the strike action of the mid-1980s (Seifert 1987). The current reform system is looking both ways: a STRB which explicitly uses comparability but which is also obliged by government to increasingly use performance-related pay type schemes. The 1994 STRB report provides a clear statement on this push-me pull-you pay determination:

> we consider the position on affordability which reflects the Government's stated approach on public sector pay. This clearly implies that any increase in pay levels will have to be funded from increased productivity and other savings. But in our view this cannot mean that there can be no increase in pay levels, regardless of other considerations. We also note the latest available information on price inflation, pay settlements and earnings which point to the need for some increase in teachers' pay if their position is not to worsen.
>
> (STRB 1994: 31)

The managerial basis for this government-inspired muddle has been powerfully expressed by Drucker:

> There are three common explanations for the lack of performance in service institutions: their managers aren't businesslike; the people are not as good as they should be; results are intangible and incapable of definition or measurement. All three are invalid and are pure alibi. The basic problem of the service institution is that it is paid for promises rather than performance. It is paid out of a budget rather than for (and out of) results.
>
> (Drucker 1989b: 31)

The essential practical components of reward management contain the points already made, shorn of their rhetoric: the determination of pay levels and relativities, reward structures, performance-related pay, and managing the system through employee relations.

Pay and labour markets

Most employers face an imperfect labour market in which the behaviour of employers and employees plays a significant role. The real issue is, as Brown noted, that 'the act of hiring an employee is not sufficient to ensure that the job in question gets done in an acceptable way' (Brown 1989: 251). The source of government thinking lies with inadequate labour market theory and the assumption that there is a simple positive link between effort and pay. This is just not the case. In general then managers can develop pay policies apart from immediate and direct market pressures, but cannot develop such policies which thwart the issue of fairness. As was argued in chapter 1 the basis for teacher pay is the ultimate tyranny of pay comparison and this is tied with the enduring notion that it is too difficult to measure the differences between teachers *qua* teachers and therefore the cheapest and least aggravating method is to pay not according to performance, that can be sorted through promotion, but by qualification, task and time.

The difficulties of applying simplistic notions of labour market adjustments to pay are especially acute for teachers in schools. Despite the overwhelming case against phoney market explanations of pay, the main textbooks encourage the unwary down the neo-classical path. Armstrong and Murlis claim that 'competitive salary levels and pay structures can only be developed and maintained if the external market is regularly and systematically checked' (Armstrong and Murlis 1988: 35). Other texts are nearer the mark when they argue that 'supply and demand remains only a partial explanation of pay determination' (Torrington and Hall 1987: 488). This was most famously expressed by Sir Henry Phelps Brown when he studied the causes of the inequality of pay as being in part associated with factors affecting the pay structure *before the market* such as class position and restrictions to entry, and those factors *within the market* such as supply and demand, status, government policy and trade union power (Phelps Brown 1977).

In practice, teachers' pay is based on national labour market norms associated with the pay levels of others. The detailed basis for this was best expressed in the Houghton inquiry into teachers' pay in 1974 and later consolidated in the IAC's terms of reference in 1987 (see chapter 2). It is the market at large and traditional felt-fair and bargained rates that drive the process and determine, along with government pay policies, the level of pay accorded to the teachers. The total pay bill for 1993–94 including oncosts was about £10.5 billion, and this paid the salaries of about 414,000 teachers in England and Wales. They ranged in September 1993 from spine point 0 of £11,244 through to the best paid head with £50,682. Such a range in levels within an occupational group further undermines labour market arguments and supports the management driven need to maintain fair comparisons and discretion by institution that overrides the market testing. A detailed analysis of pay was provided in chapter 2, but how school based management teams will set and implement their own pay systems and structures outside the national framework is a mystery.

Pay structures and grades

Pay structures, as opposed to systems, are mainly concerned with grades and salary spines. The assumed advantages of a graded salary structure include, first the maintenance of established differentials; secondly there is planning and control of career progression; and thirdly there can be greater managerial controls over starting salaries, merit pay and promotion.

The 1993 STRB recommended a new pay structure for classroom teachers. The main government objective in requiring the new structure was 'to achieve a closer relationship between teachers' pay and their individual performance, and to ensure that schools have the flexibility to recruit and retain teachers and to reward the taking on of extra responsibilities' (STRB 1993: 16).

The structure in 1992 had a ten point standard scale for all teachers other than heads and deputies ranging from £11,184 to £18,837. In addition this was supplemented by five rates of incentive allowance (£1,296, £2,097, £4,194, £5,595 and £7,692) and four rates of incremental enhancement (from £294 to £1,173), and unspecified sums for discretionary scale points up to £3,225. In most cases the pay of the individual teacher rests with the governing body within the constraints of the School Teachers' Pay and Conditions Document.

This structure, it was argued by the Review Body and others, offered a variety of ways to enhance pay to reward extra responsibilities, good performance and to resolve any recruitment and retention difficulties. In April 1992 the Review Body commissioned research into the use of the various extra payments now available to schools. The main findings of their survey were that 57 per cent of standard scale teachers received an incentive award; 86 per cent of which were given for extra responsibilities and only 1 per cent for performance; only 0.8 per cent of teachers received an incremental enhancement; 1 per cent received discretionary scale points; and only two teachers in the survey of about 55,000 had had increments stopped due to performance. In the survey 90 per cent of heads had made no use of discretionary payments other than the incentive allowances. The main reasons given for this by the STRB were lack of funds and lack of understanding of the pay structures. This latter point has been challenged by many teachers, for example, 'my own impression, substantiated with many meetings with governors, is that they understood perfectly well how the former system worked and that the only thing preventing then from using the discretionary allowances, e.g. to reward good performance, was the lack of money in the school budget' (Downes 1993a: 4).

As a result the Review Body concluded that a new simpler pay structure should be introduced. It also believed this would help achieve the government's aim of relating pay with performance (STRB 1993: 18). From September 1993 the new structure was 'a single 18 point pay spine on which placement is determined by points scores' (STRB 1994: 13). The STRB asked the OME to carry out a survey on the transition from the old to the new structure. Its preliminary findings were that the position of 86 per cent of teachers was unchanged, 5 per cent had done better and 1 per cent worse under the transfer. There was still little use of 'the discretionary provision to award excellence, recruitment and retention, or special needs points' (STRB 1994: 15).

NEOST seemed apprehensive about this proposal, believing, quite rightly of course, that it would limit employer discretion, and would be used *de facto* to reinstate more traditional teacher pay structures. Several of the unions were worried about the rather small number of points and that extra responsibility would tend not to be awarded points in future. Points are awarded on the basis of qualifications, experience, responsibilities, excellence and recruitment and retention factors. As of September 1993 53 per cent of teachers received the maximum of 2 points for qualifications while 46 per cent received 0 points. Table 4.1 provides the detail.

This may be a clearer structure and there may be slightly less discretion than before, but overall the new structure seems to raise no new principles and resolve no old problems. This type of structure appears to have elements of job evaluation and the award of points for various criteria suggests a fairly arbitrary selection. The new pay structure, however, is already being disputed as a method for resolving the problems it was meant to ease. For example, Downes claims that 'the 1993 Document removes the limits and guidelines and throws the responsibility over to governors as the relevant body. Superficially this might appear to add to the governors' management role an extra level of flexibility. In practice, it is going to make the whole operation of responsibility points more problematical' (Downes 1993b: 9).

The real issue remains the relationship between the level of funding and the labour markets faced by each school. The LMS formula tightly restricts the ability of governing bodies to reward teachers along national ideals, and even when there are monies available heads in particular seek to reward duty rather than the ever elusive excellence. In addition the main classroom unions and the majority of teachers fear and oppose the overuse of performance as the basis for pay advancement, wary of favouritism as well as demotivation. The main point is that in a static labour market with a weak economy the government's use of incomes policies and limiting funds adds up to a temporary solution to a deep seated issue, and is further

Table 4.1 Number of teachers. other than heads and deputies, with points awarded for different criteria[1] England and Wales, September 1993, unweighted sample data

	Primary		*Secondary*		*Special*		*Total*		*Full-time equivalents National distribution[2]*
	No	*%*	*No*	*%*	*No*	*%*	*No*	*%*	*%*
Qualifications Points									
0	6,651	57	5,414.5	37	439.5	62	12,505	46	47
1	87.5	1	90	1	1	0	178.5	1	1
2	4,965	42	8,997.5	62	267.5	38	14,230	53	52
Experience Points									
0	742.5	6	338.5	2	14.5	2	1,095.5	4	4
1	518	4	442	3	4	1	944	4	3
2	493	4	429.5	3	7	1	929.5	3	3
3	520	4	393.5	3	15	2	928.5	3	3
4	502	4	441.5	3	14	2	957.5	4	3
5	561.5	5	425.5	3	34.5	5	1,021.5	4	4
6	498	4	405.5	3	22	3	925.5	3	3
7	2,329.5	20	6,691.5	46	210.5	29	9,231.5	34	34
8	377	3	213.5	1	31.5	4	622	2	2
9	5,268	45	4,762.5	33	369	51	10,399.5	38	39
Responsibility Points									
0	6,747.5	55	5,265	36	390.5	57	12,403	45	45
1	3,157.5	26	2,012	14	209	30	5,378.5	19	20
2	2,095	17	3,091.5	21	78	11	5,264.5	19	19
3	231	2	1,691	11	11	2	1,933	7	7

4	26.5	0	2,026.5	14	2	0	2,055	7	7
5	10	0	609	4	0	0	619	2	2
Excellence Points									
0	11,656	99	14,480	100	674.5	100	26,810.5	99	99
1	55	1	28	0	0	0	83	0	0
2	39.5	0	4	0	0	0	43.5	0	0
3	20	0	2	0	0	0	22	0	0
Recruitment/ Retention Points									
0	11,514	97	14,330.5	99	671.5	100	26,516	98	98
1	285.5	2	122	1	2	0	409.5	2	1
2	35.5	0	72	0	1	0	108	0	0
3	6.5	0	0	0	0	0	6.5	0	0
Special Needs Points									
0	11,609.5	98	14,352	99	33	4	25,994.5	96	96
1	87	1	102	1	204.5	27	393.5	1	1
2	96.5	1	63	0	516	69	675.5	3	3

Source: STRB (1994:64)

Notes:

[1] Source: STRB, Teachers' Pay Survey, 1993 excluding sixth-form colleges

[2] Estimated national distribution calculated by weighting the sample results by local authority type and school category

evidence that the government simply does not have a coherent pay strategy for the public service sector in general and for school teachers in particular (Brown and Rowthorn 1990; see also chapter 2).

Performance-related pay

Some strong proponents of PRP have suggested, rather fancifully, that the expanded use of PRP in the UK is in part due to lower inflation and in part due to the development of the enterprise culture. Even they admit that 'there are, however, special problems in introducing performance-related pay into the public sector' (Armstrong and Murlis 1988: 177). Both the Citizen's Charter and the CBI strongly favour PRP and both do so on the basic assumption that one important way to improve performance is to link it with pay. When challenged by the evidence, which is overwhelming, that it does not operate like that at all, its proponents simply argue, as do all dogmatists, that the principle is coherent but the practice and practitioners are faulty. We need not discuss here the various schemes available, but just note that for teachers individual PRP can only be achieved through appraisal.

The experience of PRP among public service workers has been unhappy. The Inland Revenue scheme was so bad that it had to be rapidly replaced and so far there is no evidence that its reformed version is working (Marsden and Richardson 1991 and 1994); and when in 1985 Hay was used to introduce PRP for senior civil servants they concluded that for nearly £1 million extra per year there was no benefit. Indeed in 1982 the Megaw Report on the civil service favoured PRP but this was rejected at the time by the Treasury. Obvious objections included threats to team work as one member is singled out for extra pay; it may be harder to show merit in one job rather than another; judgment of excellence is too subjective and leads to the blue-eyed boy syndrome; it demotivates those who receive less than they feel they deserve while only marginally motivating the high achievers; it is an expensive system to operate; and it encourages secrecy. Despite the lack of evidence for its success and the inherent problems associated with its use in public services the government has pressed ahead. It has been introduced into local government, the NHS and the civil service, and the government favours its use for school teachers. Examples from elsewhere show the divisive nature of the system as when it was used in the USA (Johnson 1984b) and the recreation of new relationships between managed and managers. This latter point will be particularly important in schools with their high dependence on a secure relationship between all teaching staff (see chapter 5).

The current situation for the profession is that the Review Body is inching its way to introduce some kind of PRP system which goes beyond the limited recommendations in the structure proposals outlined above. The STRB members have made it clear on several occasions that this is a government driven initiative, but that they are willing to recommend some kind of application after proper study. In the 1993 report such a study was summarised based on the help of Hay (STRB 1993: 33). This contrasts with a parallel study conducted for the unions by Ruskin College TURU (1992).

The STRB concluded that in general PRP only works 'if the basic structure and levels of pay are regarded as fair' (STRB 1993: 33). Two points need to be taken up: first that the levels of pay should be fair and that the STRB along with most teachers see pay levels as inadequate and remaining so; and secondly that it is a necessary condition for the success of PRP that the levels are felt-fair – in some sense comparable.

Again the STRB is in dull support: 'on their own, PRP schemes will not guarantee improved performance' (ibid.) – hardly in line with Charter politics and free market economics. And worse – most schemes with any chance of success are those that start with senior managers and work slowly down. In addition, and here is the nub: 'without exception, the successful PRP schemes of which we heard had involved the organisation concerned in an initial increase in their paybill; they regarded this as a necessary investment' (ibid.).

The Secretary of State and the DFE both reacted to this report with a renewed emphasis on PRP for teachers in the classroom – a suggestion at odds with both Hay and the STRB. The DFE further wanted such schemes to operate without more money – another contradiction of the report. It is extraordinary that even when those sympathetic to both the government in general and to PRP produce what we and many others would see as a far too bland report anyway, the government rejects all evidence even from their allies in order to press ahead, come what may, with their trickle down and tinsel town economics.

The employers' organisations, the apparent beneficiaries of policy, were deeply suspicious. NEOST was doubtful about even the principle of PRP in schools. All six teacher trade unions presented a united position that they had grave reservations about both the principle and the practice of PRP in schools. The unions and employers oppose the scheme, the Hay consultants and the STRB are worried about the failure to agree necessary preconditions, but the government marches on. The compromise position now reached is that the STRB is monitoring pilot PRP schemes, and that the main focus of policy is on heads and deputies. The majority of classroom teachers are covered by the excellence points on the new pay structure, but, 'our pay survey has confirmed, not surprisingly, that the initial use of these points has been very limited, because of the perceived financial constraints on school budgets as well as concern and uncertainty about the principle and practicality of rewarding teachers in this way on a fair and objective basis' (STRB 1994: 29).

Although the weight of evidence is against the benefits of PRP in general and especially for school teachers some government supporters have pressed on with the case in favour. Tomlinson argued that 'in the 1980s there have been quite legitimate financial, political and legislative pressures which have led to value-for-money and market-forces arguments becoming more powerful, and necessarily so, as perhaps they always should have been' (Tomlinson 1992: 1). He acknowledged the lack of hard information to support his case, 'introducing PRP is without doubt an act of faith based on the assumption that people will perform more effectively if offered the financial incentive to do so' (1992: 2), but that did not prevent his support for PRP.

The NUT and NASUWT commissioned the trade union research unit at Ruskin College to investigate the use of PRP for school teachers. The research concluded that there is 'little or no evidence that PRP schemes resulted in improved performance' (TURU 1992: 4). For school-based schemes the main difficulty was 'quantifying performance' and, furthermore, 'there was no single indicator that was both available and acceptable' (ibid.). The research also showed that the majority of teachers, and the NUT and NASUWT, did not believe that PRP would improve education and/or motivate staff. Even the managerially minded ATL thought that 'PRP is certainly not a panacea for the education sector' (ATL 1993: 9). This is supported by a more detailed study of a system in action by Johnson in the USA. She concluded that 'not only is merit pay likely to be a poor motivator of teacher performance, it may well interfere with efforts to improve schools' (Johnson 1984b: 183). She located the impetus for its introduction not in the considered argument and evidence of school improvement but in the right-wing ideology of the Republican Party – she quoted one of President Reagan's speeches in support, 'teachers should be paid and promoted on the basis of their merit and competence' (1984b: 175).

This finding is supported by our own research. Only 14 per cent of the heads in our survey agreed that incentive allowances motivate teachers to improve their teaching, while 42 per cent felt it was unfair and 48 per cent felt it caused ill-feeling between teachers. In our detailed analysis of schools based on interviews with senior managers and governors we found general opposition to the introduction of PRP and confusion in practice between the desire and need to reward effort and this relationship with performance – these views were summed up by one head who simply said that 'payment by results is not workable'. We concluded that 'financial constraint, deep mistrust of many aspects of the reform process and relative inexperience in handling industrial relations issues would make the measuring of performance and its forthcoming link with pay a damaging activity for schools' (Sinclair and Seifert 1993: 9). An editorial in the *Times Educational Supplement* added weight to this view, 'the more Sir Graham Day and his team visited schools, the more convinced they became that few had a management system capable of running PRP' (19 February 1993: 17).

This section has rightly ended with discussion of the most pressing issue facing school managers, that of the distribution of rewards through the mixture of a deteriorating national pay mechanism and school based spinal points of which some are related to performance. The main concern for all involved with education must be that there remain serious doubts about both the principle and practice of PRP. Recent general surveys reveal that most managers are unhappy with PRP schemes in their organisations for a number of reasons. First, they are not objective; secondly they encourage the blue-eyed boy syndrome; thirdly it is easier to measure action than effectiveness; fourthly PRP was used in isolation from wider management performance; and finally there is no interest in motivating the vast majority of staff (Cannell and Long 1991). This point is taken up in schools, 'the evidence seems to suggest that PRP would actually depress overall performance by demotivating those teachers who do not receive enhanced salaries and who feel themselves unjustly dealt with' (Downes 1992: 10). This finding echoes the study of the inland revenue which concluded 'our results strongly suggest that the system . . . had . . . only a small positive motivational effect on staff. . . The net effect on staff motivation could well have been negative' (Marsden and Richardson 1994: 257).

Finally, the whole issue of managing schools better in order to improve the cost-effectiveness of education cannot be assumed, *pari passu*, to also improve the quality of education. The debate is skewed by government towards that vital link of better management meaning better education, but the management of resources driven by LMS and beggar-my-neighbour competition may well result in worse standards of education. To reward teachers on the basis of their individual performance not only goes against the notion of schools as partnerships in learning but also avoids the debate on the meaning and measurement of that performance – a debate which has moved from crude measures of performance indicators (Theodossin 1987) towards more sophisticated multi-disciplinary measures (Jesson *et al.* 1987, Woodhouse and Goldstein 1988), although the entire statistical basis for any such measures used in league tables is deeply flawed (Cuttance 1985). As a recent IPM study concluded 'the problems of external constraints on performance dogged most of the PRP systems, and none of them had worked out an effective response as yet' (Fletcher and Williams 1992: 43). There can be no greater external constraints than the influences on any group of children and the limits of the budget. The development of HRM for schools with the centrality of control over performance and pay suggests that traditional industrial relations may well have a major part to play in the future of school management. The final section of this chapter outlines these concerns.

Employee relations and industrial relations

In our view the crisis of management facing schools will emerge in a piecemeal and hesitant form at first. When, as with the trusts in the NHS, the full implications of restricted funding and market competition emerge into the daylight then large numbers of teachers and parents will come to the view that the education of children is increasingly a lottery outside their control.

In such circumstances demands from parents and reactions from teachers will put school managers and governors under immense pressure to extract ever greater efforts from ever more overworked staff. The temptation to become less of a colleague and more of a manager exercising power and control over staff will grow alongside the muddle and half-hearted adoption of some HRM policies, especially on performance and pay (Seifert 1990). In these conditions the fate of the teacher trade unions and associated collective bargaining institutions at national and LEA level will be of great importance, and the ability to control the inevitable conflict will depend to some extent upon the institutional robustness of the relevant formal procedures and efficacy of joint consultation and negotiation.

First we must be clear what industrial relations is not about and therefore reject simplistic definitions such as 'the primary aims of employee relations policies and procedures are to improve cooperation, to minimize unnecessary conflict, to enable employees to play an appropriate part in decision making, and to keep them informed on matters that concern them' (Armstrong 1991: 665). The first two objectives of policy claimed by Armstrong are related: more co-operation and less conflict. It is not obvious why these should both be objectives, although there is much assumed about workplace behaviour, but with little evidence to support it, that co-operation is somehow better than conflict. This is received wisdom but, of course, it begs all the important questions. All this is done in the name of the organisation whose goals are singular and coherent. Once the goals are known then it is preferable, on this view, to co-operate in achieving them. This rests on a series of assumptions: that all the goals are known; that everyone agrees with them; that they are not incoherent and/or contradictory; that there is enough budget to achieve them, otherwise why set them; that there is only one agreed and clear path to the achievement of the goals; and finally that we all have understood and accepted the consequences of achieving the goals, even if they have knock-on consequences for other goals.

The problem with so many personnel management handbooks and textbooks is that they assume away the goal-setting problems, and also assume away different versions of them. At one level we might just claim, the weak version, that there is general agreement on all the above although some important differences of emphasis and opinion. Such differences can be stifled by over rigorous management assertion and good ideas might be lost. This may well occur in schools where different staff may have genuine reasons for differing about goals, processes and outcomes. Our real concern, however, is to argue the strong version that the differences are in essence conflictual and are about the way power is exercised to achieve control over staff by the management as representatives of the employers' interests. In either version the position adopted by the writers on personnel management accords neither with reality nor with useful comment on how to manage anything let alone a school.

Sisson did recognise the problem of lack of analysis. He referred to the 'prescriptive approach' which is dominant in terms of material produced for managers and management students. The literature is mainly concerned with what the personnel manager does and ought to do. These works claim to be atheoretical but, as Sisson argued, 'closer inspection reveals implicitly, if not explicitly, a very particular set of ideas' (Sisson 1989: 4). These unitarist assumptions can be contrasted with the labour process approach derived from Braverman (1974) and Marx (1887). On this view, located mainly in everyday work experiences, management is seen as the exercise of power to contain conflict and exercise control. These themes of the exercise of management powers through controls over the labour process are taken up in chapter 5.

The central definition of industrial relations presented to us by Flanders (1965) is based on the cluster concept of job regulation. This term captures our own concerns: the nature of the job both as entire professional career for teachers and the exact specialist tasks and skills that together make and remake the job in the hands of the job holder and those associated with the job holder. In addition we have the notion of regulation which contains further ideas such as self-regulation (teacher autonomy), joint regulation (teacher and head and/or teacher unions and managers), and employer/government driven regulation in which discretion is removed. All of this takes place in a highly regulated profession, workplace and industry subject to the rules and laws of government and civil service, local government and independent bodies. Regulation means both power and control are involved and have been in the recent past, while job reminds us of labour market forces. Together any job regulation is partly enshrined in the contract of employment. Job regulation includes both formal regulation through collective bargaining and statute law and informal arrangements through custom and practice and professional autonomy. Teachers are well placed to exercise both formal and informal regulation over their own work. Indeed it is one of our main propositions that the LMS and national curriculum changes represent, whatever else happens, an attempt to reduce the extent of self-regulation by teachers.

This acceptance of Flanders' point on job regulation as central to our study does not flow from our acceptance of his pluralist perspective. This has been discussed in chapter 1, but it enables us to concentrate on the issues rather than the temporary institutional arrangements. Why, for example, do so many school teachers belong to trade unions? – more both absolutely and relatively than any other single profession, occupation or work group in the UK. Why does this tendency to belong persist at times when trade unions appear relatively weaker than before, and why should heads and governing bodies be concerned to deal with teacher trade unions? These questions are partly answered elsewhere in this book, but for now we can note that teachers' willingness to stay in their unions and recent evidence for support for some of their actions, as with the SATS boycott in the summer of 1993, indicates the conflict potential in schools. There is no evidence that many aspects of managerial control at school have been addressed, 'the message is that LMS solves no industrial relations issues, but will generate a range of complex and possibly intractable problems over pay and conditions of service . . . flexibility may be a long wished for practice to replace the handcuffs of national bargaining systems, but its implementation will throw up a range of grievances and disciplinary cases' (Seifert 1991a: 43). The rest of this chapter provides a summary overview of the arrangements for the institutionalisation of conflict associated with collective bargaining.

Industrial relations issues in schools, LEAs and at national level can be resolved through either consultation or negotiation. As Burchill explains

> employers may wish to recognise unions solely for consultative reasons in line with the unitary perception that trade unions might be a useful extension of the organisation's bureaucracy. In the consultative model unions can be informed of management plans and possibly come up with useful suggestions as to how these might be modified to better secure management objectives. However, in this model the ultimate decision rests with management.
>
> (Burchill 1992: 85)

In contrast joint negotiation implies 'good faith' bargaining in which both parties are prepared to make genuine concessions to reach an agreement. In this sense joint consultation and negotiation is often formalised in JNCs and JCCs. These tend to exist at the level of the LEA and local associations of the teacher unions, and at this level they are frequently formal and regular. They have in the recent past agreed LEA wide procedures on grievances and discipline, and policies on equal opportunities, redundancy and conduct during industrial action.

Until recently there was a three tier system: the national Burnham and later STRB which determined national pay issues, the second tier was LEA level, and the third tier was the school. At LEA level there were formal negotiations to both implement national agreements and to decide procedures, while at school level grievances and discipline, both formal and informal, would be initiated. Industrial action would take place at school whatever the level of decision-making, and policy implementation on equal opportunities and health and safety would take place in the school as well. They were also involved because if teacher representatives had to take time off for training and/or industrial relations activities then it was the school which lost that teacher time (Seifert 1989; Seifert and Ironside 1993).

By 1990 over 90 per cent of all disciplinary procedures in UK establishments were written and were in accord with the ACAS code of practice (Millward *et al.* 1992: 192). In those organisations where a trade union was recognised then some trade union involvement in formal disciplinary hearings was universal. In schools formal disciplinary action can only be taken in line with the relevant LEA guidance. Many exhort heads to follow the guidance or else risk loss in an industrial tribunal hearing. The procedures themselves are based on the ACAS code, but the LEA with regard to LMS schools can only press school managers down this path. Walsall education committee makes the point, 'it cannot be overstressed that advice should be sought from the outset of any formal proceedings' (Walsall LEA 1992: 19). Our survey of heads in 1993 indicated that 83 per cent would seek advice on disciplinary procedures from the LEA, with 65 per cent also seeking advice from their own head teacher association. We also found that 72 per cent of heads felt it was now easier to remove bad teachers from teaching.

Similar points can be made about grievances and disputes. A grievance in this sense goes beyond the commonsense view of feeling aggrieved. Grievances are against the management and the grounds are rooted in the claim that management has broken some rule and/or agreement (see later for a full account). Disputes occur usually when either party is dissatisfied with the outcome of a disciplinary or grievance hearing. It is often the case that disputes are settled through the intervention of third parties through mechanisms such as conciliation, mediation and arbitration. By 1990, 96 per cent of establishments in the public sector had a formal grievance procedure, and the main issues taken through such procedures were pay, grading, absence, discipline and appraisal (Millward *et al.* 1992: 187 and 205). LEAs provide guidance in these areas through model procedures in the hope that school managers will take note. As one LEA states 'they relate to school based grievances and to matters that are the responsibility of the Governing Body' (Warwickshire LEA 1992: F1).

Our survey found that 82 per cent of heads would seek LEA advice for formal grievance procedures, and the figure rose on matters such as redundancy and redeployment (87 per cent), but was lower for equal opportunities (75 per cent) and health and safety (82 per cent). When it comes to workforce reductions the most common method still used is the euphemistic 'natural wastage' – 70 per cent in the public sector, with redeployment and early retirement both at about 40 per cent. In 1990 redundancy was still limited with only 23 per cent voluntary and 4 per cent compulsory (Millward *et al.* 1992: 321). In recent years the teacher wastage rate (percentage of all teachers leaving full-time service) has hovered around the 10 per cent mark. Teacher turnover rates, which include transfers to other teaching posts as well as wastage, were 8.1 per cent overall with a variation from 9.0 per cent female primary to 7.1 per cent male secondary in 1992. In the primary sector three main causes accounting for over half of all turnover were move to another post in the same LEA, move to another post in another LEA, and early retirement. For secondary teachers the pattern was the same (STRB 1994: 74–6). We will examine the real impact and meaning of staff reduction policies in chapter 5.

As with the issues of discipline, grievance, dispute and staff reductions the matters of equal opportunities and health and safety have been traditional areas for formal agreements and trade union representation and negotiation. Health and safety issues topped our survey for the most frequent cause of contact between heads and union representatives in schools, followed by early retirements and staffing levels. This survey supports evidence from elsewhere that despite the introduction of LMS and in some cases embryo HRM the school as workplace remains a potent breeding ground for traditional industrial relations. The reforms have switched the focus and locus of bargaining away from the LEA and local association officers to the school managers and school representatives. If this change reflects power relations then we can expect real difficulties for the management of schools, if they do not reflect power realities then we can expect a black hole to form into which all forms of discontent may swirl around until they reappear as resentment, incompetence and open conflict.

The danger for employers and managers alike is the gap between the reality in the schools and the policy-making at Westminster and Whitehall. Even the relatively sensible STRB has fallen into the trap, and has this to say about personnel management:

> Headteachers, deputies and other senior teachers must be able to call on a range of personnel skills in respect of such matters as the recruitment, training, development and motivation of staff; the effective use of appraisal; the handling of poor performance, including the use of disciplinary procedures where appropriate; and dealing with unacceptable levels of sickness absence. While such personnel skills, and experience in using them, do exist there remains a need for training to be available to ensure that schools maximise the potential of their staff.
>
> (STRB 1994: 35)

CONCLUSIONS

Is that all? The bulk of government policy, STRB recommendations and employers' efforts have gone towards making teachers and schools perform better and that this should be achieved at a more cost-effective level. Pay and performance, therefore, are at the heart of operational management changes in schools. Yet with the withering away of the LEA personnel function heads are expected, in relatively small employment units, to carry out all these policies fraught as they are at every turn with possible conflicts and/or business failures. How they are actually managing and how the teaching staff and unions are responding is the subject matter of chapter 5.

This chapter has discussed the transitional situation school managers are in with regard to both the decline of the LEA personnel function and the development of school-based HRM policies including appraisal and performance-related pay. This situation has so far not been a success either in terms of government intentions of the freedom to manage at school level without LEA and trade union influence, or in terms of motivating staff in order to maintain quality standards at a time of reduced resources and greater challenges to teacher professional autonomy from central government and the imperatives of a competitive market. We have indicated that school managers will struggle to come to terms with the new requirements of HRM and that the consequences will be more school based conflict unless the LEAs and trade unions have a way back into the power system in schools.

5 The emergence of new issues in school-based industrial relations

INTRODUCTION

The main argument of this book with regard to the 1988 reforms is that the essential thrust of government policy has been to reduce funding to state schools and to remove any element of democratic control through either the profession or the elected LEA. In simple business terms this has meant downward pressure on unit labour costs as the only way to teach more children with fewer resources in a labour intensive industry. Unit labour costs are determined by some combination of pay costs (pay levels and the numbers employed) and the performance of teachers – the work and wages outlined in chapter 1. At present, despite government initiatives in the direction of PRP and STRB changes to pay structure, the pay setting mechanism for most teachers remains the national rate recommended by the STRB and enacted by government. A recent analysis of public sector pay determination concluded that despite government efforts to decentralise pay bargaining it remained an essentially national activity (Bach and Winchester 1994).

Once pay is set outside the business unit then the main vehicle for altering unit labour costs becomes the performance of the main labour force – teachers. This chapter examines three major ways in which school employers and managers have set about achieving their objectives of staying alive in a competitive market. These are job losses and the threat of redundancy; changes in skill mix through flexible use of teacher workforce allied to new pay structures; and through increased workload. These are new issues for school managers and we also discuss in this chapter how these issues might result in conflict at the level of the school and by what methods might such conflict be controlled in traditional formal procedures of industrial relations – union recognition, disciplinary procedures, and grievance and disputes procedures.

In chapter 2 we outlined the traditional Whitley system of national bargaining over pay and conditions supplemented by local joint consultation over implementation of the national agreements. At the level of the LEA most industrial relations activity was concerned with the process of implementing the agreements made in Burnham and in CLEA/ST, and with their application in practice to teachers individually and collectively. Local procedures were agreed and adopted in LEAs, with the aim of securing the orderly application of national terms and conditions. All LEAs have standing joint committees through which they consult formally with the teacher unions over the application of the national agreements and over issues affecting teachers specific to the area. Within this Whitley framework local agreements were made to regulate relations between teachers and their LEA and between teacher unions and the LEA (Stenning *et al.* 1984; Seifert 1989).

Many of these local agreements were drawn from model agreements and recommendations contained in the Burgundy Book (as the national agreement on conditions of service for teachers in England and Wales is known). Normally they would be drafted through discussion between officers of the trade unions and the LEA, being brought to the formal joint committee for ratification and adoption throughout the LEA. The Personnel Department of the LEA, whose role we discussed in chapter 4, played an important part in advising heads about teachers' terms and conditions of employment and in ensuring that heads complied with agreed procedures. Both heads and teachers would seek advice from personnel officers, and it was not unusual for workplace issues to be resolved without the involvement of trade unions. Heads played only a limited role either in personnel management or in determining teachers' conditions of service.

Similarly, at the level of the school the union representative usually played only a minor role, referring workplace problems to a local association officer or executive member (Seifert 1989). Most school-based union activity consisted of circulating union material and perhaps going to local association meetings. There was no call for trade union organisation around school-based collective bargaining, as most local bargaining took place at the level of the LEA. This included disciplinary and grievance issues which, if not resolved informally, would usually be resolved at LEA level. Thus, as we have already described in chapter 3, union organisation was focused on activity at the level of the LEA rather than the school.

Local procedures played an important role in regulating relations between teachers and their LEAs, and in maintaining a high level of stability and predictability in industrial relations (Seifert 1992a). Most substantive issues that might arise in schools were dealt with within a framework of national terms and conditions, using local procedural agreements. Job regulation was conducted jointly between LEA managers and trade union representatives, covering many aspects of teacher employment. There was considerable variation between LEAs, reflecting local political traditions and experiences of past industrial relations, especially the local impact of national industrial action. Nevertheless, the general pattern was one of stability in industrial relations at local level, both in school and at the level of the LEA. From the point of view of both managers and trade unionists in the school, most issues affecting teachers were settled elsewhere – any problems that did arise within the school could usually be shuffled off to be dealt with by LEA-level managers and union officers.

As we discussed in chapter 4, the education reforms have redistributed authority over a number of decision-making areas. Broad strategic decisions are increasingly made at central government level, through the national curriculum and through spending limits imposed on local authorities. The LMS mechanisms drive operational decisions downward to the level of the school, through delegated budgets and the transfer of some employer responsibility. LEAs have lost authority over a large range of strategic and operational issues that were previously part of their remit.

School budgets are based on two factors. First is the aggregate LEA-wide schools budget, which is decided by the LEA and is now subject to limits imposed by central government. Secondly is the share given to each school under the LEA's formula, which is related mainly to pupil numbers. A school can increase its budget share by attracting more pupils, but this is always at the expense of the other schools that might otherwise have received those pupils – a beggar-my-neighbour system. There is a fixed amount of money in the pot, and each school's share reflects the number of age weighted pupil units (AWPUs) among its pupils. If a pupil moves to another school it takes its AWPU with it. Each school's budget therefore reflects both its share of the market for pupils and the LEA's aggregate level of spending on schools.

Tight limits have been placed by central government on LEA spending. In the climate of economic recession there is downward pressure on the budgets of all schools. This puts school managers in a position where they must maximise their budget share by maximising their market share, putting them in market competition with other schools. In a recession even establishing a position as a market leader does not guarantee year on year budget stability. School managers must therefore engage in activity to obtain maximum performance while remaining within budget. This means cutting costs and, as 80 per cent of school budgets are spent on employees, it means cutting staffing costs. Cost-cutting initiatives, however, must not lead to reduced standards, as this could result in a declining market share. Under this double threat to their budget income school managers face a very clear imperative. They must cut costs to remain within their budget while maintaining or improving the performance of the school to retain their share of the market.

For the government, and for the proponents of human resource management techniques, this exposure to the force of market competition will be entirely beneficial for all concerned, most notably the taxpayer. This line of argument, fostered by the New Right, contends that with management firmly at the helm of a leaner and fitter organisation, leading a workforce dedicated to achieving the organisation's goals, making maximum use of every employee's abilities, and with everyone responding flexibly to meet the demands of the market place, then the chances of success are greatly enhanced. The government claims that the LMS reforms, along with the provision of information such as league tables to enable consumers to make their choices in the school market place, will raise standards in education (Citizen's Charter 1991: 13).

As we argued in the previous chapter, human resource management techniques contain large assumptions about goals. They are to be defined by management; and employees with the wrong sort of abilities or the wrong sort of attitudes are not wanted. 'Flexibility' means enabling the right work to be done at the right time, in the right quantity and to the right standards, all as defined by management. Goal-setting is reduced to managerialism, with no attention paid to the goals of others. Both parents and professionals in schools may have other priorities.

Private sector corporations are the model form of organisation for the new market-driven school system. Decentralised operating units are allowed to make operational decisions within their own service or product markets, having a flexible workforce, and with staffing issues settled more by line managers than by personnel departments. To argue that private sector management techniques cannot be imported into the public service sector is to miss the point. Clearly a school is different from a supermarket or a bank, and it is difficult to unpick the market relationships between government, LEAs, teachers, parents, governors, heads and pupils – who are the customers? Neither the pupils nor the parents actually pay for what happens in schools; the taxpayers do. The operating units gain their income from the LEAs, but the LEAs are not consumers as we normally understand the term. Nevertheless, the reforms have the effect of forcing schools to behave *as if* they are small businesses, or the subsidiaries of a larger company.

In the context of declining budgets then schools must follow the logic of the labour-intensive business faced with falling income and take a close look at the savings that might be made by reducing staffing costs. In short they must secure 'more for less'. The first option is a simple reduction in the size of the workforce. Secondly they might restructure the workforce, substituting some employees with cheaper ones. Thirdly they will need to make employees work harder, otherwise the saving in labour costs could be offset by a fall in output, leading to a spiral of decline. Fourthly, savings could be made by changing the payment system to secure a reduction in the total salary bill; this could include measures to tie levels of pay to employees' performance, abandoning annual increments, and tying pay increases to productivity increases to ensure pay rises at no extra cost. By 1992 the NUT was reporting that in Staffordshire high-cost senior posts had been lost, including deputy heads, teaching and non-teaching support staffing had been cut, and budgets for repairs, for books and for cover for absent teachers all had been reduced (*The Teacher*, December 1992).

These are the measures necessary for a business to stay in business, and for a school to operate without a budget deficit (as it must), when income is less than expenditure and non-staffing costs cannot be cut to make the necessary savings. They amount to an offensive against employees, attacking their job security, their pay, their working conditions and their jobs, and increasing the intensity of their work. In this chapter we identify the main issues that will arise in schools as a result of the recession/reform-induced changes, drawing from the case study and questionnaire findings of the Keele survey. We also look at the impact of the reforms on the highly formalised system of LEA-based collective bargaining and agreements, noting particularly how the old conflict resolution mechanisms become either redundant or irrelevant. We argue that the reforms induce a vacuum, leaving no obvious means of handling the inevitable school-level conflicts.

THE ISSUES FOR INDUSTRIAL RELATIONS

Job losses and job security

The application of LMS formula funding to state schools has led to redundancies amongst teachers. As this process of job loss gathers momentum, as it must, it will add to feelings of insecurity of employment among those staff that remain employed, especially the most vulnerable in employment terms – part-timers, older less well qualified teachers and those teaching some of the subjects deemed to be marginal by the government. This is, of course, one deliberate consequence of the reform programme. Why employ an older, experienced expensive teacher when the school can employ a younger, inexperienced cheaper teacher? The taxpayer, according to the government, deserves value-for-money education and therefore schools must be forced to employ at lowest possible costs. In other cases whole schools will be closed as budget constraints add to demographic change to reduce the number of small, and in particular rural, primary schools. These processes of redundancy raise issues new to most teachers and school managers: the coping with absolute job losses from schools, the resultant heavier workload, the substitution of more expensive and more skilled teachers with cheaper less skilled ones, and the ever tighter controls over existing staff.

Where an employer decides to cease operating in the place where the employees are employed, or the employer no longer requires employees to carry out all or some work of a particular kind then the employer may dismiss all or some of the employees on the grounds of redundancy. Unions likely to be faced with such circumstances usually seek a procedural agreement to protect their members in a number of related areas, and ACAS has set out advice on this (ACAS 1989b).

The union's objectives will be first to minimise the number of job losses, secondly to minimise the number of compulsory redundancies, thirdly to place limits on managerial discretion over selection for redundancy, and finally to secure the maximum compensation for those made redundant. Thus the shedding of jobs is usually accomplished over three stages, the first of which is through 'natural wastage' where employees retiring from their jobs or leaving employment with that employer are not replaced. This is usually accompanied by recruitment restrictions, or 'ring-fencing', where any vacancies which must be filled for operational reasons are filled from within the existing workforce. It may also be accompanied by procedures to redeploy employees to vacancies in other parts of the organisation, with the provision of resources to re-train redeployed employees where necessary. If sufficient reductions cannot be achieved through natural wastage, then the employer may proceed to the second stage and ask for volunteers for early retirement and for voluntary redundancy. Finally the employer will decide on the employees to be made redundant compulsorily. The law requires employers to consult with recognised unions and make certain information available, and to make offers of suitable alternative employment to displaced employees where possible.

The main concerns of the teacher unions have been to maintain staffing levels and pupil/teacher ratios, and we saw in chapter 3 that the general trend has been for the pupil/teacher ratio to fall steadily during periods of both expansion and contraction of the pupil population, although the ratio has risen slightly in recent years. Where pupil numbers were falling they sought to prevent teachers in 'overstaffed' schools from being made redundant, seeking local agreements on redeployment. In most LEAs a policy of no compulsory redundancies was agreed, but redeployment agreements took a number of forms. The most direct provided for redeployment only into vacant posts that needed to be filled. Thus if a French teacher post was required to be filled, volunteers would be sought from overstaffed schools and the post filled with the needs of the receiving school taking precedence over those of the volunteer's school.

Agreements in other LEAs allowed heads to select the candidates for compulsory redeployment, according to a range of criteria such as the curriculum needs of the school or the competency of the teachers. Under an agreement like this the needs of the 'overstaffed' school took precedence, and the LEA organised redeployment into another school, continuing to employ the teacher while searching for a vacancy in a school that was prepared to accept them. 'Safeguarding' provisions ensured that salary levels of those moved from higher to lower paid jobs were protected.

The criteria for selection, for both compulsory redeployment and compulsory redundancy, are major issues for trade unions. The law requires that selection must not be in breach of a customary arrangement or agreed procedure, unless there are justifiable reasons for doing so, and it must not be on grounds of trade union membership, race, sex or marital status. The agreed criteria must also be applied equally to all employees. In establishments declaring redundancies within the WIRS study 29 per cent used skills or qualifications as a selection criterion, 23 per cent used performance records, and 19 per cent used attendance and disciplinary records (Millward *et al* 1992: 325). The preferred criterion is last in first out (LIFO), used in half of establishments, and described by ACAS as 'objective, easy to apply, readily understood and widely accepted' (ACAS 1989b: 16).

The teacher workforce has experienced contracting levels of employment during periods of falling numbers of pupils. As we noted in chapter 3, the number of pupils in schools has been falling since the 1970s, only beginning to increase again in the primary sector in the late 1980s. The Advisory Committee on the Supply and Education of Teachers (ACSET, disbanded in 1989) predicted in 1981 that by 1991 pupil numbers would fall by 14 per cent from 8.5 million to 7.3 million, with a consequent fall in the number of secondary teachers by 60,500 (Thomas 1984: 2). The primary sector teacher workforce experienced a similar level of contraction earlier in the decade. Managing this decline in the workforce had implications for teachers.

Most writers in this area draw attention to the impact of decline on the curriculum. Expansion had presented opportunities to broaden the curriculum, drawing from the potential economies of scale. Contraction suggested the reverse might happen, resulting in a narrower curriculum, less curriculum development, more mixed age groups, less flexibility in staff deployment, and declining morale among both teachers and pupils in a climate of uncertainty. As one head in our survey commented 'teachers' morale is generally very low . . . the possible threat of redundancy because of LMS is not helping'. Furthermore, the deployment of the thinner workforce between schools is more difficult, and the unit cost of education provision tends to increase (Bondi 1989). Short-term measures to deal with contraction can lead to adverse consequences in the long term. For example, if a teacher leaves a school and is not replaced then their teaching load may be allocated to other teachers from a different specialism. This weakens the provision to the pupils, weakens the specialist department, and downgrades teacher skills (Reid 1983: 364). Reid also noted that leaving decisions about this to heads will lead to wider differences in curriculum provision between schools, and argues for a compulsory common core curriculum in secondary schools. Long-term planning for contraction may include closing schools, a method particularly favoured by the government in the 1980s who saw falling rolls as an opportunity to reduce education spending. However, closing schools presents LEAs with a range of both practical and political difficulties, and closures often reflected piecemeal responses to various competing and contradictory pressures rather than any rational objective planning criteria (Bondi 1989).

Thomas (1984: 3) lists the methods available for managing contraction, as follows: (1) reducing teacher training provision; (2) early retirement; (3) natural wastage; (4) reducing teachers' earnings relative to others; (5) non-renewal of short-term contracts; (6) redundancy; (7) redeployment; (8) in-service training. Methods (1)–(6) are aimed at reducing the number of teachers in employment, while (7) and (8) are aimed at redistributing teachers from areas of the workforce where contraction is required into areas where it is not. This redistribution may be between sectors, subjects, or geographical locations, as changes in pupil and teacher numbers can vary significantly both within and between regions.

Contraction of the workforce means a reduction in the number of higher graded posts and, as the contraction followed a period of expansion, senior teacher posts were mainly held by quite young teachers. This resulted in a reduction in the number of opportunities for promotion and a reduction in job mobility. This had an impact on job satisfaction, as opportunities to change jobs were closed down (Dennison 1979). The career path for teachers involved frequent moves between schools, and the impact of contraction was to restrict such movement. Dennison (1980) argued that the introduction of a career grade was necessary in view of the reduced number of promoted posts. Thomas offers a more clearly market-oriented version of this solution, proposing that the differentials between classroom teachers and senior teachers should be widened. Paying senior teachers more would give them an incentive to remain within the workforce, and paying junior teachers less would give the ambitious ones an incentive to seek promotion and those 'who have not demonstrated their competence to secure promotion' an incentive to leave (Thomas 1984: 10).

Wastage rates for teachers are very low, with fewer than 1 per cent of the workforce leaving it to take up other employment (STRB 1993: 76). Boosting wastage rates by reducing pay was likely to have only marginal impact, especially at a time when employment opportunities elsewhere in the economy were particularly limited. The main way to increase wastage was through increasing the number of retirements by making available incentives to persuade teachers to retire early.

Thus the LEAs organised these periods of contraction through the 1970s and into the 1980s with the assistance of incentives for older teachers to take voluntary redundancy with enhanced pension rights, or premature retirement compensation. A national scheme enabled LEAs to pay retirement pensions, with discretion to enhance them, to teachers aged fifty or over who were made redundant. There was never any shortage of takers for this scheme, and it had an impact on the age profile of the teacher workforce. In most LEAs the shedding of staff became a rather complex operation, involving the dishing out of early retirements to those who asked for it followed by staffing adjustments through a mixture of voluntary and compulsory redeployments of teachers in overstaffed schools to fill the vacancies arising from retirements, early retirements and resignations in schools that were not overstaffed. However, the scheme enabled most staffing adjustments to be made without recourse to compulsory redundancies.

In spite of the relatively trouble-free management of this shedding of jobs, in many schools morale took a downturn as teachers feared that they might be selected for redeployment, suffering the accompanying stigmatisation, and waiting for another school to agree to take them into the establishment. Heads may have welcomed the opportunity to get rid of staff perceived as 'dead wood', as troublemakers or as incompetent, but many teachers saw this as management opportunism, exploiting staffing difficulties as a way of compensating for their own inability to manage effectively. Here was a graphic illustration of the exercise of managerial prerogative at the level of the school, and many union activists gained their first experiences of seeking restraints to this during the period of contraction.

LMS has effectively formalised the school, through the governing body, as the level of decision-making over staffing levels. LEAs lose the formal powers to control the selection of staff for redundancy, and to impose a redeployed teacher onto a school. With increasing delegation of budgets they also become unable to retain displaced teachers on the central establishment. LMS schools are able to determine their own staffing levels (subject to the legal requirement to employ a 'sufficient' number of teachers) and to decide their own redundancy criteria. LEAs continue to issue dismissal notices, and they have to offer alternative employment where suitable vacancies exist, but they are not able to compel another school to take on a teacher even where a vacancy exists. However, schools cannot ignore the legislation on unfair dismissal, as LEAs will be able to deduct tribunal awards from delegated budgets where they can show that the school acted unreasonably and in contravention of LEA advice.

The net effect of this is potentially to reduce scope for flexibility. In an 'overstaffed' school redundant teachers may not find a school that will accept them for redeployment, increasing their chances of dismissal by the LEA. It is quite conceivable that teachers in one school could be dismissed while there are vacant posts in others, especially if redundancies are seen as performance related. This raises important questions about the nature of efficiency itself and any reliable measures of it. The system as devised may result in each individual school becoming more efficient in a narrow technical sense as each seeks to survive market pressures, but the overall resource allocation efficiency may be reduced on a national scale. This occurs because, for example, a redundant fifty-year-old teacher may leave a school and thereby increase the cost-effectiveness of that school, but the loss to the taxpayer (for the want of a better victim) is of the accumulated costs and value of that teacher as a practising teacher to the national education system. It must be more efficient to keep that teacher in work until normal retirement age. A corollary of this false accounting is the assumption that flexibility and increased fear of job loss makes teachers work harder. As one head explained 'security of employment is also desirable to allow people to make decisions affecting their futures and reduces stress'. The kinds of pressures generated by the new school market place on teachers appear to be counter-productive in terms of harder work, greater effort and higher performance. The evidence is that many are over stretched and over stressed and that the result is lower quality education and ultimately an inefficient education system.

LEAs responded to the possible loss of this key personnel management role, namely of some kind of human resource planning on a LEA-wide basis, by issuing comprehensive guidance to schools, setting out the statutory requirements and emphasising the status of teachers as employees of the LEA. Many have also drawn up new agreements with the trade unions, with the minimum of modification to previous agreements. These retain the LEA's role in seeking to minimise compulsory redundancy and to maximise scope for redeployment. Most importantly they also lay down the agreed redundancy selection criteria. Heads who ignore this agreement may render unfair a subsequent dismissal by the LEA, with any consequent award against the LEA being deducted from the school budget.

The following extract from one LEA's code of practice for governing bodies gives a typical example of approaches to selection criteria.

> In nominating a teacher whose post is surplus to a school's establishment and, therefore potentially redundant the following factors will be taken into account:
>
> (i) Equal Opportunities; ensuring that the nomination process is not discriminatory.
>
> (ii) The school's development plan, including the staffing structure, curricular and pastoral needs.
>
> (iii) The teacher's length of service in the school and with the Authority though this does not in itself imply a 'last in – first out' policy.
>
> In determining which staff are most appropriate to the School Development Plan individual skills or qualifications will be relevant.

This code stresses the need to avoid subjective criteria based on personal qualities, and to make judgements based on objective evidence. It expands on the above three criteria as follows.

> The following examples of detailed criteria that might be used were given in a recent industrial tribunal judgement.
>
> overall subject needs;
> subject special requirements (e.g. to support, say, improvement in maths performance in a school);
> length of service;
> seniority within the school;
> academic qualifications generally;
> particular subject expertise (e.g. recent specialist courses);
> capability to switch from subject to subject as demonstrated by current actual teaching and/or qualifications and/or past actual teaching;
> lack of qualifications in relevant subject areas;
> lack of qualifications to teach certain levels (e.g. above or below certain age groups and/or to teach particular exam standards);
> additional qualifications (e.g. administration, sports, music, counselling)

It appears to be taken for granted that in developing these criteria the management view of what constitutes 'overall subject needs', for example, will be accepted by the teachers in the school. In practice, while the decisions of managers in the workplace may be rationalised through the use of apparently neutral criteria, this may obscure the real basis for selection. Selection for redeployment/redundancy during the 1970s and 1980s took place mainly at the level of the school, and this was one of the first areas of potentially widespread school-based conflict to emerge in the post-war period. Heads played a key role in managing the LEAs' staffing reductions, and many used the opportunity to off-load unwanted teachers. However, these job losses were based mainly on falling school rolls, and the numbers were determined by decisions of the elected LEA members. The focus of discontent over staffing levels and job security was mainly at the level of the LEA.

The LMS funding formula is based on average teacher salaries throughout the LEA, which means that schools with a higher than average number of experienced teachers near the top of the salary scale have a higher than average salary bill but the same salary budget as a comparable school with a lower salary bill. This adds to the impact of declining budgets that are affecting nearly all schools as LEAs operate within government-imposed spending criteria. Many schools have found such large shortfalls in their budgets that they have had no alternative but to reduce the number of teachers, whose salaries amount to 80 per cent of school budgets. Job losses amounted to several hundred in many LEAs in 1992/3; for example, one LEA reduced the number of jobs by 450, including 300 out of 8,000 teachers. Another lost 203 teachers between 1990 and 1991, whilst the number of pupils increased by 730 (Sinclair *et al.* 1993a: 17). The Keele head teacher survey found that in the year 1992/3 a quarter of schools, including four-fifths of secondary schools, were affected by either redundancies, redeployments or early retirements.

These job losses were driven by cuts in the aggregate schools budget, forced by recessionary pressures rather than by falling school rolls. The cuts were implemented through the mechanism of the funding formula, spreading the cuts across all schools and leaving those with a declining market share with a severe budget deficit. This has led to protest strike action by either or both of the NUT and the NASUWT in some LEAs, including Staffordshire, Wolverhampton and Sandwell in the Midlands. There is some limited evidence that this has resulted in proportionally fewer compulsory redundancies among the members of these two unions.

In managing these job losses the head teacher and governors are not simply responding to an LEA decision that their school is overstaffed; they themselves are taking the decision to shed staff in order to remain within their delegated budget. Furthermore, having decided to shed staff they must then decide which ones are to go. The processes through which volunteers are sought, and candidates for redundancy are selected, raise many issues of fairness and justice. The potential for conflict is enormous. Heads may apply pressure to the more expensive teachers to leave, or they may target teachers who they believe to lack either ability or commitment. There are many possibilities for discrimination, which may be perceived as unacceptable. Teachers themselves may apply pressure to older colleagues, arguing that they should leave the available jobs to those who have family commitments and large mortgages. Finally, the cost of mistakes in this area can be substantial. The governors of a secondary school in Surrey declared three teachers redundant after finding they faced a budget shortfall of £154,000. The industrial tribunal's finding that these dismissals were unfair stressed the importance of Surrey County Council's role, as the employer, in seeking to redeploy redundant teachers to other posts (*Times Educational Supplement*, 10 January 1992). In Kidderminster a technology teacher won over £8,000 compensation for wrongful dismissal after being made redundant by his school governors (*Career Teacher*, January 1994).

Decline in jobs is thus not a new issue for teachers. Until the advent of the reform programme decline was mainly related to falling rolls and was organised by LEAs. With relatively few exceptions, conflict over job losses was institutionalised through the use of procedural agreements that were applied by personnel managers and union officers. Now job losses are business related, arising from budget deficits rather than from a reduction in pupil numbers. Many school managers are making decisions about staffing levels that raise the prospect for conflict in their schools. It is not clear what mechanisms will replace the redundant LEA procedures for containing conflict.

Workload

The evidence that teacher workload has increased throughout the 1990s is now overwhelming. Union submissions to the STRB provide sufficient examples for this, as do several national and regional surveys. This is a planned part of the reform programme. The harder teachers work, the greater the value added, and therefore government objectives of value-for-money education are met. One obvious but important objection to this argument is that harder work, *per se*, is not necessarily associated with higher performance nor with an efficient use of teacher labour through lifelong activity in the teacher labour market. Stress, increased absence rates, poorer quality in task completion and a reduction in non-teaching duties all diminish the education of pupils, weaken national standards of attainment, and reduce teacher effectiveness.

Teachers' workload has increased because of a combination of factors. First is the sheer volume of work associated with the national curriculum and pupil assessment. The general decline in budget levels is, as we noted earlier, placing downward pressure on staffing levels. Furthermore, the cost involved in providing cover for teachers absent through illness (often stress related) or for in-service training is another area where saving can be achieved. The trend is for cover to be provided from within the core school workforce rather than from either a central pool or from supply teachers. The net result of these is that all teachers are having to work harder.

The effect of running a school with fewer staff, or of running it with more pupils but the same number of staff, is to increase the overall pupil/teacher ratio. Teachers must either teach the same number of classes but with more pupils, or they must teach more classes. The evidence suggests that both are happening. Over a five year period average class sizes rose by 4 per cent and the average pupil/teacher ratio rose by 3 per cent (DFE 1992b). As the distribution of class sizes is uneven, this means that some teachers are taking very large classes, with consequent extra marking and other work. As one home economics teacher in a large comprehensive explained:

> 'In subjects where you are using craft machinery, irons and cookers, it's potentially dangerous and we like to keep groups at 20 or below, but it's now crept up to 22–24. Two years ago I had a part-timer who was not replaced, which causes me problems as I have had to deal with a number of non-specialist domestic science helpers, and I have to take account of that in the children's work. You used to have 18 scripts to mark for a class; now its 26 or more plus extra time spent on meetings and courses.'

Many secondary school teachers are also having their non-contact time reduced and their teaching load increased by being given extra timetabled teaching. Johnson noticed in her work on USA teachers that 'many teachers . . . did far more work than their contracts required, but such extra efforts were understood to be voluntary' (Johnson 1984a: 85). She also found that 'union pressure to define teachers' work obligations was, by all accounts, either a response to real administrative abuse or a defense against potential administrative abuse' (Johnson 1984a: 108). Typical comments made in the course of our own research included this:

> 'The 1265 hours . . . we just pay lip service to it. The school plan mapped this out, but with meetings stemming from the new curriculum, task groups etc so more meetings are required. You record the hours at first but it tends to fall flat. It's a vicious circle, but you don't want to let the kids down. It's a reflection of the conscientiousness of teachers, working longer hours to maintain standards.'

One head of a middle school described his own and others' workload in 1993.

> 'It has been increased due to lack of money. I spend 2 or 3 hours a night working at home. I am here late at night, sorting out the budget and going to meetings. We have 4 sub-committee meetings prior to each governors' meeting . . . so I attend 24 sub-committee meetings. For each one I have to lead the way, for example on finance, I have to do preparations. The other staff also do more outside school, monitoring, recording, preparation, work for SATS, so they all work late and are tired. The enthusiastic teacher is working longer and harder than those who rush out at 3.30, although they too often still work at home. Quality is affected if they don't do it. My teaching workload is to increase 2–3 hours a week now, and next year it will be 5 or 6; the deputy head also has a full teaching load.'

This is in spite of the codified hours of work introduced in 1987, requiring teachers to work 1,265 hours over 195 days per year at the direction of the head. Some duties, such as attendance at parents' evenings, are being made voluntary in many schools. The additional mandatory teaching hours in compensation represent an intensification of the teachers' work; they spend more time performing the more demanding work in the classroom, and less doing the less demanding work. Furthermore, 'voluntary' attendance at a parents' evening may in practice be regarded as compulsory – the consequences of non-attendance may rebound at a later date, when candidates for promotion or for redundancy are being sought. For many teachers a full day's teaching is then followed by meetings of working groups on the national curriculum, filling in monitoring reports, completing records, and preparing lessons and SATs.

In practice, the codified hours of work have become meaningless, in that they bear no relation to their actual hours worked. Duties required of them, but not directed by the head, such as administration of the national curriculum and the associated tests, have expanded at the same time as their class sizes have increased and their non-contact time has fallen. Teachers at a Hampshire school agreed that their school's budget to provide some non-contact time should be used to fund salaries. This arose because of the higher than average number of experienced teachers at the school, and the clear result of this is that the teachers will carry a heavier workload to enable the school to remain within budget (*Times Educational Supplement*, 22 May 1992). On the other hand, heads are able to use the category of 'directed time' to require teachers to undertake classroom teaching duties as and when needed by the management. This may even include the introduction of a 'twilight shift', with some teaching being done outside of standard teaching hours. This would pose particular problems for teachers with family care commitments, and had been an issue in two of the secondary schools covered by the Keele study.

Time out of the classroom because of sickness or in-service training is expensive as it must be covered by another teacher. In many primary schools cover is provided by heads as most teachers have no non-contact time. A majority of the primary heads in our survey commented on the special pressures generated in small schools by underfunding and the increased bureaucratic load. As one stated, 'budget problems mean that my class teaching commitment is very heavy and therefore management issues can be very difficult', and another added 'I know we all work harder than we have ever done'. Some teachers may be diverted from their specialist duties, such as special needs activity or duties funded under section 11, into mainstream classroom teaching. The pressure to reduce absences may result in reduced release for in-service training. In secondary schools the provision of sickness absence cover is being devolved to faculties and departments, so that teachers considering absenting themselves must also consider the impact this will have on the goodwill extended to them by their immediate colleagues. A union representative in a primary school said that 'a year ago it was implied that, when it came to losing staff, those with an absence record would be looked at' (Sinclair *et al.* 1993b: 19). One head teacher, who believed that the sick pay scheme encouraged 'malingerers', had a teacher who continued to teach his A level class while on sick leave, and later secured early retirement for that teacher. The majority view of heads was expressed by one from a middle school: 'absenteeism of teachers – a lot is caused by the extra pressures'.

Teachers' experience of these pressures is often related as 'stress'. This term is frequently used by heads and teachers when talking about the impact of changes in both staffing and workload. A secondary teacher said:

> 'Stress plays a large role especially this term. It depends on your age. Younger ones can say "I can always get out". Others like me are looking at pensions, but asking "Can I last much longer?" Lots are looking at early retirement and there is no energy.'

A deputy head in a middle school said:

> 'I have had a month off with stress caused by too many meetings. It was a build-up of hours, meetings and so on. Stress is manifest in lots of ways. Rattiness, persistent colds. You feel bitter about a system doing that to you. I considered giving up as I was getting in a state, and saw the pastoral inspector. I now duck out of things and ask myself if such-and-such a meeting is really important. I've stopped attending unnecessary meetings. Something has to give.'
>
> (Sinclair *et al.* 1993a: 24)

There are numerous examples of anecdotes to do with sickness-related early retirements. An LEA personnel officer said that he had advised one head not to use the competence procedures to dismiss a teacher recently returned from sick leave. The head agreed on realising that the procedure would take too long to resolve the immediate budget problems.

Our research in this area leaves us in no doubt that these examples of teacher responses to pressure point towards a difficult future in schools. The combination of economic recession and market-based reform is inducing in management a need to restructure both the teacher workforce and the job of the teacher. As we have seen, the experience of the classroom teacher will be one of job insecurity, loss of autonomy, and work intensification. While this experience is attributable to government policy, to underfunding, and to beggar-my-neighbour market mechanisms, the decisions necessary to live with these are being taken by school-based managers. The human resource management techniques discussed in chapter 4 are aimed at convincing teachers that these decisions are the best possible decisions in the interest of both the school and the workforce. A major part of that is development of the concept of 'flexibility' and its concomitant notions of 'reprofiling' the staff and redefining professional standards with management created standards. We discuss these next before moving on to the related topics of reward management and performance management which were identified in chapter 4 as vital management concerns.

Flexible skills in the flexible school

The central importance to the operation of the 1988 reform programme of the performance of teachers requires, *inter alia*, a greater concentration on a more flexible teacher contract, more frequent changes in the skill mix of staff, and an ideological challenge to professional definitions of performance. Under these conditions job losses and increased workload are part and parcel of the employers' human resource strategies which culminate in the application of 'flexible' working practices.

In chapter 4 we examined some of the human resource management literature, which makes much of the benefits to be derived from flexibility within the workforce. It is suggested that management should be able to draw from a variety of types of worker, introducing patterns of working that are less rigid than the usual full-time model. This, it is argued, will benefit management who will be able to draw labour from the workforce at the time when it is required, rather than having to continuously employ a fixed pool of permanent full-time labour that may not be fully engaged in productive work at all times. It is also held to offer increased opportunities for workers, who may prefer to avoid the commitment of working full-time all the time. For managers running on a tight budget there are cheaper alternatives to the well qualified and experienced full-time job-for-life professional teacher.

Such are the vagaries of the labour market that while many schools are looking to shed teachers there are also difficulties in filling vacancies. In a report by Alan Smithers, commissioned by the DES, it is concluded that there are too few applications for many vacancies, that the quality of applicants may be an issue for concern, and that some schools are suffering considerable loss of staff through a high level of wastage (DES press release, 19 August 1991). The pressures on school managers to 'make do' with what is available, even when that means a history teacher teaching English, further exacerbates the growing mismatch of supply and demand created, in large measure, by the 1988 reforms.

As well as changing patterns of employment caused by more flexible policies on hiring and firing, flexibility also embraces the nature of the job and the regulation of the job as well. Human resource management exponents urge the cultivation of a workforce with the correct mix of skills, arguing that skilled practitioners should be liberated from the more mundane aspects of their jobs. One consequence of this was described to us by an English teacher in a comprehensive school, 'competitive tendering is a great problem in this school with cleaning etc. My class which is children of 13 are currently decorating, their parents have brought in tins of paint. I said I would never do any cleaning in my class, but I get asthma now, and so I have to'. Attention is focused on both the profile of the workforce and the tasks carried out. In this section we look at the developments in this area, as school managers have sought to contain staffing costs while protecting the relevant measured educational outcomes.

According to DES statistics for schools in England in 1990 there were 375,100 full-time teachers and the hours taught by part-time teachers amounted to the equivalent of 23,400 full-timers. Part-time teaching is widespread, especially among primary schools, and many teachers would rather have a part-time job than a full-time one. However, they also give management a larger range of options for cutting the salary bill. First, a cut in hours produces an instant saving. Second, part-timers might only be employed for the hours that they actually teach, and it may be possible to avoid paying them for non-contact time and for meal breaks and assembly periods. Under these circumstances two half-time teachers might do more work at less cost than one full-time. Third, they take longer to acquire employment rights and are therefore more easily disposable than full-time teachers. Finally, they can provide a cushion against the loss of a full teaching post, enabling the loss to be spread between departments. The Keele study found examples of all of these practices – as one primary head said, 'one impact of LMS I think will be employing cheaper staff. I have been tempted, yes, to look at them. Any school denying this would be lying about this being a factor, so discrimination on age grounds is likely' (Sinclair *et al.* 1993b: 18).

There are arguments against treating part-timers in this way, ranging through practicalities, ethics, and educational value, but the cost-cutting imperative overwhelms them all. These practices are as likely to be adopted in schools as they are in other types of workplace. Only when the consequences for management of discriminating against part-timers are more severe than the consequences of not discriminating against them will such practices be stopped, and trade unions are becoming increasingly concerned about the rights of these workers. The Keele survey found evidence of an increase in the use of part-time teachers between 1992 and 1993; in the 576 schools surveyed, covering some 10,000 full-time and 1,000 part-time teachers, 26 heads said that their school employs more part-time men teachers than last year (11 said they employ fewer), and 128 said they employ more part-time women than last year (67 said they employ fewer). Three-quarters of schools employ part-timers. DES statistics show that there was an increase of 43 per cent in the volume of teaching by part-timers between 1985 and 1990.

Short-term contracts are being used in schools to an increasing degree. Over half of the schools in the Keele survey employed teachers on temporary contracts, covering a total of 600 jobs. These also provide a cushion against compulsory redundancies, enabling rapid adjustments of both staffing levels and staffing profiles to be made. Temporary workers, engaged on a series of unconnected contracts, rarely acquire employment rights. Furthermore, they are also unlikely to make progress up the pay scale so they remain cheaper than teachers holding 'permanent' posts. The use of this method of reducing staffing costs has resulted in some difficult disputes that have reached the courts. The governors of a school in the West Country agreed to £3,500 compensation after failing to renew a teacher's fixed-term contract after her maternity leave. The NUT had lodged claims of unfair dismissal and sex discrimination with the industrial tribunal (*The Teacher*, December 1992). In Dudley the employer agreed to hand over £500 compensation in respect of holiday pay to a woman teacher on a fixed term-contract, on the day before the industrial tribunal was due to hear her case based on equal pay and sex discrimination legislation (*The Teacher*, April 1994). One of the clearest cases of a governing body trying to exploit fixed-term contracts to the full occurred in Cornwall, where an industrial tribunal explicitly rejected the idea that governors could avoid a permanent appointment by claiming that they did not know 'the exact requirements of the demands of [the] business in the years ahead' (industrial tribunal verdict, quoted in the *Times Educational Supplement*, 2 April 1993).

The potential to make savings by employing cheaper teachers is notably present when filling vacancies. If an experienced teacher towards the top of the pay scale leaves the school then an instant saving is possible, first by delaying filling the post, and second by filling it with a teacher who is lower down the scale. Most teachers can relate anecdotes on this theme; teachers in a middle school gave an example of an experienced teacher volunteering for redundancy when the school was faced with a budget shortfall of £10,000. In the following financial year the head appointed a new entrant on a short-term contract, which was seen by the staff as sending some very ominous signals. Other teachers said that they believed they had been left off shortlists for jobs because of their age, and that they had been told by teacher friends that the governors said that they were too old to be considered because of the higher salary costs. This experience-related discrimination will alter the profile of the teacher workforce, favouring younger teachers and blocking moves by older ones. Some heads freely admit that this discrimination takes place, while others argue that the introduction of 'new blood' is good for the school. Discrimination on grounds of experience, or salary level, or age is not unlawful, but it would represent a break with established practice.

This reprofiling of the classroom workforce could go beyond the substitution of relatively expensive teachers with cheaper ones. It could extend to a more fundamental structural change, involving a transformation of the classroom labour process. The reform programme is aimed at challenging the grip of the teaching professionals on the process of teaching itself.

Skilled labour is more expensive than unskilled, and one of the characteristics of skilled workers is their autonomy in the practice of their craft. In the manufacturing sector of the economy the principles of scientific management, aimed at transferring the control of production from workers to managers, have been applied since the beginning of the twentieth century. The main principles of scientific management are first the systematic study of the craft by managers so that knowledge of the craft does not reside solely within the craft practitioners; second the separation of the planning of work from its execution; and third the use of this monopoly of knowledge to control the way that tasks are organised and executed (Braverman 1974: 112–20). Known as Taylorism, after the main writer on the notion of scientific management, these principles have a clear managerial logic which is being applied to the practice of teaching (*Times Educational Supplement*, 14 May 1993).

The tools of scientific management include work study. The practice rests on the assumption that managers have not only the right but also the ability to control workers and to direct the way they carry out their tasks. And the effect on work is to reduce tasks to standardised fragments and to remove the need for skilled practitioners. If the components of tasks requiring the application of skill can be removed, then the tasks can be performed by labour that is less skilled and consequently cheaper.

Skill, however, is a complex matter, defined through social, cultural and political processes rather than through objective facts. When one skill commands a higher salary than another, for example that of the engineer compared with that of the secretary, the difference reflects a range of socially defined factors, including gender. The hierarchical division of labour reflects these social factors, and is clearly visible in schools where gender divisions operate between subjects, between the primary and secondary sectors, and between heads and classroom teachers.

This provides us with a framework to examine the current attack on teacher autonomy. When teachers practise the skill, or rather the 'profession', of teaching they draw on a range of 'professional skills' which they have acquired through a lengthy period of training, study and practice. In common with other professional and skilled workers they have mobilised the concepts of professionalism and skill to defend their position in the labour market. Their skills are traditionally deployed in the classroom, without supervision and without interference by others in their teaching activity. Decisions about the content of lessons and about the teaching methods to be deployed may be located within some broad guidelines, but in large part they have been left to each professional practitioner.

Under the impact of the reforming legislation this traditional professional autonomy is being eroded. The national curriculum removes large areas of decision-making from teachers and transfers them to government, specifying in detail the content of courses. Teachers can find many ways of subverting government prescription, and they do not necessarily perform only the functions allotted them by the government. Government is not present with the teacher in the classroom (Apple 1988: 104). However, while the national curriculum is not so over-arching as to prescribe the manner in which the curriculum is to be delivered, content does impact on delivery. With the highly bureaucratic and routinised procedures for assessment making large demands on teacher time the scope for classroom innovation is reduced. When the three classroom unions imposed a boycott of the standard tests in 1992/3 this underlined the importance of autonomy and the impact of high workloads on professional activity.

Typical comments from the teachers we interviewed noted the lack of consultation by government on the introduction of the national curriculum. Most saw this, quite rightly, as an attack on their professional integrity. One deputy head noted 'there was a lack of consultation, and lack of time for analysing the documents. These reforms were just imposed on us'. A classroom teacher in a first school argued 'we feel we are getting to grips with it, but the paperwork is stupid. We can see the purpose of it but there are so many bits and inconsistencies, and the ghastly jargon in some documents; they did not ask enough teachers to get involved first, particularly in primaries'. Another teacher added a point which summarised the general frustration 'I get bad temper when I have to do all this. I have just started smoking again after 20 years!'

American teachers have had some experience of standardised learning programmes. Here the teachers no longer practise the key traditional skills of developing lessons and teaching methods, but they are enskilled to become 'classroom managers', supervisors of a predetermined classroom production process . . . . keeping students 'on task', disciplining or excluding those who disrupt the production process, and keeping track of production records – primarily through administering and recording standardized test data' (Carlson 1987: 290). The process as a whole promotes the cheapening and increased substitutability of teachers' labour, as 'skill kits' are designed to be taught by less qualified, lower paid, inexperienced teachers, particularly in urban, poor areas. While there has not yet been any significant adoption of these techniques in British schools, there is a trend in this direction in the vocational training sector, with private consultants playing an increasing role in the development of programmes to be delivered by unqualified trainers and instructors.

Nevertheless, the demands of the national curriculum have already had some impact on the division of labour between teachers along scientific management lines. Some teachers have been given a brief to ensure the national requirements are followed throughout a school or department, acquiring titles like 'subject co-ordinator'. This has frequently been the basis for the award of pay enhancements, introducing a formal hierarchy based on skill where none previously existed. It has the effect of concentrating knowledge about the curriculum in the hands of senior teachers, giving them a degree of control over the content of lessons and consequently some control over the activities of classroom teachers. This trend provides a basis for the NASUWT's demand for increased differentials for teachers taking on managerial tasks.

For rank and file classroom teachers these developments signify a deskilling of their jobs, moving them towards a role of classroom minder and curriculum deliverer, with little role in curriculum development and with limited access to the knowledge necessary to challenge the decisions of the senior teacher. A further result of this trend is that teachers' work is intensified – as they are removed from lesson planning so they can spend more time in the classroom, leaving them with less respite from the demands of ensuring the delivery of the curriculum to pupils. One head told us that his main objective since LMS 'has been to protect the staff to enable them to concentrate on their performance in the classroom'. In short, the combination of the national curriculum, the assessment procedures and increased workload have meant less work on lesson content and more work on classroom and administration routines, which represents a general degradation of the job – the Taylorisation of teaching.

As the content of lessons is more closely specified by agents outside of the classroom there is more scope for classroom teachers to diversify and to teach additional subjects. The pressure of shortages of some subject teachers has meant that teachers have covered by teaching subjects other than the one in which they qualified. Under LMS the pressure is increased by tight budgets; a school representative in a secondary school said that 'geography teachers are doing science as there have not been many appointments and there are more highly paid people here at the top of the scale'. Another secondary school had lost nine posts, out of forty, and had been restructured at every level. A physics teacher had escaped redundancy by agreeing to teach chemistry, and a secondary school PE teacher said 'my concern is . . . we will be teaching more of our second subject to compensate for lack of staff; I don't want to teach more geography, but it will be a fact I think' (Sinclair *et al.* 1993a: 15). One LEA, in its advice to governors (agreed by all the unions), includes 'capability to switch from subject to subject as demonstrated by current actual teaching and/or past actual teaching' as an acceptable criterion for selecting candidates for redundancy. The multi-skilled, or rather the generalist and non-specialist teacher, who can move between years and between subjects, would provide much scope for flexibility but, like the multi-skilled handy-person compared with the skilled craftsman, would be a cheaper form of labour than the skilled professional. Early efforts were made by the government to introduce licensed and articled teachers' schemes from 1989. Fifty LEAs took part in the first two years of operation, training some 617 people, of whom 60 were awarded Qualified Teacher status (*Times Educational Supplement*, 19 July 1991).

Introducing another stratum of lower-qualified staff into the classroom hierarchy would pose a significant threat to the skilled professional. In nursery schools inadequate teacher staffing levels have long been managed by ensuring that nursery nurses carry out some of the duties of the teacher. This is being extended by substituting increasing numbers of classroom assistants for teachers, intensifying the work of the teacher and reducing the salary bill. Non-teacher classroom workers in nursery classes are now expected to prepare pupils for the national curriculum. In primary schools unpaid volunteers, usually parents, are playing an increasing role in normal classroom life. One primary school head said:

> 'I have 20 parents a week who work regularly in school as voluntary helpers. They take cooking, classwork, help with artwork and special needs. One mother has two hours a week recording assessment for a statement over the child's performance. Another goes swimming with the children',

and another told us:

> 'we have larger reception classes now and rely on a volunteer helper 4 days a week. I know she should certainly be paid. Also we have parents – small groups just to play with the children, make things etc, and we have loads of volunteers – at least 2 parents plus 4 classroom helpers, and students who get training here.'
>
> (Sinclair *et al.* 1993a: 19)

The licensed teacher scheme provides a route into the teacher workforce without the usual qualification and at a lower rate of pay. The government has floated a number of possible schemes to dilute the role of the teaching profession, including opening access for parents into a one-year training course to qualify them for classroom work.

In their 1990 report the Interim Advisory Committee on School Teachers' Pay and Conditions commented on the skill mix requirements of schools, noting that many teachers 'appear to be part-time secretaries, clerical assistants, furniture movers and general factotums' (IAC 1990: 47). Their argument that resources should be targeted, using the increased flexibility generated by LMS delegated budgets, suggests a shift of resources away from teachers and towards cheaper types of labour. Many teachers appear to believe that increased classroom support worker provision will automatically enhance their status. The reality of a skill mix adjustment is more likely to mean the transfer of the high-skill components of teachers' jobs, such as development work on both curriculum and teaching methods, away from classroom teachers to senior teachers; the transfer of the low-skill components to non-teachers; fewer qualified classroom teachers and more classroom supervisors; and a more intensive classroom-based workload for the rank and file classroom teacher.

This suggests a radical departure from the traditional organisation of schools on the basis of teams of professional teachers operating as colleagues. Rather than promoting flexibility through professional teamwork, the logic of recessionary pressure and market vulnerability leads to the fragmentation of the workforce into a rigid hierarchical division of labour. Human resource management techniques will be needed to keep control over this, as each new group in the hierarchy competes for an increased share of resources. School managers will engage in a complicated balancing act, trying to develop reward strategies that will ensure the motivation of all segments of the divided workforce. They will also have to manage the performance of all staff, seeking to direct activities towards the desired objectives.

For industrial relations, the implications are for increased grievance activity around a number of issues. Senior teachers will require enhanced pay differentials to reflect their newly acquired responsibilities (and also their enhanced bargaining power). Disputes about job descriptions are likely to surface among many teachers, as they try to regain some control over their classroom work. Demarcation disputes may arise as teachers act to protect their job territory. As managers implement the reforms they are pushed into making structural changes that transform the very nature of the teacher labour process. This attack on the job of the classroom teacher is not desired by most heads, but most heads will be unable to find any alternative. It is this destabilising aspect of the reform process that will create the most severe difficulties for managers and trade unions alike, presenting them with a new range of discipline and grievance issues and testing the mechanisms for resolving conflict.

Pay structures and systems

It has already been argued in chapters 2 and 4 that the development of a national pay rate for teachers irrespective of differences based on gender, qualification and sector depended on a strong sense of fair comparison among the teachers themselves, the reluctance by school managers and employers to become the arbiter of their own colleagues' pay, and the expense and time involved in workplace pay setting. A heavier workload, some job losses and changes in skill mix based on flexible contracts and working practices outlined above are the best and main management tactics in generating the low cost education system desired by government. Tinkering with the pay structure and introducing performance-related pay will add little to management effectiveness, but may well provide the issues that create both unrest and a resurgence of teacher trade unionism, especially within the NUT.

We should anticipate that new pay structures will reflect the context of both declining school budgets and competition in the market for pupils. Linking pay to performance is usually aimed at meeting two management objectives – first securing the motivation of employees towards the goals of the enterprise by enabling them to achieve their own goals at the same time, and secondly ensuring that pay determination is taken out of collective bargaining and placed in the hands of management. Appraisal systems are used to lend legitimacy to management decisions on the award of performance pay, by giving the appearance of equitable treatment of all employees through a neutral set of bureaucratic rules.

The operation of performance related pay is underpinned by the assumptions of scientific management – not only can the organisation of work be reduced to a set of technical requirements to be met through the application of techniques like work study, but also human motivation can be reduced to the simple pursuit of economic gain. When tied to notions of affordability then unilateral management discretion over pay is asserted. Issues of comparability and fairness in pay determination are cast aside. In this section we discuss some of the problems that school managers encounter as they are required to exercise their new discretionary powers.

One of the central features of the government's policy on public sector pay has been to move pay determination away from national level towards the local level. As we saw in chapter 2, national bargaining over teachers' pay was abolished in 1987, and the Teachers Pay and Conditions Act gave the

Secretary of State the right to decide. He introduced a new main scale to cover all classroom teachers, supplemented by a range of five incentive allowances to be awarded by LEAs and LMS schools. Incentive allowances could be awarded to teachers who fulfil one or more of the following criteria:

(a) undertaking responsibilities beyond those common to the majority of teachers;
(b) demonstrating outstanding ability as a classroom teacher;
(c) employment to teach a subject for which there is a shortage of teachers;
(d) employment in a post which is difficult to fill.

(School Teachers' Pay and Conditions Document)

The number of allowances at each level available to each school was determined according to a formula based on pupil numbers. Governors were free to exceed the number given in the formula, but these additional allowances would not be funded by the LEA. The DES estimated that in March 1991 there were 183,500 teachers with allowances, over 40 per cent of the teacher workforce.

More 'flexibilities' were added in 1991, allowing governors to give individual teachers accelerated increments or part increments (subject to the maximum of the scale not being exceeded). Where LEAs agreed, additional points could be added to the top of the pay scale, subject to a ceiling. These pay supplements were intended to be used for rewarding the best teachers, recognising extra responsibilities, providing recruitment incentives where shortages exist, promoting retention of the best staff, and motivating all teachers. We deal with each of these issues below; however, the STRB itself was soon forced to recognise that the provision of a number of overlapping criteria covering a number of mechanisms all designed to deal with all aspects of incentives was a 'recipe for confusion' (STRB 1992: 22). It was also a cause of industrial relations issues and trade union resistance.

In 1993 a new scale was introduced, consisting of a single pay spine with the point on the spine being determined by adding together points for qualifications, for service, for responsibility, for recruitment and retention purposes, and for excellent teaching. Points for service may be withheld from a teacher whose performance is deemed unsatisfactory; points for recruitment and retention may be reviewed after two years; and points for excellence are awarded on an annual basis. The notion of tying pay to performance is being expanded and diluted at the same time.

Successive Secretaries of States' remits to the IAC and then to the School Teachers' Review Body have included a direction to have regard to 'the Government's view that school teachers' pay and conditions of service should be such as to enable maintained schools to recruit, retain and motivate sufficient teachers of the required quality'. The government also believes 'that flexible pay systems which allow the targeting of additional payments are the most effective way of addressing any problem of recruitment and retention'. More recently the government has asserted 'that the most effective way of improving teachers' performance is by establishing a regular and direct link between an individual teacher's contribution to the education of pupils and his or her reward', in line with the Citizen's Charter. Furthermore, 'resources for performance related pay should be found by devoting to that purpose an increasing proportion of the pay bill' (STRB 1992: 46–7). The basis on which additional payments are given to some teachers and not given to others is potentially a major issue for workplace industrial relations.

By 1992 nearly 60 per cent of teachers received one of the five incentive allowances, and of these nearly 90 per cent were awarded on the basis of extra duties and responsibilities (STRB 1993: 17). This replicates the system before 1987, where a number of different scales were in use. The Review Body accused some head teachers of avoiding friction in staff rooms by awarding allowances on the basis of phoney additional duties, and further suggested that heads did not understand the way that the incentive allowance system was supposed to work. However, the Review Body had already acknowledged the difficulties built into the use of the range of pay supplements – 'pay enhancements will have little chance of serving their purposes if the messages conveyed by their award are blurred or confused' (STRB 1992: 22).

On the surface, the use of additional payments to deal with labour market difficulties appears straightforward. If a vacant post is difficult to fill, either because there is a shortage of a particular type of teacher or because the job has some undesirable characteristics, then a local supplement may be sufficient to attract recruits. On the other hand, if a member of staff has skills or qualifications that are in demand then an additional payment may be sufficient to retain the teacher in the school. However, this must take place within the context of tight budgets; only a limited number of pay enhancements are possible. Furthermore, pay differentials on the basis of labour market forces are resented by teachers who believe themselves to be equally experienced and to work just as hard. The managerial freedom to award market pay supplements carries with it the possibility of dissatisfaction and resentment among those who do not receive them.

Any pay supplement that is rooted in market conditions must, by implication, carry the possibility of termination if the market conditions that gave rise to it cease to exist. The scale introduced in 1993 makes this possible, as the number of scale points awarded to each teacher is subject to review each year. A head may wish to retain a particular teacher one year but not the next, and extra points given in the first year could be withdrawn in the second, leading to a salary cut. There is little incentive for managers to take these risks, especially in the context of declining budgets. School managers have so far shied away from using these flexibilities. A total of only 2 per cent of incentive allowances were awarded in recognition of recruitment and retention difficulties (STRB 1993: 17).

The Keele study found that the Review Body's statistics may not give a complete picture of the ways that allowances are actually being used. Our detailed case study findings reveal a complex but unsystematic use of the allowances as heads seek to award them while avoiding some of the pitfalls. Some heads said that after failing to fill a vacancy through advertising they would add an incentive allowance and justify it by adding some duties to the post, rather than clearly stating that the allowance was for the purpose of securing recruitment.

Heads report that in virtually all cases incentive allowances have been awarded in recognition of additional duties, but the manner in which this is done is overwhelmingly *ad hoc*. Many school teachers found the way that these allowances was distributed between them was unfair and arbitrary. One NUT representative told us how the head handled the award of allowances in two comparable situations. 'One went through on the nod whilst the other had to be justified and the person was interviewed and kept waiting around for a decision.' A secondary head boasted of having poached a language teacher from a nearby school. Another told how he had kept a teacher in the school by using an allowance as a 'golden handcuff – he had applied elsewhere and this is to retain his services'. This same head had 'reduced someone on a "D" to a "C", with his agreement, as he had not been coping'. In another school a probationer teacher was given an 'A' allowance in recognition of 'enthusiasm'. In practice it is not clear to individual teachers exactly how they might acquire enhanced pay, and they often express the view that head teacher discretion can be shrouded in mystery.

The mystery deepens with the idea of merit pay. The government has made it clear that it sees performance related pay as a major plank of its public sector pay policy, giving it a prominent place in the Citizen's Charter announced in 1991. Contrary to all the evidence, this claims that action towards improving performance had already been taken across the public sector, including 'in schools, heads and deputies receiving more pay for improved performance', and 'extra payments available for the best classroom teacher'. The Charter declares an intention of 'extending rewards for performance – and, equally important, penalties for failure – as part of the normal package of pay and conditions' (Citizen's Charter 1991: 35).

There are two forms of performance related pay that could be introduced into schools. First it could be based on the performance of the school as a whole, as measured by a range of performance indicators. These would include the data that go to make up the league tables based on truancy and examination results for example. The Review Body considers that 'the best means of relating teachers' pay more closely to their performance, at least in the short term, would be through a scheme which rewards schools which demonstrate a year-on-year improvement in performance' (STRB 1992: 15), focusing on annual improvements rather than on absolute levels of achievement. It is, however, silent on the way that school performance bonuses would be distributed between the teachers in the school, on the size of the bonus as a proportion of pay, and on the proportion of the total pay bill that would be used in this way.

The government has however rejected this approach and insists on merit pay for individual teachers, perhaps linked to appraisal, but without separate or additional funding. This is preferred to a school-based approach 'because of the desirability of rewarding good teachers in poor schools but not poor teachers in good schools' (STRB 1993: 34). We discussed the use of performance related pay as a management tool in chapter 4, noting that only 1 per cent of teachers received incentive allowances for classroom performance in 1992 (STRB 1993: 69). Provisions for other pay enhancements were also little used. The Review Body estimates that 2.3 per cent of eligible teachers received incremental enhancements, and that 20 per cent of those (about 1,600 teachers in the whole of England and Wales) were paid for classroom performance. Discretionary scale points had been awarded to 1.5 per cent of eligible teachers, and only two teachers out of their sample of 54,600 had an increment withheld from them (STRB 1993: 70).

Our head teacher survey, covering schools with some 10,000 teachers, found only 200 teachers in receipt of pay enhancements other than incentive allowances in 1992/3, a proportion comparable to that found by the Review Body's survey. Both heads and union representatives believed performance related pay to be divisive in principle and unworkable in practice. The incentive allowance system as a whole was regarded unfavourably, with half of heads and two-thirds of union representatives agreeing that it causes ill-feeling between teachers. Heads had been approached directly by teachers requesting allowances, using arguments about their workload, about their outstanding performance, and even about their long journey into work – as one head put it, 'the begging bowls are out'.

Nevertheless, heads argued clearly that payments on the basis of performance were not a viable option. While a small number would have liked to award payments for excellence, they had not done so for two reasons. First was their tight budget situation, with performance pay taking a much lower priority than other more pressing problems such as repairing the school and buying books. Indeed, in many schools with tight budgets we found that the full complement of allowances, as specified in the Pay and Conditions Document, had not been awarded. In one LEA there was tacit agreement that no formal action would be taken by the trade unions to enforce the provisions of the Document, for fear of provoking a budget crisis that may result in redundancy. Secondly, even the heads who had some enthusiasm for the idea in principle realised that putting it into practice needed considerable caution. They recognised the potential for teachers not receiving performance payments being demotivated, and they would not want to award performance related enhancements unless they were sure that such problems could be avoided. Most heads argued that the main reward for high performance was promotion. As the Review Body reported, teachers see career advancement through assuming extra duties rather than through improving their classroom teaching (STRB 1993: 18).

Most school representatives were similarly opposed to the idea of performance related pay, as confirmed by the findings of the Keele survey reported in chapter 6. However, there is a significant minority of younger teachers who appear to believe that if performance bonuses are available then they will be the ones to receive them. Typical of some of the unreflective comments made on this theme was the NUT representative at a secondary school who said that his members favoured performance related pay 'as we felt that we would do well out of it, and people say "yes – let's have it – that will teach those dossers who go home at a quarter past three"'.

While heads were generally not keen on performance related pay enhancements for teachers they took a different view when it came to their own pay. The Review Body reported that 'pay progression for heads and deputies is one of the discretions which schools have used significantly in the last couple of years', estimating that 'around 30 per cent of heads and . . . . deputies have been awarded additional spine points since this discretionary provision was introduced in January 1991, and that on average these individuals have gained between 3½ and 4 extra spine points' (STRB 1993: 28). An increase of four spinal points represents a pay increase of about 7 per cent, on top of their annual award.

Wide regional variations were found, with 35 per cent of heads gaining increases in the South-East and 6 per cent in Yorkshire and Humberside. The Keele survey found similar variation between LEAs. In one only 4 per cent had received extra spine points. Most of the heads interviewed in this LEA had not asked their governors for extra pay. In another, all heads had been awarded one extra point, subject to not exceeding the maximum point of the normal range for their school's group number. The third LEA issued guidelines recommending governors to award between one and three points. A primary head in one of our case study schools asked her governors for an increase in line with this and was refused, leading to a rift between her and the governors. At a school in Hounslow the governors agreed a pay increase for the head, only to withdraw it when the adjourned meeting reconvened. The NAHT took the case as far as the High Court before the governing body conceded, agreeing to pay the increase of £2,000 per annum while the LEA agreed to pay back pay and court costs amounting to some £15,000 (*Times Educational Supplement*, 16 July 1993).

Pay differentials between heads and deputies and other teachers were an issue that could lead to acrimonious debate in LEA Joint Consultative Committees, and within the Teachers Panels. Nationally, the head teacher associations have called for separate pay determination arrangements for themselves. At school level they can call for enhanced payments for themselves without opening up divisions between teachers in the school. However, the opportunity plainly exists for heads to use pay movements in neighbouring schools to justify a claim to their governors, and this opens up the prospect of leapfrogging claims. Heads have considerable bargaining power relative to their governing body – governors who lose the co-operation of their head will find themselves in for an uncomfortable ride.

According to all the available evidence there is little support among school managers and union representatives for school-level pay determination. There is no indication that managers believe the development of local payment systems to be a priority issue. In one of our LEAs there was tacit agreement between the teacher unions and LEA and school managers that there would be no union action against schools awarding a smaller number of allowances than the number required under the Pay and Conditions Document if their budget was tight. Both managers and union representatives prefer the local stability rooted in a nationally negotiated rate for the job.

However, the new pay spine for classroom teachers is forcing school-based managers to review the pay of each teacher individually, and to have more regard to the award of salary points for performance. The breakup of the national pay structure may have profound implications. For the unions it undermines the basis for strong national organisation around national negotiations on the rate for the job. For teachers it represents a further step away from felt-fair comparisons with other occupational groups in setting their pay, and a step towards comparisons between individual teachers. The lower-paid majority will be keeping one eye on the job and the other on their chances of catching up with the better-paid minority who have had discretion exercised in their favour – fertile ground for grievances to grow.

Performance and appraisal

Appraisal as introduced as part of a wider scheme of professional development has generally been welcomed by the majority of teachers and their unions. However, the pressures on managers to lower unit labour costs has meant a shift in the use made of appraisal. It can now be used as a tool of control, to blame poor performing teachers for the school's failures and to use the outcome of the appraisal interview to determine both pay and job security. This process of hijacking appraisal is part of a wider debate on control over definitions of what constitutes professional attitudes and behaviour among teachers. Ball used his own empirical research to conclude 'this, and other, data suggest the emergence of a stark division of values and purposes, of professional culture if you like, between managers, oriented to the budget, the market, entrepreneurial activities and the drive for efficiency, and teachers, oriented to the National Curriculum, teaching and learning, student needs and the drive for effectiveness' (Ball 1993: 115).

Since the publication of the white papers *Teaching Quality* and *Better Schools* the issue of teacher appraisal has been the subject of protracted argument, with the teacher unions arguing strongly against the use of appraisal for any purpose other than professional development. The Education (School Teacher Appraisal) Regulations 1991 came into effect in 1992, requiring the introduction of a two year cycle of appraisal to cover all teachers in LEA maintained and grant-maintained schools by 1 September 1995. The regulations give the main purposes of this statutory appraisal system as being to identify: (1) ways of improving skills and performance; (2) where a change of job would be appropriate; (3) candidates for promotion; (4) training needs; and (5) poor performers.

These purposes are entirely managerial, having no explicit reference to education other than being directed towards the appraisal of school teachers. They could apply equally to any other employee, manual or non-manual, skilled or unskilled, professional or technical. The regulations give heads the sole authority to appoint appraisers (other than for their own appraisal), and the basis is created for appraisal by teacher-managers with an orientation towards the fulfilment of business criteria. In other words, appraisal, as with other management techniques of control, is not neutral as to its application. It can be either part of professional development, or part of management control, but not both.

The regulations state that appraisal procedures must not form part of disciplinary or dismissal procedures. However, they do require the preparation of a written appraisal statement, recording the main points made by the appraiser and the appraised, the conclusions reached, and the targets for action. This statement may be used 'in advising those responsible for taking decisions on the promotion, dismissal or discipline of school teachers or on the use of any discretion in relation to pay' (Regulation 14). Even though the regulations themselves try to reassure teachers that there is no direct link between appraisal procedures and either pay or dismissal, school managers will be able to use appraisal records in arriving at decisions about performance related pay enhancements and about performance related redundancies and other dismissals.

The purpose of appraisal makes a difference to the way in which it is carried out. An appraisal that is meant to enable a teacher to build on strengths and to identify training needs to tackle weaknesses is distinct from an appraisal that is carried out in order to decide which teachers are to be denied merit pay or to identify candidates for redundancy. The person carrying out the appraisal will be seen by the teacher being appraised quite differently, depending on the purpose. In the former case the appraiser is seen as a supportive colleague working to enable the teacher's professional development. In the latter the appraiser is seen as a resource manager making tough decisions about either pay or job security on a basis that is not entirely clear. The teacher being appraised will not know exactly what the appraisal is for, and is likely to behave during the appraisal in line with the cautious assumption that the appraisal statement might in future be used against them in either salary or redundancy discussions. The following words of an ATL member give clear expression to the way that teachers feel about this:

> 'The majority of staff are not happy about appraisal – they feel vulnerable about who is doing the appraising due to the personalities here and whether they are properly trained. If it is seen as staff development its OK – but fears may get in the way. Some of us were keen to be appraised but the majority of staff don't want it.'

In his remit to the Review Body the Secretary of State stated that 'the Government's view that the most effective way of improving teachers' performance is by establishing a direct link between an individual teacher's contribution to the education of pupils and his or her reward' (STRB 1993: 47). This implies adopting some sort of procedure to place teachers in a hierarchical order of their contribution. Those who make the lowest contribution are to be paid the least and are to be the first to be dismissed as redundant, while those ranked highest are to be paid the most and get promoted.

There is no good evidence that teachers can be so ranked on any systematic basis. Experience in America suggests that individual school managers might place their staff in a rank order, but that different managers stress different criteria. Furthermore, the same manager might place the top ranking teacher above the second for one set of reasons, and the second above the third for another set. There is no escaping the use of subjective criteria when trying to place teachers in a hierarchical order. Johnson used her study of American schools to conclude that using performance-based criteria for redundancy selection has a number of consequences for management: the role of the head as 'protector, provider and instructional leader' is altered; co-operative and collegial relations among staff are jeopardised; and the effectiveness of teacher supervision is diminished (Johnson 1980: 216).

Payment systems that claim to reward outstanding performance might work over a sustained period if the relationship between effort and pay is clear and easily understood. Employees may, under some circumstances, increase their effort if they are certain that the increased effort will result in increased pay. This may mean the diversion of effort towards the high-scoring performance indicators like exam results, and away from low-scoring activities like voluntary sport and cultural activities. The link between effort and reward is very complex. The government's assumption of a straightforward relationship between pay and motivation is every bit as crude as that enshrined in the writing of F. W. Taylor, the founder of the movement towards scientific management and work study in the first decade of the twentieth century (Taylor 1911). Moreover, increased effort is not the same as high motivation; the direction of effort towards hitting performance targets in order to gain higher pay or to avoid dismissal does not necessarily result in better teaching. As we outlined in earlier chapters, where performance related pay acts against teachers' strong attachment to felt-fair comparability the outcome can only be division, demotivation and demoralisation, the contrary to the claims of its proponents.

In schools the individual teacher has little control over crude performance indicators like truancy rates and exam results; a range of other people and socio-economic factors are likely to overshadow the impact that any one teacher might have. Using appraisal statements has the potential for introducing huge areas of subjectivity. How would one teacher's appraisal be compared with another's? When a small minority of teachers in a school get their performance bonuses will it be clear to the majority what they have to do to win a bonus in the next round? Will all teachers have the same opportunities to win bonuses? What action will be taken by teachers who believe that they deserve the bonus that was given to another? These questions add further ingredients to the cocktail of discontent being mixed in schools, providing fuel for grievances. And while teachers may turn to grievance procedures to seek redress, managers may be turning to disciplinary procedures as part of their quest to secure the maximum performance from every member of staff.

The job regulation issues brought to the fore by the reform programme would normally be dealt with through the use of jointly agreed procedures, but these too have been affected by the restructuring process. We turn shortly to grievance and discipline as issues in themselves, but first it is necessary to look more closely at the relationship between management and unions. Union recognition, largely taken for granted in schools, also stands to be transformed by the reform process.

THE PROCEDURES FOR INDUSTRIAL RELATIONS

Union recognition

As school budgets are squeezed so the pressure will mount to secure ever greater performance from the teacher workforce. We have seen above how job loss, increased workload, flexible approaches to skill mix and new pay structures are likely to generate a set of issues at the level of the school. We saw in previous chapters how conflict was often avoided at school through the LEA and national industrial relations system removing the resolution of the conflict from the school to a higher level of decision-making. In this way the head, and to a lesser degree the governors, could be left free to manage the school on the basis of colleagues from the same profession operating in the agreed interests of the children and the wider community. These conflict avoidance mechanisms relied on the three pre-conditions outlined by Clay (1929) for the successful operation of a national collective bargaining system, namely, a high level of union membership, that the employer recognised unions for bargaining purposes, and that both parties accepted the benefits from 'good faith' bargaining. If, and when, these conditions wither away then it is doubtful whether conflict can be avoided in ways designed to minimise the disruption of pupils' education. We have seen in chapter 3 that union membership remains high among teachers and that the balance between the largest three classroom unions may be swinging back to the NUT. What we discuss now is the extent to which unions are recognised for bargaining purposes within school policies and whether the managers still accept the benefits from the operation of the main conflict avoidance mechanisms: disciplinary, grievance and disputes procedures operating under a general recognition and facilities agreement.

A recognition agreement lays down the agreed basis for the conduct of business between the union and the employer, and is mainly concerned with the rights of union representatives to take part in negotiations and to make representations on behalf of individual members. Negotiations may be allowed on the whole range of procedural and substantive issues, or they may be more limited in scope. For example, a procedure for granting access to in-service training may be jointly determined by negotiation, while the allocation of work between teachers may be unilaterally determined by management.

At present both LEAs and schools are required to recognise all of the unions recognised at national level. This is usually taken to mean that the unions are recognised for the purposes of both collective bargaining and representing their members, but it is rarely set out in a formal written agreement actually detailing the scope and extent of collective bargaining. The written provisions that do exist are usually in the form of the constitutions of joint consultative committees and in the local grievance, disputes and disciplinary procedures (the latter are outlined below). Practice therefore varies between LEAs, reflecting differences in approach by individual LEAs and local union associations and the different histories of industrial relations and the trade unions within both the LEAs and the wider communities. In this respect, the conduct of industrial relations during strikes and other industrial action has had a powerful impact in determining the scope of recognition in practice.

Variation in collective bargaining practice includes both the scope and content of the agreement. Meetings between management and union representatives may consist of little more than management communicating their decisions to representatives, or it may involve joint decision-making between them on the basis of compromise and negotiation – 'good faith' bargaining. Bargaining may encompass a larger or smaller range of issues. Thus in a school recognition might simply mean the representation of members in grievance and disciplinary hearings, and attendance at short meetings where the head passes information about management decisions to the school representative. Alternatively, it could mean the deep involvement of school representatives in regulating the conditions of employment of their members, through formal meetings of negotiating committees, through informal dealings with departmental heads, and through upholding custom and practice arrangements. Both the scope and content of collective bargaining may alter over time, reflecting shifts in the prevailing balance of forces. Management and union are constantly pressing on the 'frontier of control' (Goodrich 1920) as union representatives seek to restrict managerial authority.

Recognition agreements establish a right for union representatives to organise around negotiations, which militates against unilateral management authority. Negotiation means compromise through union involvement in joint decision-making over job regulation. This represents an erosion of managerial prerogative – the human resource management literature stresses communication as the preferred means of involving employees in decision-making, perhaps extending to consultation when necessary.

Recognition has the effect of imposing on employers a duty to consult with representatives of recognised trade unions on a wide range of issues, including health and safety and redundancy. Union representatives acquire legal rights in a number of areas; employers must provide them with facilities necessary to represent members in negotiations, and they must provide information on matters related to collective bargaining. The recognised union in the school must be given access to information that may include the school's budget, its forward plans, its accounts, and its staffing plans. However, there is no general legal right to union recognition, and the right of unions to be recognised by LEAs and schools is contained within the education legislation rather than the employment legislation.

The right of union representatives to carry out their duties is usually regulated by means of a facilities agreement. This sets out the range and scope of entitlements of union representatives to enable them to perform their functions. In law employees who are the representatives of trade unions recognised by their employer have the right to take reasonable time off for duties concerned with negotiations on the following industrial relations issues: (1) terms and conditions of employment and working conditions; (2) recruitment and selection policies, human resource planning and redundancy and dismissal arrangements; (3) allocation of work, job gradings and job descriptions; (4) matters of discipline; (5) representation of employees; (6) provision of facilities to union representatives, such as telephone, office space, use of office equipment; and (7) machinery for negotiation and consultation and other procedures (ACAS 1991: 6–8). Union representatives are also entitled to take time off to undergo training on these issues (ACAS 1991: 9).

The national agreement (Burgundy Book: Appendix V) sets out the agreed facilities to be given to teacher union representatives by LEAs. Local association officers are entitled to: (1) time away from school without loss of pay; (2) lists of new teachers, and arrangements for communicating directly with them; (3) a list of teachers employed by the LEA; (4) use of premises for meetings; (5) use of the LEA's distribution system; and (6) deduction of membership subscriptions by the LEA. School representatives are entitled to: (1) use of a notice board; (2) access to a telephone; (3) use of a room for meetings of members; and (4) use of school typing and photocopying equipment.

Local agreements at the level of each LEA were developed to spell out in more detail the arrangements for both enabling and constraining the above facilities. For example, the upper limit of the amount of facility time might be expressed as a number of hours each week, on a scale that would give more time to the representatives covering the largest number of members.

No mention is made in the national agreement of the provision of cover for union representatives while they carry out their union duties, other than a recognition by CLEA that 'it may be necessary for LEAs to provide additional staffing resources in individual schools' (Burgundy Book: 42). Normally the school staff would cover for a school representative, but local officers with responsibilities for negotiating at the level of the LEA are frequently released from all teaching duties, becoming effectively full-time union officials while remaining LEA employees. For example, in one LEA each teacher union is allowed between 1 and 7 days' release from teaching per week, to be shared out between the union's officers. In another the maximum is 2 days per week, and in another 15 teacher-days are allowed each week, to be divided between and within the teacher unions. These allowances are taken into account when determining school staffing levels. Some LEAs give guidance as to the amount of time considered reasonable for school representatives, but in practice this issue is more likely to be decided more or less informally at the level of the school itself. The WIRS studies found that in general 'around nine out of ten workplace representatives in 1990 (manual and non-manual) reported an arrangement with management covering their trade union duties and activities' (Millward *et al*, 1992: 122).

Under LMS these arrangements may be reviewed as the extent of financial delegation increases. So far, the usual practice is to retain the pre-LMS agreement, with a central budget being used to reimburse schools with teachers entitled to facility time under the terms of the agreement. Schools may be provided with supply cover funded from this central budget, or they may be provided with an addition to the school budget which they may use to buy cover if they choose. This sort of arrangement may break down as further delegation takes place. If funding for facility time is delegated to individual schools it will become difficult for LEAs to meet the salaries, or part-salaries, of teachers involved in union duties outside of the school in which they work. Heads will not want to pay the salaries of teachers who are spending time out of the school, working on matters not directly related to the school.

Experienced union representatives may therefore be confined to their schools as heads refuse to release them in the absence of either cover or financial compensation, as is already happening in grant-maintained schools. They will be withdrawn from activity both at the level of the LEA and in other schools. Some union officials are already reporting a marked decline in the number of school representatives attending union training courses, perhaps reflecting both a reluctance on the part of heads to grant time off, and the reluctance of teachers to take time off in the face of their own heavy workload. All of this helps to destabilise industrial relations, removing the most experienced union representatives from activity in the broader area of rule-making. It also restricts their scope for involvement in representing members in schools, individually or collectively, other than those in their own school. Under these circumstances experienced union representatives may turn their attention to issues in their own schools, building up membership activity and organising around workplace grievances. Other schools will be left to manage without these representatives and without their skills in using the conflict resolution mechanisms – both union members and managers will find that handling workplace conflict will be affected by their absence.

In small primary schools, especially in rural areas, formal union recognition and the use of formal procedures within the school will be either irrelevant or unnecessary. Several of the heads in our questionnaire survey took the view that their schools were too small and that the staff were not interested in trade unions as workplace organisations, but they did agree that in the case of an incident then they would call in the LEA. It is in larger primary schools and secondary schools that some heads have begun to understand what is at stake and are acting in a variety of ways. One head told us that 'we consult all staff regularly and recently concluded an in-depth survey of their attitudes to the organisation and management of the school. No desire to formalise procedures with unions was in evidence'. The current situation is that the vast majority of schools retain school-level union recognition as part of the LEA and national system, but a small number of larger schools are edging their way to a situation where the unions may not be recognised for bargaining purposes.

Disciplinary procedures

The maintenance of discipline in the workplace is a key feature of industrial relations. Where all else fails, and sometimes before, managers desire the ability to impose sanctions against employees whose conduct or performance is believed to be unsatisfactory. As we discussed in chapter 4, the question of teacher performance is brought to the fore by the reforms, suggesting that there will be a trend towards increasing use by management of disciplinary action to enforce the imposition of heavier workloads, flexible skill mix changes and performance.

A disciplinary procedure sets out the ways in which employers and managers make decisions about whether or not to impose sanctions against an employee, and the range of sanctions that may be imposed. The statutory code of practice on disciplinary practice and procedures in employment sets out a framework, identifying the main elements that should be incorporated into a disciplinary procedure. The main concern is to uphold the principles of natural justice, such as the right to representation, the right to a hearing, the right to a proportionate penalty, and the right of appeal. According to the official ACAS code:

> Disciplinary procedures should:
> (a) Be in writing.
> (b) Specify to whom they apply.
> (c) Provide for matters to be dealt with quickly.
> (d) Indicate the disciplinary actions which may be taken.
> (e) Specify the levels of management which have the authority to take the various forms of disciplinary action, ensuring that immediate superiors do not normally have the power to dismiss without reference to senior management.

(f) Provide for individuals to be informed of the complaints against them and to be given an opportunity to state their case before decisions are reached.
(g) Give individuals the right to be accompanied by a trade union representative or by a fellow employee of their choice.
(h) Ensure that, except for gross misconduct, no employees are dismissed for a first breach of discipline.
(i) Ensure that disciplinary action is not taken until the case has been carefully investigated.
(j) Ensure that individuals are given an explanation for any penalty imposed.
(k) Provide a right of appeal and specify the procedure to be followed.

(ACAS 1977: 3)

The code of practice goes on to set out the main operating principles of disciplinary procedures. Further detailed guidance, including model procedures and practical suggestions for handling disciplinary matters, is given in the ACAS handbook (1987b). This represents a summary of good practice based on ACAS' experience after ten years of operation of the statutory code.

Compliance with the code is not a statutory requirement, but should an employee be dismissed either through some other procedure or without the use of any procedure the employee will be able to argue at an industrial tribunal that this is strong evidence that the dismissal was unfair. This makes the procedures used in dismissal particularly important – if employers are to maintain a defence against claims for unfair dismissal they must use procedures that accord with the principles of natural justice. According to WIRS, over 80 per cent of private sector, and virtually all public sector establishments, have formal procedures covering discipline and grievances (Millward *et al.* 1992: 187). This reflects the trade unions' successful protection of the individual worker in cases of alleged breach of contract, but the wider issues of authority relations within the workplace as upheld through disciplinary rules are matters for collective resolution.

There is no national agreement on a model disciplinary procedure in schools, although a procedure is laid down for dismissal (Burgundy Book: paragraph 8). The law on the appointment and dismissal of teachers gives rights and responsibilities to both LEAs and schools. Consequently disciplinary procedures for teachers are often very long-winded documents, reflecting both a desire for bureaucratic tightness, the legal requirements on dismissal, and frequently misunderstanding of the dynamics of workplace discipline. One LEA provides for four stages of warning (oral, written, severe written and final written), with the provision for heads to give oral warnings without any record being kept. There is no provision for appeal against these oral warnings, contrary to the principles of natural justice. Another LEA's procedure provides for appeals to be determined through written submissions, leaving no opportunity for cross-questioning.

Other examples of misunderstandings of disciplinary procedures are contained in handbooks and textbooks aimed at school governors. One such booklet, produced for the governor training organisation Action for Governors Information and Training, contains a number of errors. It sets out a model procedure which contains the provision for heads to issue 'verbal warnings', which are not to be recorded. In spite of this lack of any concrete existence they can be followed by a written warning within six months (Hume 1990: 29). Under this procedure a teacher could be set on a path to dismissal, initiated by a warning that is unrecorded but, since it is the first step in a formal procedure, has formal status. No provision is made for representation, for cross-questioning, or for appeal, all contrary to the principles of natural justice. This publication makes no mention at all of the detailed advice contained in the ACAS handbook.

In most LEAs there are two sets of procedures, one for misconduct, and one for incapability or incompetence. The latter procedures are for use when management believes that the teacher is unable to meet the requirements of the post. The purpose of a hearing would be to establish whether or not, on the balance of the evidence, the teacher is capable of doing the job. If the teacher is found to be not capable, then the outcome might be transfer to a post within the teacher's capability or, if such a course of action is not available, then dismissal. In cases of misconduct the purpose of a disciplinary hearing would be first to establish whether or not, on the balance of the evidence, the teacher's conduct had been in breach of applicable rules and, if so found, to decide on the appropriate penalty to be chosen from the range of penalties specified in the procedure.

The distinction between misconduct and incompetence is not always clear. If management believe a teacher's performance to be unsatisfactory then this may stem from a refusal to carry out reasonable instructions or from the teacher's inability to attain a satisfactory level of performance. Or it may arise from a combination of factors. Gaining hard evidence of unsatisfactory performance raises a number of problems, not least that teachers are unsupervised for most of their time in the classroom. Among teachers, disciplinary action frequently cannot be reduced to a question of whether or not simple rules were broken.

There are obviously many examples of disciplinary action taken against teachers, although the majority leading to dismissal tend to be for misconduct. These cases are themselves of a varied nature, but those that tend to be reported in the media are associated with relationships between staff members and pupils. Our concern is to see how the exercise of disciplinary activity by the management involves and may well develop into serious industrial relations issues.

In one case, for example, the head wanted to introduce a new GCSE into the school and asked the relevant head of department to start preparations for the new course. The head of department subsequently refused on the grounds of workload and lack of adequate resources. The head took informal disciplinary action against the head of department and instructed another teacher to set up and operate the new GCSE. As a result the head of department took out a grievance against the head for unreasonable behaviour on the grounds of both the issuing of the disciplinary warning and the use of a more junior teacher to run the new course. The case reached a full formal hearing of the LEA at which the head teacher was represented by his union, the head of department by her union and the other teacher by yet another union representative. In addition the LEA officials were out in force. It was clear from the hearing that the level of understanding of all concerned of their own procedures, let alone of the industrial relations issues, was minimal (we discuss grievance procedures below). The result was that the matter was referred back to the school to be sorted out between the head teacher and the head of department, and that the LEA officials and union representatives were urged to become conversant with their own formal procedures.

In another case a German language teacher in a secondary school was asked to take on extra duties which she refused. Quite soon after, the head issued her with an informal disciplinary warning and suggested that she seek redeployment to another school. The next appointment to the school in question was a deputy head who could also teach German, and soon after that the German teacher was redeployed to another school. In this case the head had used disciplinary measures without good reason in order to persuade a teacher to leave. In another case a long-serving primary school teacher was given a disciplinary warning by the head without his having followed any of the procedures in place. He subsequently withdrew the warning but soon after gave her a series of severely delivered informal warnings after which she took sickness leave of absence. This continued to be the pattern of behaviour and finally the head sought to dismiss the teacher due to her absence record!

In all cases the unions were involved but either failed to understand the mechanisms involved or were powerless to stop oppressive behaviour. This partly reflects the difficulties teacher unions have in representation when the cases are so bound up with other staff issues, and partly that the teachers involved may be reluctant to take union advice as it may mean further unpleasantness. Most cases of poor performance are associated with lengthy periods of absence relating to some physical or psychological problems.

There are additional complications in the practice of discipline when the head teacher is the subject of the action. Here the governing body along with LEA officers are involved, but the real difficulty is discovering the problem and getting the evidence. It usually requires a remarkable breakdown in school life before teachers will take action against the head, and under LMS this seems less likely. We came across a dozen examples in our survey of action being taken against heads by the LEAs, but in most cases the governors and the LEA officers were reluctant to act decisively. The evidence so far is that while LMS may make it easier for heads to discipline and dismiss other teachers, it may be harder to dismiss heads.

Most LEA procedures provided for initial disciplinary action short of dismissal to be taken by heads and/or governors, for dismissal proceedings to be instituted by the chief education officer, and for appeals to be determined either by a subcommittee of the LEA or by a joint panel of LEA and teacher representatives. The outcomes of the disciplinary process have dramatic implications for teachers, contrary to Hume's assertion that 'it is not a punishment' (1990: 25). A disciplinary record represents not only a step towards dismissal, either through further disciplinary action or through selection for redundancy, but also a blighted career (promotions and references for other posts may be influenced) for as long as the record remains on file, with possible repercussions for the remainder of the teacher's life. Protection from disciplinary action is one of the main reasons for the high level of teacher union density, and the teacher unions secured considerable protection from arbitrary management action through LEA-level stages in the procedure.

As with most procedures, the formal written agreement provides a framework for a range of more or less formal activities by both managers and union representatives not explicitly provided for in the written document. The fact that written procedures contained stages involving LEA officers enabled those officers to involve themselves in disciplinary issues before the formal stages were actually reached. Similarly, a union representative might call on a LEA official to intervene informally before reaching the formal stage. Thus the provision of a formal stage involving LEA officers could enable disciplinary issues to be resolved before actually invoking the formal procedures. Furthermore, once formal procedures had commenced, LEA officers were often able to ensure negotiated outcomes that were acceptable to those involved at the level of the school. That is not to argue that the penalties imposed on teachers were necessarily less harsh. The point is that the outcomes of disciplinary action could be more likely to be perceived as fair when they have been determined through a quasi-judicial process where the decisions are taken by officials less directly involved in the workplace situation.

Under LMS the governors can take decisions over the whole range of both disciplinary matters and sanctions. The LEAs are sending detailed guidance to schools on this potentially very difficult area. Most LEAs are setting out the main legal requirements along with recommendations, after consultation with trade unions, although some are issuing model procedures and stressing that they are collectively agreed with the unions. Most recommendations provide for appeals to be heard by the governing body or a sub-committee, although the unions are pressing for an appeal stage outside of the school.

In chapter 4 we argued that the reforms drive school-based managers towards a deeper concern with teacher performance, and earlier in this chapter we noted that where teachers fail to meet the standards of performance required by management, or where they do not perform in the manner required by management, then managers are likely to turn to disciplinary procedures. What is required of teachers is being increasingly codified. The logic of the reforms tends towards the wider use of job descriptions, setting out individual teachers' duties in more detail. The national curriculum requires attention to both the content and the outcomes of classroom activity, and appraisal provides the opportunity for regular examination of performance. Heads seeking to ensure the desired classroom activity and to enforce the performance of job descriptions will have to rely on disciplinary measures. The use of disciplinary action may become the main method of enforcement of management control over employees' performance in the workplace.

Heads and governors invoking disciplinary proceedings against one of their staff enter murky and uncharted waters. Most heads wishing to secure change in the behaviour of an individual member of staff will try informal measures first, before invoking formal procedures. Many heads may believe that they can resolve problems with staff behaviour without recourse to formal action, preferring to keep the unions out of school affairs. For many managers the commencement of a formal disciplinary hearing represents a failure to exercise effective management skills on their part, leading them to try to muddle through. This has two effects. First it leaves issues of control unresolved, and second it excludes the union from the rule-making process. Burchill (1992: 88) points out that the disciplinary process includes subprocesses – not only the identification of breaches of the rules and the application of sanctions but also the establishment of the rules and the establishment of the sanctions.

Heads may seek deliberately to exclude the unions from the disciplinary process in order to exercise unilateral authority, or they may exclude them under the muddled notion that effective managers can modify staff behaviour through leadership, example, exhortation or persuasion. Either way, exclusion of the unions represents a managerial attempt to exercise unilateral control over both the establishment and the enforcement of the rules at work, breaking with the notion of joint regulation. As we noted in chapter 3, security of tenure and freedom from arbitrary management action were key organising principles of the early NUT. Prominent among the original nine aims adopted at the founding conference of the NUET was the gaining of a right of appeal against dismissal beyond an appeal to the school managers (Tropp 1957: 113 and 120). There is great potential for disruption within the school if teachers perceive management action to be unjustly harsh or unreasonable or simply muddled. No longer can the focus of conflict be shifted to the level of the LEA – it can only be resolved within the school.

Grievance procedures

In chapter 4 and in this chapter we have identified new directions of management action arising from the reform programme. School managers have acquired considerable authority over the determination of teachers' working conditions, over the organisation and deployment of the teacher workforce, over the activities of teachers in the classroom, and over some elements of the remuneration package. All of this provides fertile ground for the growth of grievances among teachers. The reforms have introduced a further destabilising element by removing a central component of the traditional conflict-resolution mechanisms of the Whitley system.

Employees believing themselves to have been unfairly or unjustly treated may feel aggrieved, and may wish to take the matter up. Grievance procedures exist to enable this to happen, but they cannot deal with all issues. A grievance is more narrowly defined than a complaint, and a worker who is genuinely aggrieved about something to do with work may not have a grievance. The International Labour Organisation Recommendation 130, adopted in 1967, contains a useful definition of the circumstances which may give rise to a grievance:

> the grounds for a grievance may be any measure or situation which concerns the relations between employer and worker or which affects or may affect the conditions of employment of one or several workers in the undertaking when that measure or situation appears contrary to provisions of an applicable collective agreement or of an individual contract of employment, to works rules, to laws or regulations or to the custom or usage of the occupation, branch of economic activity or country, regard being had to principles of good faith.

Thus a grievance is always about the right of the employee, and is always against the employer; it cannot be directly against another employee. For example, a teacher who is assaulted while at work may take action against the attacker directly through the courts, but not through the grievance procedure. Any grievance would be against the management for failing to prevent the assault, in contravention of their general duty towards employees under common law and of their more specific duty under the health and safety at work legislation to provide a safe place of work. One of the contributions made by experienced personnel officers and union representatives when discussing alleged grievances is in untangling what rights exist under a particular set of circumstances, and in identifying whether or not managers have acted in breach of those rights.

Individual grievances usually relate either to some incident between one member of staff and another such as racial and sexual harassment, or to some friction between a member of staff and their line manager about some aspect of work. Some grievances emerge from the oppressive behaviour of other teachers – 'bullying' is sometimes used to describe such behaviour at work. We found significant evidence of the widespread 'bullying' of staff by line managers. In these cases the formal mechanism for dealing with it is through the grievance procedure. This will nearly always involve the union, but there are major stumbling blocks to a successful outcome. As noted in the examples on discipline given above there is a criss-cross of relationships not made clear by formal procedures, many teachers are reluctant to become involved for fear of souring relationships permanently, and unless the matter can be dealt with outside of the school the pressure not to act is immense.

The other main area of grievances other than those relating to some failure by management to implement agreements or due to behaviour is over general relations between staff and management on issues such as consultation. Several union representatives complained to us that the head teacher was autocratic in decision-making, and in one school the head did not allow questions at staff meetings. In this sense the grievances are collective and are dealt with under the next section. The general impression was that too many teachers felt that under LMS the head would decide more and tell less in terms of the industrial relations issues in schools than ever before. This itself would then become an issue.

During 1990 grievance procedures were activated in over a quarter of the establishments covered by WIRS, including a fifth of the smaller establishments of 25–49 employees (Millward *et al.* 1992: 205). If these proportions were reflected in schools this would involve thousands of heads in formal grievance hearings each year. We argue here that the reforms both create the basis for a massive increase in grievances among teachers and may destroy the main mechanisms for resolving them.

The issues more frequently subject to formal grievance procedures include pay and conditions, working conditions, performance appraisal, and job grading (Millward *et al.* 1992: 205). As we identified above and in chapters 2 and 4, issues such as these are brought to the fore by the reforms as management is constrained to act in implementing the reform programme. The deployment of HRM techniques to secure staffing adjustments, to fend off budget deficits, and to gain control over teacher performance, all have consequences for industrial relations. Issues of job security, working conditions, workload, pay supplements, pay differentials, and performance management are familiar territory for grievance activity. With such increased scope for perceived injustices to multiply we may expect the number of aggrieved teachers to increase also.

Grievance procedures are designed so as to allow employees formally to confront management with their grievance and to seek redress. There is no state guidance on the operation of grievance procedures, the Code of Practice on Industrial Relations issued under the terms of the Industrial Relations Act 1971 having been withdrawn in 1991. The national agreement gives the following as the basis for a model procedure for teachers: a teacher with a grievance should first raise it with the appropriate line manager. If not resolved, the teacher may refer the matter formally to the head, who will arrange a hearing before 'the managers or governors, in consultation, where appropriate, with the chief education officer or his representative', and will seek to settle the matter. There is then a right of appeal to 'such standing or *ad hoc* body as may be agreed locally in consultation between the authority and the organisations of teachers' (see Burgundy Book: Appendix II).

The teacher has the right to union representation at the hearings, and time limits are specified for each stage. The procedure for hearing appeals varies between LEAs, with some of them being management only bodies and others being joint bodies, consisting of equal numbers of LEA and union representatives. An *ad hoc* body normally consists of one union representative, one LEA representative, and an independent chairperson acceptable to both parties.

LMS schools determine their own grievance procedures, and again most LEAs are recommending governors to adopt procedures that introduce the minimum of change. However, the new procedures will be stretched as they are applied to the new circumstances, facing difficulties that may prove insurmountable. The old procedures operated within a framework where the main issues at stake centred on the local application of national terms and conditions of employment. For example, individual teachers might invoke the grievance procedure if they believed that the LEA (or the head acting as a manager on behalf of the LEA) had acted contrary to the provisions of the sex discrimination legislation, or contrary to the LEA's equal opportunities policy. The grievance would have been against the LEA.

Under LMS the issues will be very different, potentially involving disagreements about pay differentials, about allocation of work, about performance related pay and about job security. The reforms deliberately set out to ensure not that managers treat teachers uniformly but that they discriminate between them. Some teachers will receive enhanced pay and others will not. Some will be made redundant. Some will be given extra work to do. Inevitably, some teachers will feel that they have been unfairly treated, and there will be a general desire to ensure that discrimination between teachers is not on the basis of unilateral exercise of arbitrary managerial authority but on the basis of jointly agreed procedures and rules.

These rules do not exist, and grievance procedures may not be effective in determining new rules. Grievance procedures can deal quite effectively with disputes of right, where the disagreement focuses on the rights and entitlements of the parties. In disputes of interest, however, where either or both of the parties is seeking to establish an entitlement, grievance procedures may be less effective. As school managers work to implement the reforms they will encounter dissatisfaction among teachers who may seek redress through grievance activity, and it may be the case that the school procedure will not resolve the grievances. The formal procedure, in its written form, offers 'no precise guidance as to the nature of the resolution process' (Hyman 1972: 38).

The legitimacy of a grievance procedure rests on whether or not it is perceived by those aggrieved as fair in operation. The resolution of grievances is often 'political' rather than technical in nature; it is not just a question of establishing exactly what rights the employee has and whether or not those rights have been infringed. The outcome of a grievance action over a dispute of right can set lasting precedents with which either party may have problems in coming to terms. When this happens the participants in industrial relations may take up entrenched positions and fail to reach a mutually acceptable settlement of the issue. For example, a grievance about selection for redundancy may become a dispute about management's right to declare redundancies, with management claiming the right to decide staffing levels and the union requiring a guarantee of no compulsory redundancies.

Under circumstances such as these a settlement is difficult. Under the old system an unresolved grievance would be referred to the next level of management, removing it from the school and putting it in the hands of LEA personnel managers and teacher union officers. LMS schools no longer have this escape route. One LEA's recommended procedure provides for grievances to be heard first by the head, then, if unresolved, by the chair of the governing body, and then by a joint arbitration panel. The panel would consist of three governors and three union representatives, and they would aim to 'reconcile the differences giving rise to the grievance'. If they fail to achieve this then they may make a recommendation, which will be binding if the parties so agreed at the start of the hearing.

Very few heads or governors or school-based union representatives have had any experience of handling grievances. Procedures like the one just outlined give little indication of the processes through which a head or a governor would actually resolve a grievance. The ways that the head, the union representative and the aggrieved teacher would set about reaching a negotiated settlement are not obvious. Nor is it clear how the parties involved would set about deciding whether or not to commit themselves in advance to accept a joint panel decision as binding. The old procedures had the effect of transferring conflict arising from teachers' grievances away from the school to the LEA – from the school managers' point of view they disappeared. These procedures no longer apply to LMS schools, leaving heads and governors to struggle with the consequences.

Disputes and their resolution

We saw in chapter 4 that school managers are being required to implement the reforms at the level of the school, and that this leads to the use of human resource management techniques. In chapter 2 we discussed the transfer of managerial authority away from LEAs as budgets and pay were set elsewhere. The focus of conflict over terms and conditions of employment has shifted away from both national and LEA levels to the school, because the long standing Whitley mechanisms for setting pay and for resolving disagreements are being dismantled.

The experiences of most classroom teachers and head teachers are likely to be that the majority of issues are settled without reference to 'industrial relations machinery'. Only 10 per cent of school representatives and 1 per cent of heads covered by the Keele survey disagreed with the statement that 'most issues affecting staff at my school are settled amicably without union involvement'. There is a significant difference between the heads' and reps' responses, but the general picture is one of relatively harmonious industrial relations with such events as industrial disputes belonging to other spheres of employment. Such a view glosses over the important role played by the LEA-level institutional arrangements in enabling stability and industrial peace. The reform package has the effect of dismantling those institutions at the same time as creating new bases for conflict.

Disputes procedures are intended to enable the parties to collective bargaining to resolve their differences without having recourse to the application of sanctions, such as 'industrial action' by employees and 'withdrawal of privileges' and/or 'lock-outs' by managers. Disputes fall into two categories: disputes of right and disputes of interest. The former are similar to grievances, in that the application or the interpretation of an existing provision is under question, and they are usually resolved through a procedure similar to the grievance procedure. Disputes of interest are concerned with issues where there is no clear framework of rights or responsibilities. For example, a group of teachers may express their concerns about teaching a particularly disruptive pupil, and request management to remove the pupil from their classes. In the absence of a clear procedure to deal with such an issue, and if the management disagrees with the request, the teachers may call in their union and seek to invoke the disputes procedure, to try to get the issue resolved in their favour before having recourse to industrial action, perhaps in the form of refusing to teach classes in the presence of that pupil.

Thus the main element of a disputes procedure is that which seeks to resolve disputes of interest and avoids either side having to impose sanctions on the other. It is explicitly recognised that disputes may arise, setting out a formal procedure for resolving them. This often relies on the intervention of a third party acting either as a conciliator or as an arbitrator. A conciliator's main function is to hear the arguments of both parties, to make suggestions, and to help the parties arrive at an agreement. An arbitrator hears the arguments and then decides the issue – usually both parties have agreed in advance that they will accept the arbitrator's decision. Most pay and conditions procedures (typically 90 per cent in the public sector and 70 per cent in the private sector) contain a provision for some sort of third party intervention into dispute resolution (Millward *et al.* 1992: 193).

The Burgundy Book contains a recommended procedure for regulating collective disputes between teachers and LEAs (Burgundy Book: Appendix II). This is based on conciliation, through the independent chairperson of an *ad hoc* body consisting of nominees of the parties to the dispute. In the event of failure to resolve the dispute the parties are recommended to refer the matter to a national conciliation body. While arbitration has played an important part in national disputes over pay, as described in chapter 2, there is no provision for arbitration over local disputes. Arbitration at local level can only take place with the agreement of both parties to the dispute.

Many local agreements make no reference to disputes procedure at all, leaving them to be dealt with under grievance procedures. These may be adequate to resolve many disputes of right but, as we argued above, they are unlikely to contain disputes of interest. Under Burnham most disputes arose either nationally or at the level of the LEA, and there was little experience of school-based disputes. However, school-based disputes were not unknown – we have already mentioned some in chapter 2, such as Poundswick where the teachers of one school took strike action against management decisions. Such school-based disputes can only increase under LMS. Detailed figures are hard to come by, but there is much evidence of an increase in protest strike activity at local level, especially at the time when LEAs decide their aggregate school budgets. Schools in Sandwell saw strikes by teachers when the LEA produced an aggregate budget that implied the loss of hundreds of jobs.

One of the most revealing school-based disputes was in 1980, when Nottinghamshire LEA suspended Mrs Eileen Crosbie from her teaching post because she had refused to teach her class of forty children since that breached the limit allowed for in NUT policy. She was disciplined and then sacked. As a result, the union called a local strike which lasted for twenty weeks while her case went to an industrial tribunal. At the hearing several mistakes by the management emerged, for example, the county's relevant senior adviser had never visited Mrs Crosbie at her school. The dispute started when the education committee had cut back on staff numbers and escalated to become the worst industrial action ever by Nottingham teachers. The chairman of the industrial tribunal said in his conclusions 'it is sad that it should have come to this. It is a pity that the whole matter could not have been settled by negotiation' (quoted in Seifert 1987: 161). Our rather pessimistic view of the future of such issues under LMS is that there will be many more Mrs Crosbies and that if the disputes procedure cannot resolve the matter then either strikes will follow, or the issue will remain unresolved to fester.

As we have seen serious difficulties arise at the level of the school when deadlock arises. Under the old system with its high degree of standardisation – the rate for the job, national conditions of service, and LEA-level collective agreements – there was a basis for conflict but over a limited range of issues only. With the breakdown of standardisation, and with most important employment matters settled at the level of the school, the range of issues that might generate conflict has expanded dramatically. The parties to school-level disputes, however, have little experience, and therefore little competence, in finding solutions to disputes. Burchill clarifies some frequently misunderstood points about the dynamics of arbitration when he argues that 'arbitration is used on an *ad hoc* basis when both parties see the continuation of the dispute as mutually destructive' (Burchill 1992: 106). The party that believes itself to be winning will not agree to arbitration, so arbitration only occurs when neither party believes it can win. It must be the case that, in the absence of any experience or knowledge of the dynamics of industrial conflict resolution, the parties to school-based disputes will find it difficult to resolve deadlock.

There have already been some examples that illustrate the seriousness of this issue. The governors of a school in Birmingham found themselves facing both strike action and legal action over some of their actions (*Career Teacher*, February 1994). A Huddersfield head was suspended by governors as teachers and groups of governors fought for control of the school (*Sunday Times*, 7 November 1993). What measures can governors take when their staff take strike action against school management because they 'are unable to work with them'? This happened at a school in Bradford, where the teaching staff passed a vote of no confidence in the head and deputy, going on to take strike action when the governors failed to find a solution to the dispute (*The Guardian*, 5 February 1994; *Career Teacher*, February 1994). With no LEA intervention disputes like this could blight a school for years.

CONCLUSIONS

This chapter has presented evidence and information to support our view that schools will become the centre for conflict-laden issues determined by the development of LMS and restricted school budgets. The pressures on school managers and employers will gain pace as market competition forces schools to out-perform their rivals on indicators decided far away by government ministers and their civil servants. This general aspect of government policy has peculiar and distinctive applications when used in schools. The new line management authority of the head will mean that a school-based individual will be transparently responsible for decisions that directly influence the working lives of every member of staff. The entire staffing profile of the school, the workload of the teachers, the performance assessment of colleagues, and their pay enhancements, are now in the hands of the heads. The issues generated by a more arbitrary system and the tensions created by having the decider of such issues on the premises will intensify what is already a fraught situation in many schools. The test is whether the traditional methods of avoiding conflict will remain, and this depends on the continued presence of well supported trade unions, the continued use of the LEA personnel function and the cautious approach to such matters taken by most heads. Evidence from examples of whole-school pay policies and governing body procedures is that the dominant trend is to stay within the LEA-union brokerage system.

School managers are required to drive a process of reform and change which has a direct impact on teachers, affecting their pay, their workload, and their job security. Heads are also required to give close scrutiny to the performance of all teachers. These issues are the substance of workplace discipline, of workplace grievances, and of industrial disputes. The experiences of managers and trade unionists throughout all the major sectors of the economy have led them to build institutional arrangements with the aim of handling these industrial relations matters and producing outcomes acceptable to both employers and employees. The industrial relations machinery in the schools sector, however, is being slowly dismantled, which will leave the managers of 25,000 workplaces with nowhere to turn if they find themselves in conflict with their staff. The final outcome remains unclear, and in the final chapter we provide some evidence of the most likely developments and arrangements in industrial relations in schools.

6 Workplace industrial relations: management and unions

INTRODUCTION

In this chapter we examine the responses of managers and trade unionists in the workplaces to the changes brought in by the 1988 reform programme. Our evidence is taken from the Keele surveys of head teachers and school representatives, which provide us with a substantial amount of data. Our research was conducted in three LEAs in the Midlands using a variety of methods. Activity at the level of the LEA was studied through analysis of LEA and trade union documents, through interviews of LEA and trade union officers, and through observation of LEA, trade union, and joint meetings. School-level activity was studied through case study analysis in seventeen schools, representing a mix of primary and secondary schools covering a range of different communities across the social, economic, political and cultural spectra. There are 899 schools in the three LEAs covered by the survey; 776 are primary schools, and 123 are secondary. Questionnaires were sent to the heads and to the teacher union representatives in all of them. The responses gave us data from 580 heads and 600 school representatives, which are very large survey samples of workplace managers and trade union representatives in a neglected area of industrial relations activity.

Our concern here is to evaluate the evidence and to draw together the main points made in the preceding chapters. In this section we review the issue of management's right to manage, considering the impact of collective bargaining on managerial decision-making. In the next sections we consider the responses of school managers to the reform programme, followed by an examination of the union responses at school level. We look in detail at management and union activity, drawing from our survey data. Our analysis leads us to conclude that the reforms have undermined the basis for the orderly resolution of conflicts between teachers and their employers over industrial relations issues, and that there is no evidence of the emergence of any new stabilising order.

One of the advertised benefits of the reforms was to be increased freedom for heads to manage. Many heads felt themselves to be constrained by pressures which were seen as originating from outside of the school. LEA decisions were perceived as being imposed on schools without due regard for the consequences for school managers, resulting in 'harassment by document' (Taylor 1983: 281). Trade unions allegedly acted as a brake on management freedom – one report on the findings of a survey of heads contains the following:

> Heads' freedom to manage increasingly appeared to be at the mercy of a series of pincer movements – between DES and LEA, between LEA and teacher associations, and, in some cases, between individual members of teacher associations and governing bodies. In their union guise it was the associations which aroused the greatest concern, because they were always physically proximate, on occasions self-evidently irresponsible, and, at worst, destructive of crucial relationships. The LEA . . . . appeared singularly unable or unwilling to protect its managers against the grosser manifestations.
>
> (Taylor 1983: 283)

Johnson's (1983, 1984a and 1984b) analysis, referred to in earlier chapters, challenges this negative view of trade unions. She presents evidence about the impact of union organisation and collective bargaining on schools in the USA. Her conclusion, that 'the school site effects of teacher unionism proved to be far less extreme, uniform, and unmanageable than many suppose' (Johnson 1983: 311), is rooted in three main factors. First is the distinctive nature of schools, which contain professionals as the numerically dominant occupational group. Teachers and teacher-managers share the same qualifications, and many other aspects of their relationships are reciprocal. Furthermore, teachers' relationship to their work, and the value that they place upon it, is also quite distinctive. It cannot be assumed that collective bargaining in schools will be the same as collective bargaining in other spheres of employment.

Secondly, school managers themselves play a key role, as individuals, in determining the nature of relations in schools. The ways that heads work, and the ways that school staff regard them as individuals, have an influence on union activity in schools. The head's own approach to managing the school has a significant impact on the teachers' working lives. Thirdly, collective agreements are not necessarily rigidly adhered to by either heads or union representatives. Johnson found that while some aspects of collective agreements were enforced in all schools other aspects were not.

Johnson examined in depth the interplay of these factors in the context of the American education system, finding considerable variation in practice within the apparently highly regulated system of determining teachers' contracts through collective bargaining. Her analysis gives collective bargaining a central importance in regulating teacher activity in schools, without seeing it as an over-riding constraint on either management authority or teacher professionalism. Johnson stresses three factors in explaining school-level outcomes – the interdependence between teachers and their managers, the nature of teacher concerns, and teacher attitudes to collective bargaining. The first of these makes the simple but important point that the activities of *both* heads and teachers are important for a successful school, and that each one depends on the other. Teachers need managers to provide them with the conditions that make good teaching possible, while managers rely on the commitment and performance of the teachers. When resources for schools are in decline then this places the relationship under a strain. Management freedom to decide on spending is meaningless if there is nothing to spend, and teacher commitment can ebb away as staff face redundancy, workload increases, and limited resources force a reassessment of provision by downgrading the professional definitions of standards.

The second point about teachers and collective bargaining is the fact that not all of their concerns can actually be addressed by it. Collective bargaining can cover some of their main concerns, such as salaries, job security, class sizes, and non-contact time. It will not ensure, however, parental support, or student discipline, or, importantly, effective managers. Johnson found that heads who used collective bargaining effectively were attentive to all teacher concerns, and not just to those that were negotiable. Again, quite a simple point is being made here, but it is important to draw it out. Before the LMS reforms, most of the teacher concerns that might be addressed by collective bargaining were determined at either national or LEA level. As Johnson states, 'the relationship between teachers and principals extends well beyond the relationship of labor and management' (1983: 323), and schools are heavily reliant on the administrative skills of the head. Shifting employer responsibility to the level of the school also shifts the locus of teacher concern about employment issues to that level, and these issues were previously resolved through collective bargaining rather than by the mobilisation of administrative skill. Johnson makes a link between effective schools, effective administrators, and effective collective bargaining. In the American system teacher contracts are negotiated at the district level, covering teachers in all schools in the district. This gives a strong role for the district in industrial relations, while in England and Wales the LEA role, which was always subordinate to Burnham, is being weakened almost to the point of disappearance.

School managers are now expected to deal with the full range of teacher concerns, and to resolve them at the level of the school, gaining more responsibilities rather than more managerial freedom (Stenning 1989). Indeed this reveals that when managers call for more *freedom* to manage they are in fact calling for more *power*. With LMS power is centralised to the government and the DFE, while responsibility is decentralised to school managers.

Finally, Johnson considers teacher attitudes to collective bargaining and to unionism. Broadly speaking, American teachers endorsed strong union action at the level of the district, but had reservations about it at school – it is worth quoting to make this point:

> Collective bargaining was viewed as a useful and necessary means to achieve narrow objectives rather than a cause deserving constant and

> unconditional commitment. At the district level, where the voice of one teacher might be inaudible, teachers accepted the necessity of pursuing their interests collectively. However, at the school site, where teachers were known individually and where they had the opportunity to act on their own behalf with administrators, they were far less likely to stress their union identities.
>
> (Johnson 1983: 325)

This meant first that teachers placed importance on the fact that their contracts were negotiated by their union. Secondly, however, teachers were willing to be flexible at the level of the school in order to accommodate to the needs of their principals. This flexibility is open to them within the framework of the district-level collective agreement, which gives protection from administrative abuse but allows for school-level variation from the letter of the contract. Here the unions, and collective bargaining, are seen as constraints on management in that they establish rights for teachers. There is still scope for flexibility at the level of the school, for teachers to co-operate with managers without seeking recourse to grievance procedures.

Johnson's main concern was to examine the impact of collective bargaining on American schools, and in doing this she uncovered the concerns of both teachers and principals. Her main findings informed the conduct of our research into the impact of the reforms of the school system in England and Wales. The abolition of national collective bargaining, the virtual ending of the LEAs' role as employers, and the shift of employer-like responsibilities and duties to some 25,000 schools, places a considerable burden on school managers as outlined in chapter 4. Heads have always played a vital role in school administration and in generating teacher enthusiasm and commitment. Can they sustain this vital role while also being required to extract more work from fewer teachers, within tight budgets, and with reduced levels of job security? What will replace national-level and LEA-level collective bargaining, which played such an important role in maintaining stable relations between teachers and their employers under Burnham?

The reform programme gives a large range of new responsibilities to school-based managers, reducing the influence of the LEAs and making redundant the agreements between the LEAs and the unions. In our analysis we pose questions about how these new responsibilities can be fulfilled in practice. One example is sufficient to illustrate the point – the responsibility for pay determination.

As we have already seen in previous chapters, governing bodies have a range of discretionary powers, and they are coming under increasing pressure to use them. In practice, heads will play the most significant role in discriminating between teachers when pay supplements are awarded as part of the annual review process. The fact that this opens up potential problems, which could cause disruption of the school, has resulted in the development by LEAs of model 'whole-school pay policies'. The National Association of

Governors and Managers (NAGM) has argued with the government that pay discretion is not workable in practice under tight budgets and in the absence of objective criteria (*NAGM News*, Issue 1 1992). However, in principle the operation of governor-level pay discretion is seen as workable through the use of whole-school policies.

These policies set out the range of pay discretions, based on the School Teachers Pay and Conditions Document, and they give the circumstances under which awards might be given to one teacher and not to another. There is usually a notion that the process of implementing the policy should be open and fair. For example, one LEA advises that the award of responsibility points has an impact on staffing structures, and that 'governing bodies should ensure that any judgements they make about the management structure of a school are reasonable, [and] that appropriate consultations have taken place'. Within the formalised LEA structures it was clear what such a policy would have meant in practice. Experienced personnel managers and union representatives would have met on several occasions to discuss a range of options, concluding with a negotiated agreement as to what constitutes a 'reasonable judgement', and finalising the agreement in a formal joint negotiating committee. But what would it mean at the level of the school? Would negotiations take place? Who would be involved? Should there be a formal negotiating committee? What would happen in the event of a failure to agree? Or, if pay is not to be agreed by employer and employee representatives through a process of negotiation, and if it is not to be determined by management acting unilaterally and in secret, then what exactly is the process to be used instead?

THE MANAGERS IN THE SCHOOLS

In looking at heads as a group of managers it is important to recognise that they are very highly unionised. Table 6.1 shows a union density of 99 per cent, putting head teachers among the most highly organised employees in Britain. As expected the NAHT predominates in the primary sector, with 85 per cent of heads, while SHA has 59 per cent of secondary heads. A significant minority of heads retain membership of their classroom union, with some 12 per cent remaining in either the NUT or the NASUWT (ATL does not recruit heads). Just over 95 per cent of all heads had been members of trade unions before becoming heads. Half of them had been in the NUT,

Table 6.1 Union membership among heads

Sector	*Union membership (% of heads)*						
	NUT	*NASUWT*	*ATL*	*PAT*	*SHA*	*NAHT*	*None*
All (N=576)	8	3	<1	2	9	76	1
Primary (N=493)	9	4	<1	2	<1	85	1
Secondary (N=83)	7	1	0	0	59	30	2

a quarter in the NASUWT, and one in eight were in ATL. Head teachers are rooted in classroom teacher union membership, with a significant minority of one in ten retaining membership of the TUC affiliates and the remainder belonging to the head teacher organisations.

This union orientation is reflected in heads' attitudes to trade unions. Only a quarter agree with the statement that 'those who supported the 1984/5 teacher strikes were misguided', and only one in ten agree that 'strikes by school teachers should be prohibited by law' (see Table 6.2). While the head teacher organisations, in particular the NAHT, have welcomed some aspects of the reforms that strengthen their managerial role, union membership also has the effect of damping managerial hostility to the classroom unions. While nearly all heads agree that most issues are settled amicably without union involvement, a majority agree that negotiating with union representatives is beneficial, and nearly all have a good relationship with the union representatives in their school. However, it is our view that in most schools this good relationship lacks depth in industrial relations, being based on shared professional concerns rather than on a history of bargaining over workplace rights. The reform process places this relationship under strain, as heads' activities become more tightly focused on costs and on teacher performance. Heads are becoming human resource managers and budget resource allocators, rather than senior figures among teams of like-minded professionals.

Heads' attitudes on a range of other related issues are set out in Table 6.2. Here it can be seen that heads *qua* managers welcome the new authority given to them by the reforms. Three-quarters agree that they have more authority under LMS, and over half agree that the efficiency of the school has increased. Two-thirds agree that teacher appraisal improves the performance of the school, and three-quarters agree that it improves the performance of individual teachers. Nearly half of heads agree that the best teachers should be rewarded by higher pay.

However, heads *qua* teacher professionals are less enthusiastic. Three-quarters of them agree that the LMS funding formula is inherently unfair, and nearly half agree that compulsory redundancies are inevitable. Well over two-thirds reject any link between appraisal and pay – and of those who agree that the purpose of appraisal is to establish such links many made a comment to the effect that there ought to be no link. Half of heads agree that the incentive allowance system caused ill-feeling between teachers, only one in seven agree that the system has encouraged improvement in teaching, and nearly all heads agree that the reforms have made teaching more demanding. Our case study investigation confirms that most heads believe that the best teachers should be rewarded through higher pay gained through promotion into a higher-paid post rather than through pay supplements.

Our evidence suggests very strongly that heads are not convinced that the recession and reform-induced changes are beneficial to anyone. They give no real powers to managers, no real benefits to teachers, and they do nothing to improve the pupils' education. As human resource managers they have

Table 6.2 Head teachers' attitudes

Statement	*Attitude (% of heads, N=576)*				
	Agree strongly	*Agree*	*Neither agree nor disagree*	*Disagree*	*Disagree strongly*
Those who supported the 1984/5 teacher strikes were misguided	7	17	30	30	15
Strikes by school teachers should be prohibited by law	3	7	16	43	31
Most issues affecting staff at my school are settled amicably without union involvement	54	43	2	1	0
School management can benefit from negotiations with teacher unions	11	43	38	7	1
School managers lose authority if they get involved in negotiations with teacher unions	1	4	38	45	12
I have a good relationship with the union representatives at this school	34	53	13	1	0
One of the main purposes of teacher appraisal is to establish a link between teachers' performance and their pay	5	15	15	28	39
One of the main purposes of teacher appraisal is to enable school managers to remove bad teachers from the school	2	6	19	38	36
Teacher appraisal improves the performance of the school	16	51	27	4	2
Teacher appraisal improves the performance of individual teachers	19	54	22	3	2
It should be easier to remove bad teachers from teaching	21	51	21	5	2
Under LMS I have more authority to manage the school	22	52	16	8	2
The efficiency of the school has increased under LMS	15	39	33	10	3
LMS has resulted in improved performance of the school	9	23	46	19	4
The LMS funding formula is inherently unfair	39	34	14	8	4
Compulsory redundancies are inevitable under LMS	13	35	22	24	6
The head should have the right to refuse the redeployment of individual teachers into a school	51	42	4	3	1
The incentive allowance system has encouraged teachers to improve their teaching	1	13	29	43	14
The incentive allowance system is unfair	12	30	30	24	3
The incentive allowance system causes ill-feeling between teachers	11	37	30	19	2
The best teachers should be rewarded by higher pay	11	36	27	19	8
The education reforms have made teaching more demanding	78	20	1	1	1
There should be more control over teachers' activities in the classroom	3	17	41	33	7

acquired some new responsibilities, some of which they have welcomed, but they are deeply sceptical about the human resource management techniques, such as appraisal without staff development, appraisal related pay and appraisal related dismissals which they are being required to implement. Nevertheless, somehow they have to deal with the industrial relations consequences of their new management role.

Much of the human resource management literature places great stress on the importance of communications in maintaining good relationships with employees. Regular staff meetings are a normal feature of school life in virtually all schools. Table 6.3 shows that 95 per cent of heads hold meetings of all school staff at least monthly. Even in the larger secondary schools, meetings at least once a term are the norm. In larger schools these might be augmented by meetings of faculties and departments. Given the extent to which these practices are a part of the normal life of the school it is no surprise to find that issues relating to staffing, timetables, appraisal, in fact the whole range of issues with industrial relations implications are discussed at staff meetings. In some cases the industrial relations matters are tacked onto the end of the meeting when the union representatives are asked to comment or just to inform the meeting as to developments. The extent to which this can be regarded as consultation depends on the intricate nature of the school situation and the intention of the head.

Table 6.3 Frequency of staff meetings

Sector	*Frequency of meetings (% of all schools)*					
	Never	*Less than yearly*	*Yearly*	*Termly*	*Monthly*	*Weekly*
All (N=576)	<1	<1	<1	4	15	80
Primary (N=493)	<1	<1	<1	<1	10	88
Secondary (N=83)	1	0	2	22	41	34

This might appear to have parallels with the human resource management technique of holding team briefings or organising quality circles in order to bypass trade unions. However, in this case it is simply the extension of the past practice of professional colleagues meeting to plan and discuss the work ahead. Furthermore, there was no workplace organization to bypass – the issues had not arisen in the same way before the reforms. Nevertheless, the effect of this is to inhibit the development of an ordered approach to collective bargaining. An ATL representative said

> 'There is not really a forum [for negotiations]. I would like to see a union-based staff committee with direct liaison with senior management. You can raise things as an individual and you might get support, but if we went in as a committee it would be different. We have so many committees though – for the curriculum and for LMS – and you tend to deal with things there.'

At a staff meeting in one school the head informed the staff of a budget crisis and offered them the choice of either redundancies or larger class sizes and less non-contact time, going on to put this to a vote. Another head told how he organised consultation over changes to the length of the school day through his faculty managers. The senior teachers in each faculty then held meetings with groups of staff. This method of 'sounding out' staff gives the appearance of a systematic approach to obtaining their views. In reality it amounts to no more than a vehicle for passing messages from senior management to staff about their intentions. The messages that get passed back to senior management, filtered through the layers of middle management, have little real value, giving no indication as to which trade-offs would actually prove the least unacceptable, if not the most acceptable. In short, under this method change is decided by management unilaterally rather than through negotiated *agreement*.

Nevertheless, the large majority of heads indicate a positive support for management through formally agreed (at the LEA level) procedures. As we saw in chapter 5, LEAs are issuing guidance to schools on employment issues, including model procedures that have been subject to either negotiation or consultation with the teacher unions. Table 6.4 shows a high level of satisfaction among heads with the advice given to them by LEAs, but there is a noticeable lack of interest in teacher representation through formal consultation arrangements, and facilities for union representatives is not an issue for many heads.

Table 6.4 Heads' views on LEA guidelines

Procedure	*Heads reporting guidelines as 'helpful' and 'very helpful' (%)*		
	All (N=576)	*Primary (N=493)*	*Secondary (N=83)*
Appraisal	89	88	93
Redundancy and redeployment	89	88	93
Disciplinary procedures	87	86	94
Health and safety	87	87	84
Grievance procedures	83	83	88
Equal opportunities	78	79	71
Parental complaints	64	65	60
Pay policy	64	64	59
Professional competence	49	48	51
Recruitment	49	49	48
Consultation arrangements	48	48	46
Promotion procedures	46	47	36
Facilities for union representatives	31	32	28

This pattern is confirmed by Table 6.5, which records the sources that heads said they would use for advice after full delegation of their school budget. Almost all heads giving an answer intended to continue to use the LEA for

Table 6.5 Sources of advice to heads after full delegation

Issue	*Heads using this source of advice (%) (N=576)*							
	LEA	*Lawyer*	*Management consultant*	*Designated staff member*	*Specialist governor*	*Head teacher association*	*Other*	*Don't know/no answer*
Appraisal	88	0	<1	11	9	41	6	12
Redundancy and redeployment procedures	87	2	<1	4	16	50	4	11
Disciplinary procedures	83	2	<1	4	18	65	5	10
Grievance procedures	82	2	<1	3	18	59	5	13
Health and safety	82	1	<1	19	15	34	5	15
Professional competence	76	1	1	5	14	51	7	21
Parental complaints	76	2	<1	4	27	48	8	17
Equal opportunities	75	1	<1	12	13	33	7	25
Recruitment	69	0	1	4	23	24	10	30
Pay policy	68	<1	1	4	22	46	8	26
Promotion procedures	65	0	0	5	20	31	9	31
Consultation with unions	53	<1	<1	16	8	49	5	48
Facilities for union reps	46	<1	<1	14	6	40	7	51

Note: (Rows add up to more than 100% where heads indicated use of more than one source)

advice, with hardly any considering using other sources outside of the school. The exception to this is their own association, which is seen as a useful source of advice by a significant number of heads over a range of issues. The handful of cases of schools using outside management consultants and/or other experts has led to rapid disillusionment with both the quality of advice and the cost.

When asked which sources of advice they would use on consultation with unions and on facilities for union representatives, half of heads either did not know or gave no answer. A significant number, about one in seven, would designate a member of staff to deal with these issues. This also suggests a relatively low level of concern for institutional arrangements to support a formal system of industrial relations.

Further confirmation of this low level of concern is brought out in Table 6.6, which shows the responses of both heads and school representatives when asked if the governors in their school had adopted procedures covering a range of issues. The proportion of heads replying in the affirmative was consistently higher than the proportion of school representatives. For the key industrial relations procedures covering pay determination, discipline and grievances the difference is up to 25 per cent. The difference is mainly accounted for by school representatives who did not know if procedures had been adopted. This suggests a low level of concern among school representatives about the importance of formal procedures.

In chapters 2 and 5 we have argued that the national and local systems of industrial relations have been rendered redundant by the reform provisions. We further argued that the removal of the LEA-level mechanisms for institutionalising conflict creates the basis for intractable problems in schools. Here we consider the extent to which school-based institutions have been created to deal with conflicts in schools. As we noted earlier, the role of the LEA in job regulation, formalised through procedural agreements with the trade unions, has been weakened by the transfer of legal duties from LEAs to governing bodies under LMS. This evidence suggests that the formal trappings of the LEA procedures have been imported into the schools but without including the basis to operationalise them at the level of the school – regular meetings of a standing negotiating body, with established rights for union representatives to organise.

Most schools have adopted the procedures recommended in guidelines issued by their LEA. These were discussed within the usual LEA-level bodies for negotiation and consultation, and the normal practice is for the guidelines to have been agreed by the teacher unions. Our case study findings suggest that in the large majority of schools the LEA/trade union recommended procedures have been adopted, with many heads recognising that trade union agreement helped to give the procedures legitimacy among teaching staff. The trade union objective of securing the adoption of model procedures in schools appears to have met with a high degree of success. However, this has been achieved through organisation at the level of the LEA. In many schools,

Table 6.6 Procedures adopted by governing bodies, as reported by school representatives and heads

Procedure adopted	*School representatives (%)*			*Heads (%)*		
	All (N=595)	*Primary (N=417)*	*Secondary (N=178)*	*All (N=576)*	*Primary (N=493)*	*Secondary (N=83)*
Appraisal	67	62	78	57	55	56
Health and safety	63	62	64	78	77	80
Parental complaints	58	58	60	72	72	74
Equal opportunities	52	44	69	72	70	79
Redundancy and redeployment	48	41	64	71	67	90
Grievances	45	41	53	72	70	82
Pay policy	44	39	55	60	58	76
Discipline	39	33	53	65	63	80
Promotion	33	28	45	46	43	60
Recruitment	33	29	42	47	43	71
Recognition	27	19	44	—	—	—
Consultation	23	13	44	27	24	43
Professional competence	22	21	24	32	40	34
Facilities for union representatives	10	6	20	13	11	21

heads appear to have adopted the union-agreed procedures without the workplace union representative knowing about it. All of this suggests that there is a concern among heads to ensure that institutional arrangements are in place, but these do not include arrangements that would bring teacher union representatives into joint decision-making over conditions of service issues. Teacher union participation in school-level decisions seems to be accepted in principle, but on an *ad hoc* basis in practice rather than on a formally constituted basis.

In only one of our case study schools was there a formal consultative committee, with some signs that one could emerge in another. Procedures for consultation at the level of the LEA are well established, and the practice at school level has been to deal with issues as they arise, within the national and LEA frameworks. Prior to LMS the LEAs played a crucial role in resolving disputes, and our case studies show that this role was generally highly valued. Virtually all disputes between teachers and their managers were referred to LEA officers and to local teacher association officers to resolve, and usually heads were satisfied with the outcomes of that process. The ability of the LEA-based system to make school-based problems vanish from the school helps to explain the widespread adoption of LEA guidelines in LMS schools.

Our case study observations and interviews confirmed the intensity of the pressures faced by heads. The continual battle to achieve more with dwindling resources, while school buildings were deteriorating further after many years of neglect, exacted a considerable toll. One fieldwork problem was that, in spite of clearly expressed support among heads for the research project, arranging appointments to interview them was difficult. Furthermore, once arranged they often had to be rescheduled to enable heads to meet other demands, and during interviews frequent interruptions occurred as heads were called on to deal with a wide range of unforeseen urgent issues. This sort of fieldwork problem is not unusual, but our overall impression is that heads in all schools, both large and small, carried a very large workload and were unable to plan their own work programme because of constant demands on their time from a variety of sources. Many questionnaire survey respondents made unsolicited written comments on this aspect of their jobs, often remarking that they were filling in the form quite late at night.

Under these circumstances it is not surprising that there is little in the way of strategic thinking about the management of human resources in schools. Most governors do not have the inclination, or the skills, or the time to involve themselves in any systematic fashion in school management. Heads rely heavily on the commitment of teachers to teaching and on their willingness to do work beyond that required in the Pay and Conditions Document. While they welcome the freedom to manage under the reforms, they would prefer someone else to make the tough decisions about selection for dismissal or about a pay cut for a struggling teacher. Heads might see themselves as taking the helm and steering their school towards a bright new self-managed future, but they positively welcome the LEA's involvement at the 'mucky' end of industrial relations. It is by no means clear that attempting to force heads to get their hands dirty with decisions about redundancy and pay will have any benefits for the school. Rather it would further damage teacher morale, intensifying the divisions between heads and classroom teachers and adding yet more to the burden carried by heads.

Our evidence points towards a troubled future in schools, with institutional arrangements to deal with school-level conflict being put in place in only one of our case study schools. The fact that this particular school had some history of difficult disputes may give a pointer as to why school-level institutional arrangements are unlikely to appear. We might start with the question as to why they should appear anyway. From the point of view of the majority of heads and teachers in the schools most of the time there is no need for conflict-resolution mechanisms, as virtually all conflicts are in reality resolved through discussion between the teacher professionals. Collective bargaining arrangements do not just happen because some clever people perceive that this is the best way forward. They become established because employees demand them, applying trade union pressure to gain a foothold in job regulation. They arise out of struggle over job regulation, rather than through management initiative – thus a LEA's advice to set up procedures to consult with trade unions may be seen as interesting and worthy, but also as abstract and unnecessary in the absence of anything to actually consult about that has not been managed previously through staff meetings. So our next question is whether or not the teacher unions are likely to engage in activity that will make the establishment of school-level bargaining more likely.

THE UNIONS IN THE SCHOOLS

In Chapter 3 we charted the development of the teacher unions, locating the three main classroom unions within a broad taxonomy. The NUT is most closely associated with the wider concerns of the labour movement, in particular with the establishment of a national rate for the job; the NASUWT is craft-like in its concern for differentials and in its narrow sectional concern for career teachers in secondary schools; and the ATL, with its focus on managerialism and professionalism, is most like a business union. We noted the main structural changes and the main policy positions taken up by the national unions in response to the reform programme. Here we look more closely at the responses locally, at the levels of the LEA and the school.

The gender composition of the Keele respondents, summarised in Table 6.7, shows clear divisions between the sectors and the unions. In the primary sector three-quarters of respondents to the Keele survey were women, while in the secondary sector three-quarters were men. ATL has the highest proportion of women representatives – nine out of ten representatives in the primary sector are women, compared with half for the NASUWT. This suggests that ATL's expansion in the primary sector is mainly among women

Table 6.7 School representatives, by sex

Trade union	*Men and women (%)*					
	All (N=595)		*Primary (N=417)*		*Secondary (N=178)*	
	M	*W*	*M*	*W*	*M*	*W*
All	40	60	26	74	73	27
NUT	35	65	26	74	66	34
NASUWT	61	39	46	54	84	16
ATL	28	72	9	91	67	33

teachers. Although nearly half of the secondary teacher workforce is female only a quarter of the representatives are women. Less than a fifth of NASUWT secondary school representatives are women.

Table 6.8 shows the distribution between LEAs and between the primary and secondary sectors of the school representatives responding to the Keele surveys. This data confirms the predominance of the NUT in the primary sector, with 45 per cent of respondents, and of the NASUWT in the secondary sector, with 39 per cent. There is some variation in the distribution of representatives between the three LEAs. In LEA2 the NUT is particularly strong in primary schools, where the NASUWT is weakest, while in the secondary sector the ATL is particularly strong and the NUT is weakest. ATL is weakest in secondary schools in the urban metropolitan LEA3, where the NUT is strongest. NASUWT is at its strongest among the primary schools in this LEA.

Our survey did not trace the historical background of the unions in the three LEAs, but our general point made in chapter 3, about the roots of the NUT

Table 6.8 School representatives, by LEA, sector and trade union

LEA	*Sector*	*School representatives (%)*		
		NUT	*NASUWT*	*ATL*
All	All (N=595)	41	29	30
	Primary (N=417)	45	25	29
	Secondary (N=178)	30	39	31
LEA1	All (N=358)	40	32	28
	Primary (N=250)	44	28	28
	Secondary (N=108)	30	41	30
LEA2	All (N=148)	43	21	36
	Primary (N=105)	51	15	34
	Secondary (N=43)	26	35	40
LEA3	All (N=89)	39	32	28
	Primary (N=62)	40	31	29
	Secondary (N=27)	37	37	26

in the primary sector and the NASUWT in the secondary sector, is in line with these figures. It appears that ATL has made some gains in expanding from its secondary sector base into the primary sector, although the presence of a school representative is not necessarily indicative of an organised membership. The high response to our survey suggests that the teacher unions have large numbers of representatives in place in schools. As we have noted in earlier chapters, their role traditionally has been to ensure the passage of information from the national union to the membership and to refer members with problems to experienced branch officers or full-time officials. Our concern here is to establish whether these representatives are becoming more involved in school-based activity.

One measure of organised union activity is the extent to which representatives undertake training. The 1990 Workplace Industrial Relations Survey contains data on the number of establishments having worker representatives trained in the year prior to the survey. In 1989 the non-manual representatives in 45 per cent of public sector establishments and in 38 per cent of all establishments, and the manual representatives in 39 per cent of public sector and in 37 per cent of all establishments received training (Millward *et al.* 1992: 119). The WIRS surveys cover workplaces with twenty-five or more employees, which rules out most primary schools. Our evidence suggests that school teacher representatives attend union training in numbers comparable to the workplace representatives of other unions.

Table 6.9 shows the extent of attendance on union courses, revealing differences between the primary and secondary sectors and between the unions. Secondary school representatives are more than twice as likely than primary school representatives to have been on a basic course and more than three times as likely to have been on an LMS course.

In the primary sector, a quarter of NASUWT representatives have attended a basic course, compared with a fifth of NUT. ATL representatives are significantly less likely to have attended a basic course for representatives, but significantly more likely to have attended one on LMS. In the secondary sector NASUWT representatives show a high take-up of training – half have attended a basic course and over a quarter a course on LMS. NASUWT representatives are seven times more likely than NUT representatives to have attended a course on LMS. A third of ATL representatives have attended basic training.

Much of this training is provided by the unions themselves. The NASUWT has used TUC provision to strengthen its LMS training programme, and our evidence suggests that this has paid off with a relatively high rate of take-up in the secondary sector. Levels of attendance on basic courses, particularly among the TUC affiliates in the secondary sector, suggest a widespread commitment to performance of the school representative's role. Our findings suggest that most secondary school representatives are acquiring at least some basic knowledge about their union, about LMS, and about the role of the school representative. Primary sector representatives are much less keen

Table 6.9 School representatives attending union courses

Course	*School representatives attending (%)*								
	All reps	*Primary reps (N=417)*				*Secondary reps (N=178)*			
	(N=595)	*All*	*NUT*	*NASUWT*	*ATL*	*All*	*NUT*	*NASUWT*	*ATL*
Basic	25	18	20	26	10	42	42	49	32
Advanced	3	1	0	1	2	8	2	17	4
Health and safety	7	6	6	10	5	7	4	12	4
Equal opportunities	2	1	1	1	2	3	9	1	0
Teacher governors	4	4	6	5	14	2	2	4	0
Local association officers	3	1	1	2	3	8	13	9	2
LMS	9	5	2	9	15	17	4	28	18

Table 6.10 School representatives attending local association meetings

Attendance rate	*School representatives (%)*								
	All reps	*Primary reps (N=417)*				*Secondary reps (N=178)*			
	(N=595)	*All*	*NUT*	*NASUWT*	*ATL*	*All*	*NUT*	*NASUWT*	*ATL*
Never	37	41	31	36	62	26	23	13	43
Less than once a year	27	30	35	26	27	20	31	9	23
Yearly	12	12	16	13	4	11	10	10	13
Termly	16	11	10	18	3	29	21	46	14
Monthly	9	7	8	7	5	15	15	21	7

to attend union courses, and this means that in many primary schools there is likely to be little union organisation around LMS issues. The very low level of attendance at LMS courses by NUT representatives stands out in both sectors.

Another measure of union activity is the extent to which members attend branch meetings. School representatives included in the Keele survey were asked how often they attended meetings of their local associations. Their answers are summarised in Table 6.10, showing clear differences between both sectors and unions. 'Infrequent attenders', that is those who answered 'never' and 'less than once a year', can be compared with 'frequent attenders' – those who answered 'termly' or 'monthly'. Seven out of ten primary school representatives are infrequent attenders, compared with half of secondary. Nine out of ten ATL primary representatives are infrequent attenders.

The variation between unions is very high in the secondary sector. Two-thirds of NASUWT secondary representatives are frequent attenders, compared with a fifth of ATL. This evidence suggests that NASUWT representatives are much more involved in their local associations, and that only a minority of ATL representatives, even in the secondary sector, are active in their branches.

Union structures may be a factor here, with ATL branches having their boundaries coterminous with the LEA. NUT and NASUWT local associations are geographically much smaller, with boundaries reflecting the smaller LEAs of many years ago. In large rural counties the smaller, more localised associations are more easily accessible. Furthermore, the NUT and NASUWT have established traditions of organising activity in support of collective bargaining, including industrial action, through their local associations. The higher rate of participation among NASUWT representatives reflects this union's established tradition of organising around local conditions of service issues. On the other hand, the ATL's preoccupation with managerial/professional issues needs much less in the way of local organisation.

Participation in union activity can be considered in more detail by looking at union representatives' contacts with other trade unionists, with their members, and with managers. Table 6.11 summarises their contacts with other trade unionists and with managers, as revealed by the Keele survey. Respondents were asked to record their contacts as occurring 'often', 'sometimes' or 'never', and the tables give the totals for 'often' and 'sometimes' replies.

In the secondary sector nearly three-quarters of school representatives reported contacts with other school representatives. As the unions operate normally on the basis of one representative per school this means contact with representatives from other schools. An even higher proportion of 86 per cent reported contact with the representatives of other teacher unions, which may occur mainly in their own school. Half of primary school representatives have similar contacts. The WIRS survey reports that in workplaces with more than one representative 36 per cent of non-manual representatives have meetings

Table 6.11 School representatives' contacts with others

Contact	*School representatives reporting contact 'sometimes' or often' (%)*								
	All reps (N=595)	*Primary reps (N=417)*				*Secondary reps (N=178)*			
		All	*NUT*	*NASUWT*	*ATL*	*All*	*NUT*	*NASUWT*	*ATL*
Other members of union	88	83	85	85	78	98	98	100	95
Other school reps	55	47	48	55	36	72	75	79	61
Local association officers	68	62	65	59	61	81	90	85	66
Full-time officials	38	28	33	29	21	58	69	67	36
School reps (other unions)	65	56	51	66	52	86	90	87	82
Non-teacher stewards	8	4	6	5	1	17	15	21	13
School managers	44	32	32	39	25	70	81	75	54
School governors	52	52	63	46	42	51	44	64	43
Managers and governors	23	22	23	23	19	24	8	25	20

with other representatives of the same union (Millward *et al.* 1992: 131). There appears to be a very high level of contact between teacher trade unionists, which can be only partly explained by the often close working relationships between teachers. Meetings between school representatives from the same union usually are meetings between representatives from different workplaces.

Contact with full-time officials is more marked among secondary school representatives and less marked among ATL representatives. Over two-thirds of NUT and NASUWT secondary school representatives meet their full-time officials, nearly twice the proportion of ATL representatives. Secondary school representatives are as likely to be in touch with their outside officials as are other union representatives; the WIRS survey recorded contacts between 69 per cent of all senior non-manual representatives, and 61 per cent in the public sector (Millward *et al.* 1992: 129). The much lower figure for ATL may partly reflect the absence of local structures in this union. However, the proportion of ATL representatives reporting contact with local association officers is also significantly lower than for the other two unions, particularly for the 90 per cent of NUT secondary representatives.

Relatively low levels of contact were reported with representatives of non-teacher unions. This is not surprising, given the large differences in terms and conditions of employment between teachers and other workers. Nevertheless, it is clear that there are contacts between teacher and non-teacher activists in a significant number of secondary schools. These contacts are, however, not formalised. In our case studies we found no evidence of formalised workplace union activity in the shape of workplace committees, joint union committees, or regular workplace union meetings. It would be most unusual for these to exist in such small workplaces in any case. The WIRS survey of establishments bigger than most schools found workplace joint stewards committees and single-employer combine committees in about a third of all establishments, (Millward *et al.* 1992: 131–4). Within the highly organised system of bargaining in local authorities most inter-union activity occurs at the level of the local authority and at the level of the local authority department, rather than at the level of the small workplace. In most LEAs it is standard practice to hold regular joint teacher union meetings, and in many LEAs there are joint committees of unions including teachers and both manual and non-manual non-teacher employees.

Our evidence suggests that teacher union organisation at LEA level is highly developed, being well organised and stable. Co-operation between the main unions is variable, but generally relations are friendly; most inter-union disputes are resolved through negotiation, and open hostility is rare. The exception is the PAT, which is usually frozen out of meaningful participation in formal negotiations. In one case the NUT and the NASUWT refused to sit down with the PAT and subsequently found them sitting across the table on the management side at the negotiating committee meeting. At workplace level both NUT and NASUWT representatives take part in a range of trade union activities and participate in wide networks of workplace-based trade union contacts. ATL representatives are much less likely to take part in workplace-based activity. However, there are no formal workplace trade union structures.

Having looked at school representatives' contacts with other trade unionists we now consider in more detail their contacts with their members and with their managers. The 1990 Workplace Industrial Relations Survey recorded 76 per cent of non-manual representatives having meetings with managers (Millward *et al.* 1992: 130). In schools, 32 per cent of primary representatives and 70 per cent of secondary representatives report having such meetings (Table 6.11). Over three-quarters of NUT and NASUWT secondary school representatives reported meeting managers, but only half of their ATL counterparts were similarly active. There is a much higher degree of activity in secondary schools and among the two TUC unions.

The Keele survey reveals a considerable amount of information about the issues that were taken up by school representatives. We asked about a range of specific issues – whether members raised them never, sometimes or often, and whether the representatives then raised them with management never, sometimes or often. The main concerns of teacher union members, and the extent to which they raise them with their workplace representatives, are listed in Table 6.12. This shows a similar pattern between the two sectors, although secondary school representatives are significantly more likely to be contacted about a much broader range of issues.

ATL primary representatives report fewer contacts than the other two unions by a margin of more than 5 per cent for half of the issues listed. NASUWT and NUT primary representatives report broadly similar levels of contacts for most issues, with NUT representatives reporting higher levels more frequently. In the secondary sector the NUT and ATL show quite similar patterns of contact, while the proportion of NASUWT representatives reporting contact is significantly higher than both of the other two unions for over three-quarters of the issues listed. This may reflect NASUWT's tradition of issue-driven militancy in its secondary sector heartland. ATL representatives in the secondary sector report significantly lower levels of concern than the other two unions over salaries, workload, pensions, appraisal and stress. NASUWT representatives report significantly higher levels of concern than the other two over all issues except salaries, early retirement, pensions, appraisal, training and race discrimination.

Table 6.13 sets out the issues reported by school representatives as sometimes or often taken up with management. The differences between Tables 6.12 and 6.13 show that issues that can be resolved in the workplaces are more likely to be taken up with management. For example, while contact by members over salaries and pensions is reported by 81 per cent and 63 per cent of representatives, they are only taken up by 42 per cent and 17 per cent of representatives respectively. On the other hand, where appraisal, staffing levels and job descriptions are raised by members among 60 per cent of

Table 6.12 School representatives contacted by members about issues

Issue	*School representatives reporting contact 'sometimes' or 'often' (%)*								
	All reps (N=595)	*Primary reps (N=417)*				*Secondary reps (N=178)*			
		All	*NUT*	*NASUWT*	*ATL*	*All*	*NUT*	*NASUWT*	*ATL*
Salaries	81	80	84	85	68	82	90	85	69
Early retirement	69	59	70	51	45	86	82	87	89
Workload	66	63	61	73	55	73	69	87	58
Pensions	63	58	65	47	53	74	77	81	62
Incentive allowances	61	58	62	55	51	68	63	75	64
Health and safety	61	57	56	58	58	67	61	77	62
Appraisal	61	56	48	66	63	70	73	75	62
Staffing levels	60	56	56	64	49	67	63	75	60
Job descriptions	57	50	51	55	45	67	61	75	64
Redundancy	54	47	48	48	45	66	53	75	65
Stress	53	50	54	45	47	58	57	71	42
Working hours	48	46	43	56	42	52	45	65	40
Cover	48	34	39	36	24	71	65	79	67
Redeployment	41	39	44	38	30	46	41	53	40
Disciplinary action	34	25	26	32	18	50	41	63	40
Promotion	33	28	27	33	24	43	37	53	37
Leave of absence	33	28	31	30	18	41	37	50	33
Sickness absence	32	28	33	27	18	40	39	47	31
Temporary contracts	32	29	33	25	23	38	33	46	33
Part-time contracts	31	28	33	25	21	37	28	47	33
Maternity leave	31	23	28	23	15	44	45	50	35
Training	29	25	24	36	17	36	31	38	38
Ill-health retirement	28	23	29	25	12	36	29	49	27
Professional competence	22	19	46	15	19	28	20	37	23
Sex discrimination	20	16	18	19	8	28	29	35	17
Holidays	18	16	20	16	8	22	12	28	23
Travel allowances	16	15	19	12	9	17	6	24	20
Race discrimination	11	11	14	8	5	12	18	10	10

Table 6.13 School representatives contacting management about issues

Issue	*School representatives reporting contact 'sometimes' or 'often' (%)*								
	All reps	*Primary reps (N=417)*				*Secondary reps (N=178)*			
	(N=595)	*All*	*NUT*	*NASUWT*	*ATL*	*All*	*NUT*	*NASUWT*	*ATL*
Salaries	42	40	47	40	30	46	44	52	20
Early retirement	42	33	40	26	28	58	46	67	58
Workload	64	62	66	67	51	68	58	84	56
Pensions	17	16	20	14	12	19	22	20	14
Incentive allowances	58	56	61	58	47	61	54	73	54
Health and safety	61	58	61	57	56	66	62	70	64
Appraisal	69	67	64	73	66	72	66	77	71
Staffing levels	68	63	67	50	59	78	74	84	75
Job descriptions	70	69	69	71	69	70	58	72	79
Redundancy	46	37	35	45	34	62	56	72	56
Stress	46	43	50	39	35	51	46	64	40
Working hours	45	42	43	39	32	52	42	64	46
Cover	54	47	53	44	41	66	54	75	67
Redeployment	36	29	34	32	20	49	44	55	46
Disciplinary action	30	22	24	28	15	45	30	63	37
Promotion	40	36	38	41	29	49	46	48	52
Leave of absence	32	28	27	41	19	39	34	42	40
Sickness absence	30	28	30	33	20	33	34	38	27
Temporary contracts	25	23	29	15	19	28	20	36	27
Part-time contracts	24	22	26	18	19	28	22	30	33
Maternity leave	18	14	17	14	10	25	16	33	23
Training	51	53	49	55	27	47	38	48	54
Ill-health retirement	20	15	18	15	10	28	22	36	25
Professional competence	31	30	29	35	25	33	28	39	31
Sex discrimination	14	12	14	15	7	18	22	19	12
Holidays	15	11	12	19	3	22	18	25	21
Travel allowances	15	16	17	19	11	14	10	17	14
Race discrimination	10	10	12	12	6	9	8	8	12

representatives, they are taken up with management by 70 per cent. Table 6.13 shows that over two-thirds of school representatives raise a number of issues with management.

The distribution between unions follows the same pattern as previously, with ATL primary representatives being somewhat less active than the other two, and NASUWT secondary representatives reporting considerably more activity. There also appears to be more activity in the secondary sector than in the primary. Particularly important to note is the nature of the issues that give rise to the most activity between representatives and management – they include issues related to job security, to pay and to workload. These issues are frequently the subject of grievance and disciplinary activity, as we discussed in chapter 5, and we might expect some concern with school-based formal procedures. However, we saw earlier in this chapter that many representatives did not know whether or not their school had adopted formal procedures.

The national unions provided local representatives with model procedural agreements, and urged representatives to ensure that both LEAs and schools adopted them. Table 6.14 shows that this advice was found either helpful or very helpful in most cases. Union advice on pay policy was found helpful by 80 per cent of representatives in both sectors and in all unions, reaching 90 per cent for NUT representatives in secondary schools. Similar figures apply on the issue of appraisal. Advice on health and safety, redundancy and redeployment, discipline, grievances, equal opportunities and consultation was found helpful to a higher proportion of secondary school representatives. Advice on consultation and on facilities was found helpful by less than half of the respondents.

However, two-thirds of NASUWT representatives in secondary schools found their union's advice on both facilities and consultation helpful, compared with about two-fifths of NUT representatives. Examination of Table 6.14 shows the NASUWT's advice on many procedural issues being favourably rated by more representatives than both ATL's and NUT's, with NUT being regarded least favourably of all on a significant number of issues. This is particularly true of procedures on discipline, grievance and job security in both the primary and secondary sectors. The relatively low rating given to NUT advice by many school representatives in this union's primary sector heartland poses some urgent questions for this union.

More broadly, our survey material raises some major questions for both managers and unions in schools. The reforms have handed school budgets to school governors, giving them many of the responsibilities of employers. Heads have also been given a range of managerial responsibilities, but their power to manage has been heavily restricted by central control over the curriculum, over aggregate school budgets, over teacher performance requirements, and over salary payment systems. No consideration has been given to the implications of the reforms for industrial relations; such consideration is now urgent.

Table 6.14 School representatives' views on union advice

Procedure	*School representatives reporting union advice as 'helpful' or 'very helpful' (%)*								
	All reps (N=595)	*Primary reps (N=417)*				*Secondary reps (N=178)*			
		All	*NUT*	*NASUWT*	*ATL*	*All*	*NUT*	*NASUWT*	*ATL*
Pay policy	82	81	82	80	81	84	90	83	80
Appraisal	82	79	77	84	78	87	90	83	90
Health and safety	77	75	80	77	64	81	84	83	75
Redundancy/redeployment	76	71	65	76	75	90	88	95	84
Discipline	64	60	51	70	65	73	61	81	73
Grievances	62	59	51	73	59	68	59	75	69
Equal opportunities	57	54	57	59	46	64	67	69	55
Recruitment	50	50	45	60	50	51	33	63	53
Consultation	48	44	39	46	51	54	45	64	51
Facilities	48	47	44	56	44	51	39	67	43
Professional competence	42	43	38	48	45	39	35	47	33
Parental complaints	38	39	31	46	43	35	31	39	35
Recognition	41	39	31	45	44	46	45	50	43
Promotion	35	34	28	41	37	39	35	44	37

The teacher unions do not face hostile managers, but they do face management practices that have major implications for teachers' pay and conditions. Our analysis leads us to conclude that effective union organisation around these school-based issues involves a new role for branches. Practical support for school representatives means the development of new networks and new structures with a focus on workplace activity. In other spheres of employment the union representatives have formed both informal and formal networks, in the forms of stewards committees, working parties, task groups and so forth, with the aim of sharing information, providing support, and developing and co-ordinating local strategies. Activity of this nature will emerge spontaneously but sporadically, and the actions of the national unions will play an important part in either promoting or stifling the revitalisation of local associations. It is clear that the development of a cohort of local negotiators is necessary if the school-based issues are to be taken up effectively.

Salaries, workload, staffing levels, staffing structures and working time are issues to be settled largely at the level of the school, raising the potential for division and discrimination between teachers and for conflict between teachers and their managers. Industrial relations practice will be determined by the issues as and when they arise in the school. Outbreaks of conflict look set to be met by *ad hoc* responses rather than by well planned agreed procedures, introducing an element of unpredictability and instability into industrial relations. Our evidence suggests that when conflict does occur, as it inevitably will in many schools, then in some cases it will be resolved peacefully but by accident rather than by design. In other schools the disruption resulting from conflict will inflict lasting damage, destroying careers and casting a pall over the pupils in the classroom for years to come. We reject the managerial vision of peace and harmony in conflict-free schools through the application of HRM and TQM techniques in the pursuit of excellence. Urgent action is necessary to plan for ways of resolving the coming school-based conflicts between teachers and their employers.

CONCLUSIONS

The Keele survey data confirms that teacher trade unions are deeply embedded in schools in the 1990s as they have been for many years. They may have been denied a major role with the ending of national bargaining but, especially in the NUT and the NASUWT, local organisation remains strong. Local union organisation and activity reflects the origins and the traditions of the three main unions; NUT having the broader base of both membership and activity, NASUWT having the narrower base among career men and acting vigorously on local conditions of service issues, and ATL continuing to act mainly as a national pressure group on managerial/professional issues.

However, the main focus of local union activity is at the level of the LEA rather than the workplace. Strong bargaining relationships continue to hold between LEA officers and local union leaders, but there is little evidence of formalised union activity at school level. The three main classroom unions have found ways of working together at LEA level, with particularly the NUT and the NASUWT co-operating in their negotiating strategies in many cases. Indeed, the existence of multi-unionism may have strengthened the union teams by enabling more activists to become involved in bargaining activity. At school level, especially in primary schools, multi-unionism makes much less sense and may militate against the development of stable forms of organisation and representation.

The national union strategy of using LEAs to secure the adoption of procedures in schools has met with some success. The union organisation necessary to operationalise these procedures is only partially developed. In the schools most representatives have neither the skills nor the inclination to become negotiators. Most school representatives see themselves as teacher professionals first and as the point of contact between the union and the members second. Few see themselves as representing the members by making deals with management on their behalf. It is still the local association officer or the regional full-time official who undertakes the difficult negotiations on behalf of individual teachers facing problems at work. Furthermore, in negotiating over issues like job security it is still the case that LEA officers are likely to play a part.

School-based managers have also looked to the LEA to deal with their problems. While many of them have welcomed the LMS reforms in principle, in practice they have not welcomed the outcomes that the reforms were introduced to deliver – reduced spending in schools through cutting labour costs under the discipline of market forces. They are deeply sceptical about the value of appraisal-related pay, and they do not wish to dismiss teachers on grounds of redundancy. LEA support on issues like these continues to be highly valued, with heads relying heavily on the expertise available among LEA officers. Heads value their relationships with their staff, recognising that the interdependence between teacher professionals, both in the classroom and in the management team, is a key component of a successful school. They protect this reciprocal relationship by involving the LEA in managerial decisions that have adverse consequences for teachers in the school. Heads have always been shielded from the consequences of redundancy, disciplinary action, pay cuts and other employment issues, and they want to keep it that way.

This has resulted in the LEAs being involved in staffing issues to a much greater extent than was anticipated by many observers. Both the classroom unions and the heads have, each for their own reasons, acted so as to ensure a continuing role for the LEAs. The LEAs also retain some important residual powers; they continue to operate some core services, they hold the detailed knowledge of and expertise in the complex requirements of both education and employment law and, crucially, they are still the teachers' employers.

This chapter has provided evidence for the ways in which school managers, mainly heads, and school union representatives intend to cope with the mounting pressures caused by the emergence of the industrial relations issues discussed in chapter 5. The pattern that emerges is one in which teacher trade unions are unusually well served by membership strength and local lay activity in both schools and LEAs. This has not diminished under LMS, although the balance as between school sector and unions may be changing with the NUT regaining ground lost to ATL. Most representatives surveyed dealt with a stream of inquiries from members on the whole range of issues in schools, and most continued to deal with them through a mixture of informal discussions in schools and formal advice seeking and negotiation outside the school with LEA officers and union officials and/or local association officers.

The heads also had overwhelmingly adopted a cautious and pragmatic approach to the emergence of new and potentially damaging issues in their schools. Hence most still sought LEA advice and adopted LEA procedures with some notion that this should be checked out with their own unions. The majority saw the classroom unions as an extension of their staff and wanted them to be there to co-operate with the day to day problems of school management while recognising their rights to independent representation and the more serious and urgent nature of the problems they now face. In other words the teachers in the schools were getting on with the job of educating their pupils within their resources and with every attempt to avoid disruption. Of course the test of any system is not so much with the application of the routine but with the definition of the crisis.

The evidence points to an increase in the oppressive behaviour of some heads, and sometimes other teachers, towards those staff perceived as possible targets for removal from the school. This is mainly an unwilling activity as the pressures build up, but for some heads it may be seen as a chance to enforce long cherished aims of forcing out certain colleagues. Whatever the personal reasons, the new market place requires heads to be tougher, not fairer, in this respect. The withering away of the LEA–local association brokerage system of conflict avoidance, despite the best intentions of the parties, may result in more individual cases going to industrial tribunals, and more collective disputes remaining unresolved waiting to erupt into walk-outs.

7 Conclusions

We have used traditional industrial relations analysis to try to make some sense of the impact of the LMS reforms on maintained schools. We have emphasised the key role played by the system for the determination of wages and conditions of service for school teachers, and the central aspect now played by teacher performance in the regulated market invented by government. This demonstrates continuity with historical discussions about the nature of job regulation, and with the importance of fairness in the determination of a national rate for the job for teachers. The fear raised by Routh (1980), discussed in chapter 1, is that when national pay setting based on fairness is abandoned then the result will almost certainly be managerially determined 'rough justice'. What is particularly important in schools is that the decisions on pay, conditions of service and other staffing issues were traditionally taken away from the level of school management. Any resultant conflict was resolved at the level of the LEA. One of our main concerns has been to demonstrate that as the national system collapses and the LEAs are squeezed so the mechanisms for resolving conflict will disappear, leaving a dangerous vacuum at the heart of the institutional arrangements in school industrial relations.

We have raised a number of questions about the ability of an LEA-based system to deal with school-based industrial relations issues. The combination of recession and market mechanisms have implications for teachers that become apparent through the decisions of school-based managers. These managers face an urgent imperative to maintain the school's share of the market for pupils, and to be seen to protect quality standards while cutting costs to stay within dwindling budgets. The assertion of control over teacher performance at work has become a crucial management concern. This is reflected in the staff rooms, with teacher workload, staffing levels, staffing structures, and job content becoming the main workplace concerns of classroom teachers. A survey carried out for AMMA, NAHT and SHA concluded that 'conditions of work and pressure are as important as financial reward in improving the morale of the profession' (Varlaam *et al.* 1992: 47). The boycott of compulsory tests by all three classroom unions in 1993 also showed the importance of the workload issue as a source of conflict.

Furthermore, there are other additional sources of conflict that are generated by the reforms; the requirement to review each teacher's pay annually, regular appraisals, recruitment practices, disciplinary action and dismissals, to itemise a few that are new issues at the level of the school. Without the protection of LEA-level negotiations, and with no school-level substitute, it is not clear how disputes arising from these issues will be resolved.

Our conclusion is that school-level disputes about management decisions are bound to increase, both in number and in intensity, as the issues of teacher pay and teacher performance become school-level issues. The loss of the LEA-based system leaves heads dependent on finding school-based solutions to potential conflicts. Heads have never seen themselves as business managers. Even if they now see themselves as the chief executives of their schools, especially in the cases of large secondary schools with multi-million pound budgets, the reality is that most of them do not have either the experience or the inclination to become business managers. They still see themselves first and foremost as the heads of institutions devoted to the education of pupils – as head teachers, and as first among equals rather than as 'the management'. As the progress of the reform process deepens then more and more heads will find themselves making difficult, budget-driven managerial judgements that have more to do with business criteria than with educational ones. There are not the resources to support heads in such a system. Moreover, heads are not skilled in collective bargaining, and it is not easy to see how heads could set about establishing effective negotiating relationships with local union leaders. The weakening of the LEA role in dealing with bargaining issues has resulted in a managerial vacuum.

In the absence of strategic planning, heads are turning to human resource management techniques in their attempts to shape teacher commitment to the market-driven goals of the LMS school. We have argued in chapter 4 that such an approach, resting on a set of management-oriented unitarist assumptions, will not guarantee peace in schools. Indeed when workplace conflict does erupt then this approach contains no means to resolve it, as one of the central assumptions is that conflict is irrational. Even under the traditional LEA-based system some conflicts about control in schools were very bitter and protracted affairs. The rhetoric of HRM provides shelter for managers confronted with crisis, offering visions of a bright future if they only follow the leadership of the latest best-selling management guru. Our analysis is that the recession and reform combination makes workplace conflict inevitable, even with the best managerial will in the world. School managers are being driven to act as if they are managing businesses, seeking to extract maximum performance from staff at minimum cost. The new school-based issues discussed in chapter 5 are emerging to affect all schools, increasing greatly the scope for potential conflict.

What we are left with is a very uncertain future. Traditional collective bargaining has played an important role in stabilising industrial relations in schools and, although it has been weakened, LEA-level bargaining continues to resolve many of the difficulties faced by school managers. However, its continued existence looks precarious, coming under threat from two government-driven initiatives. First is the further extension of budget delegation which may result in the collapse of central services such as personnel and staffing sections. Surviving personnel departments will operate on a consultancy basis, transforming the predictable bureaucratic relationship between school and LEA into a contractual one based on service-level agreements. The full consequences of this are not obvious, but they are likely to include a few governing bodies deciding to make budget savings by not renewing contracts (and schools that need to make budget savings are the ones that are most likely to need personnel support), disputes between school managers and LEAs about the terms of the contract and its performance, and disruption to the role of the LEA as broker between school managers, individual teachers and the teacher unions. The second threat to LEA-level bargaining lies in the abolition of many LEAs and the creation of new ones. The review of local government, with the introduction of smaller unitary authorities, may break up the strong bargaining relationships that exist in the large counties. The responses of the teacher and head teacher organisations have a central importance in determining the outcomes of these developments.

The smooth operation of Burnham for over half a century, under the dominance of the NUT, vindicated Clay's view that for most of the time the Whitley system would contain conflict while assuring fairness through representation in collective bargaining. The long crisis of the Burnham system detailed in chapter 2 created widespread disillusionment with national collective bargaining and government interference, helping to forge the attitudes to pay setting and school management freedoms that became so important in the 1990s. The abolition of national pay bargaining left the national unions without a clear role, having a particularly severe impact on the NUT. The concept of the rate for the job has been subjected to a concerted attack, with the introduction of market and appraisal-related supplements. Further inequalities are likely to be opened up as the reform process gathers momentum, between primary and secondary sectors, between full- and part-time employees, and between women and men teachers. The loss of the rate for the job will represent a major setback for the majority of classroom teachers. A few teachers in managerial positions will benefit from the introduction of a more or less codified hierarchy of teacher managers, teachers essential to the core business, and teachers involved in peripheral work. The establishment of pay differentials between teachers breaches the fundamental principle of the rate for the job. A divided and fragmented profession will be in a poor position to resist the managerial offensive.

However, at the national level there is little evidence of strategic development among the unions. ATL has no experience of organising local collective action around traditional trade union concerns. Professionalism is the sole organising principle for this union. The former teachers and education officers drafted in as their case-workers will provide individual members with support in the form of advice and advocacy, but there is no intention that these semi-detached officials will play any role in organising collective action to establish workplace rights for teachers. Branch officials have little experience of either national or local campaigning activity in support of collective bargaining.

The NASUWT's steady growth is continuing, although showing signs of slowing, and its tradition of workplace-based militancy is likely to continue to be attractive to teachers looking for a clear policy of resistance to managerialism. Furthermore, the NASUWT's apparent lack of internal dissent indicates a degree of unity not present in the NUT. This unity stems from a range of factors. First and foremost is the absence of a democratic tradition, an absence which can be traced back to the union's origin as a breakaway movement. Unity is aided by a highly centralised command structure and by the union's sharp organisational focus around a narrow range of concerns. Its traditional sectional concern with differentials, now under the banner of 'collegiality', leads to a narrow and exclusive focus on pay and conditions for 'career' teachers, mainly in secondary schools, and to opportunist policy reversals typified by its switch from support for free collective bargaining to support for pay review. Sectionalism and opportunism do not amount to a strategy sufficient to destabilise the DFE's hegemonic position.

For the NUT the picture is one of long-term decline which may at last be about to end. The defeat of 1985 had a profound impact on the union, leaving it bitterly divided. Abolition of collective bargaining over pay created a vacuum that affected the NUT more than the other two unions, removing its ability to act around the rate for the job. Defending the basic rate of pay has been the NUT's key organising principle, and the continuing existence of the Review Body has prevented the development of a campaigning focus. The grouping that has gained ascendancy within the union has become a prisoner of its own success in suppressing the divisive ultra-left in the 1980s. In breaking up the ultra-left the leadership has become over-cautious, abandoning militancy over pay and conditions and reflecting the wider move towards 'new realism' in the aftermath of successive defeats of several large strikes. Instead it has turned to professionalism, aiming to influence education policy through building school-level alliances between teachers, parents and governors (Barber 1992a and 1992b). Under this leadership the union has seen declining membership for the last nine years.

More recently the debate within the NUT has become sharper again, and the conservatism of the last few years is giving way in places to a stronger reaction to the LMS issues. This may gather momentum with the more rigid application of appraisal and the introduction of performance-related pay. These are the conditions for the re-emergence of strong trade unionism within the union, generating opportunities for the NUT to give national leadership to both national and local campaigns.

We have argued that, as in the American system, collective bargaining has been a stabilising component of the school system in England and Wales. Collective bargaining is itself an outcome of union pressure – it only takes hold where union activity is sufficient to ensure both its establishment and its continuation. The teacher unions do not appear to have grasped the significance of this point. A replacement for LEA-level bargaining will only be established as a result of local union pressure, and there is no evidence of any national strategy to secure such local bargaining. The way forward for the unions, especially the NUT, is to restate their commitment to collective bargaining around a fair national rate for the job – the Webbs' analysis is still relevant in the 1990s. The upheaval of the school system, induced by recession and reform, is generating forces that are dividing the teaching profession. A strong platform for teacher unity around the standard rate for the job, coupled with successful representation and negotiation at school and LEA levels, would directly address the concerns of the classroom teachers.

Turning to the level of the school, we argue that management concern with teacher performance means that struggle over the classroom labour process is a key issue for local teacher trade unionists. We have seen in chapter 3 that the unions have taken some steps to strengthen their local structures and to divert resources into providing support at regional level. While there is evidence of strong and active union branches, particularly among the NUT and NASUWT local associations, these are focused primarily at the level of the LEA. Chapter 6 showed that there is little evidence of school-based union structures emerging and, given the small size of most schools, it is difficult to see how stable units of workplace organisation could be sustained over the longer term. Nevertheless, it is certain that local activists will devote their considerable energies towards setting up school-based support networks, and the impact of such initiatives in generating workplace power should not be under-estimated. On the other hand, the continuing existence of multi-unionism presents real difficulties in building workplace organisation.

There have been many teacher union successes, not least the continued recruitment and retention of nearly all teachers into union membership in spite of the enormous pressure. However, in the absence of national trade union militancy there are few grounds for optimism at present. The government has a policy of saving money, but has no national strategy on teachers' pay. Teachers pursuing their professional jobs are going to come into conflict with heads seeking to implement cuts in unit labour costs. Such conflict takes on special meaning and form when it occurs within the state education system because of the special features of that system: high levels of union membership, small size of employing unit, senior managers sharing a profession with most of those managed, and the nature of the service itself – the education of the majority of the country's children. As the conflict avoidance and resolution mechanisms wither away, then the consequences for teachers and their pupils will be very serious.

The reformed education system is crisis-prone, generating conflict that will surface in schools in a random and unpredictable fashion. The spirit of co-operation is very strong in the school environment, but the market system favours individuality above the collective. Sooner or later most school managers will be faced with issues that can tear schools apart.

Bibliography

ACAS (1977) *Code of Practice 1: Disciplinary Practice and Procedures in Employment*, London: ACAS.

ACAS (1983) *Collective Bargaining in Britain: Its Extent and Level*, London: ACAS.

ACAS (1985) *Introduction to Payment Systems*, Advisory Booklet 2, London: ACAS.

ACAS (1987a) *Labour Flexibility in Britain*, Occasional Paper 41, London: ACAS.

ACAS (1987b) *Discipline at Work: the ACAS Advisory Handbook*, London: ACAS.

ACAS (1988) *Employee Appraisal*, Advisory Booklet 11, London: ACAS.

ACAS (1989a) *Job Evaluation*, Advisory Booklet 1, London: ACAS.

ACAS (1989b) *Redundancy Handling*, Advisory Booklet 12, London: ACAS.

ACAS (1990) *Employment Handbook*, London: ACAS.

ACAS (1991) *Code of Practice 3: Time Off for Trade Union Duties and Activities*, London: ACAS.

ACAS (1992) *Motivating and Rewarding Employees*, Occasional Paper 51, London: ACAS.

Adam, R. (1982) 'The future of teachers' unions', *Comparative Education*, vol. 18(2).

AEC (1963) *The Burnham Story*, London: Councils and Education Press.

AGIT-LDBS (1991) *Teachers' Salaries*, London: AGIT-LDBS

Allen, V. (1966) *Militant Trade Unionism*, London: The Merlin Press.

AMA (1961) *Seventy Years of Progress*, London: AMA.

AMA (1974) *The Assistant Masters' Salary Memorandum to the Houghton Committee of Inquiry*, London: AMA.

AMMA (1989) *Teacher Appraisal*, London: AMMA.

Apple, M. (1988) 'Work, class and teaching', in J. Ozga (ed.) *Schoolwork: Approaches to the Labour Process of Teaching*, Milton Keynes: Open University Press.

Armstrong, M. (1991) *A Handbook of Personnel Management Practice*, fourth edition, London: Kogan Page.

Armstrong, M. and Murlis, H. (1988) *Reward Management*, London: Kogan Page.

ATL (1993) 'Performance-related pay', *Report* (journal of ATL), January.

Bach, S. and Winchester, D. (1994) 'Opting out of pay devolution? The prospects for local pay bargaining in the public services', *British Journal of Industrial Relations*, vol. 32(2).

Bagwell, P. (1963) *The Railwaymen: the History of the National Union of Railwaymen*, London: George Allen & Unwin.

Bailey, R. (1994) 'British public sector industrial relations', *British Journal of Industrial Relations*, vol. 32(1).

Bailey, R. and Trinder, C. (1989) *Under Attack? Public Service Pay Over Two Decades*, London: Public Finance Foundation.

Bain, G. (1970) *The Growth of White-Collar Unionism*, Oxford: Clarendon Press.

Bain, G. (ed.) (1983) *Industrial Relations in Britain*, Oxford: Blackwell.

Bain, G. and Price, R. (1980) *Profiles of Union Growth*, Oxford: Blackwell.

Ball, S. (1987) *The Micro-Politics of the School*, London: Routledge.

Ball, S. (1993) 'Education policy, power relations and teachers' work', *British Journal of Educational Studies*, vol. 41(2).

Banfield, J. and Fearn, E. (1987) 'Nine by two: guidelines for job applicants and for selectors in schools and similar education organisations', *School Organisation*, vol. 7.

Barber, M. (1992a) *Education and the Teacher Unions*, London: Cassell.

Barber, M. (1992b) 'A union of interests', *Managing Schools Today*, vol. 1(7).

Baron, G. (1954) 'The teachers' registration movement', *British Journal of Educational Studies*, vol. 2(2).

Batstone, E., Boraston, I. and Frenkel, S. (1977) *Shop Stewards in Action*, Oxford: Blackwell.

Beare, H., Caldwell, B. and Millikan, R. (1989) *Creating an Excellent School*, London: Routledge.

Beatson, M. and Butcher, S. (1993) 'Union density across the employed workforce', *Employment Gazette*, January.

Beeton, D. (1989) 'How pay is determined in public services: some recent research evidence', in D. Beeton (ed.) *Trends in Public Service Pay*, London: Public Finance Foundation.

Bland, S. (1994) 'An investigation of the methods used to select primary school headteachers and deputy headteachers', unpublished MBA thesis, Keele University.

Blyton, P. and Turnbull, P. (eds) (1992) *Reassessing Human Resource Management*, London: Sage.

Blyton, P. and Turnbull, P. (1992) 'HRM: Debates, dilemmas and contradictions', in P. Blyton and P. Turnbull (eds) *Reassessing Human Resource Management*, London: Sage.

Bondi, L. (1989) 'Selecting schools for closure: theory and practice in "rational" planning', *Journal of Educational Policy*, vol. 4(2).

Braverman, H. (1974) *Labor and Monopoly Capital*, New York: Monthly Review Press.

Brown, A. (1985) *The Trials of Honeyford*, London: Centre for Policy Studies.

Brown, W. (1989) 'Managing remuneration', in K. Sisson (ed.) *Personnel Management in Britain*, Oxford: Basil Blackwell.

Brown, W., Ebsworth, R. and Terry, M. (1978) 'Factors shaping shop steward organisation in Britain', *British Journal of Industrial Relations*, vol. 16 (2).

Brown, W. and Rowthorn, R. (1990) *A Public Services Pay Policy*, London: Fabian Society Tract 542.

Bryant, R. and Leicester, C. (1991) *The Professional Association of Teachers: the Early Years*, London: Buckland Publications.

Buras-Stubbs, M. (1994) 'Teacher appraisal: development or control?', unpublished MBA thesis, Keele University.

Burchill, F. (1992) *Labour Relations*, London: Macmillan.

Burchill, F. and Seifert, R. (1993) 'Professional unions in the NHS', paper to the University of Wales College of Cardiff Employment Research Unit conference.

Burke, V. (1971) *Teachers in Turmoil*, Harmondsworth: Penguin.

Burnham Management Panel (1984) *Management Panel Submission to the Arbitral Body on Teachers' Pay from 1st April 1984*, London: Management Panel.

Burnham Teachers' Panel (1984) *The Teachers' Panel Submission to the Board of Arbitration on the Salaries of Teachers from 1 April 1984*, London: Teachers' Panel.

Cambridgeshire County Council (1991) *Education Personnel Management*, Essex: Longman.

Cannell, M. and Long, P. (1991) 'What's changed about incentive pay', *Personnel Management*, October 1991.

Carlson, D. (1987) 'Teachers as political actors: from reproductive theory to the crisis of schooling', *Harvard Educational Review*, vol. 57(3).

Carpenter, M. (1988) *Working for Health: the History of COHSE*, London: Lawrence & Wishart.

Casey, B., Lakey, J. and White, M. (1992) *Payment Systems: a Look at Current Practice*, Sheffield: Policy Studies Institute for the Employment Department.

Chapman, S. (1990) *116 Not Out*, Leicester: SHA.

Chitty, C. and Simon, B. (1993) *Education Answers Back: Critical Responses to Government Policy*, London: Lawrence & Wishart.

Citizen's Charter (1991) Cm 1599, London: HMSO.

Clay, H. (1929) *The Problem of Industrial Relations*, London: Macmillan.

Clegg, H. (1971) *How to Run an Incomes Policy and Why We Made Such a Mess of the Last One*, London: Heinemann.

Clegg, H. (1972) *The System of Industrial Relations in Great Britain*, Oxford: Blackwell.

Clegg, H. (1979) *The Changing System of Industrial Relations in Great Britain*, Oxford: Blackwell.

Clegg, H. (1980) *Standing Commission on Pay Comparability*, Cmnd 7880, London: HMSO.

Coates, R. (1972a) 'The teachers' associations and the restructuring of Burnham', *British Journal of Educational Studies*, vol. 22.

Coates, R. (1972b) *Teachers' Unions and Interest Group Politics*, Cambridge: Cambridge University Press.

Cohen, G. (1988) *History, Labour and Freedom*, Oxford: Clarendon Press.

Cole, S. (1969) *The Unionization of Teachers*, New York: Praeger.

Conway, F. (1962) 'School teachers' salaries 1945–1959', *Manchester School of Economic and Social Studies*, vol. 30(2).

Conway, F. (1967) 'Salary indices for school teachers', *Manchester School of Economic and Social Studies*, vol. 35(1).

Cooper, M. and Goodier, J. (1989) 'Changing the climate: self-appraisal', *Teacher*, February.

Curson, C. (1983) 'Thoughts on contract of employment and collective agreements', *Education*, September.

Cuttance, P. (1985) 'Methodological issues in the statistical analysis of data on the effectiveness of schooling', *British Educational Research Journal*, vol. 11(2).

Daniel, W. and Millward, N. (1983) *Workplace Industrial Relations in Britain*, London: Heinemann.

Dash, J. (1969) *Good Morning Brothers!*, London: Lawrence & Wishart.

Demaine, J. (1993) 'The new right and the self-managing school', in J. Smyth (ed.) *A Socially Critical View of the Self-Managing School*, London: Falmer Press.

DES (1983) *Scales of Salaries for Teachers: Primary and Secondary Education, England and Wales*, London: HMSO.

DES (1989) *School teacher Appraisal: a National Framework*, London: HMSO.

DES (1990) *Projecting the Supply and Demand for Teachers*, London: HMSO.

DES (1991) *LMS: Further Guidance*, Circular 7/91, London: DES.

Dennison, W. (1979) 'Teachers and shrinking schools', *The Durham and Newcastle Research Review*, vol. 9 (43).

Dennison, W. (1980) 'Falling rolls and Burnham alternatives', *Secondary Education Journal*, vol. 10(1).

DFE (1992a) *Choice and Diversity: a New Framework for Schools*, Cm 2021, London: HMSO.

DFE (1992b) *Written Evidence from the Department for Education to the School Teachers' Review Body*, London: DFE.

Donovan (1968) *Report of the Royal Commission on Trade Unions and Employers' Associations 1965–1968*, Cmnd 3623, London: HMSO.

Downes, P. (1992) 'Just reward', *Managing Schools Today*, vol. 2(3).

Downes, P. (1993a) 'A teensy bit of hope', *Managing Schools Today*, vol. 2(6).

Downes, P. (1993b) 'Where's the incentive', *Managing Schools Today*, vol. 2(8).

Drucker, P. (1989a) 'The spirit of performance', in C. Riches and C. Morgan (eds) *Human Resource Management in Education*, Milton Keynes: Open University Press.

Drucker, P. (1989b) 'Why service institutions do not perform', in C. Riches and C. Morgan (eds) *Human Resource Management in Education*, Milton Keynes: Open University Press.

Durcan, J., McCarthy, W. and Redman, G. (1983) *Strikes in Post-War Britain*, London: George Allen & Unwin.

Education, Science and Arts Committee (1990) *Second Report*, London: HMSO.

Edwards, B. (1974) *The Burston School Strike*, London: Lawrence & Wishart.

Edwards, P. (1992) 'Industrial conflict: themes and issues in recent research', *British Journal of Industrial Relations*, vol. 30(3).

Evetts, J. (1991) 'The experience of secondary headship selection: continuity and change', *Education Studies*, vol. 17(3).

Fidler, B. (1989) 'Staff appraisal – theory, concepts and experience in other organizations and problems of adaptation to education', in C. Riches and C. Morgan (eds) *Human Resource Management in Education*, Milton Keynes: Open University Press.

Flanders, A. (1965) *Industrial Relations: What Is Wrong with the System?*, London: Faber.

Fletcher, C. (1993) 'Appraisal: an idea whose time has gone?', *Personnel Management*, September.

Fletcher, C. and Williams, R. (1992) 'The route to performance management', *Personnel Management*, October 1992.

Foot, M. (1973) *Aneurin Bevan vol. 2 1945–1960*, London: Davis-Poynter.

Fox, A. (1966) *Industrial Sociology and Industrial Relations*, Research Paper 3, Donovan Commission, London: HMSO.

Fox, A. (1974) *Man Mismanagement*, London: Hutchinson.

Fredman, S. and Morris, G. (1987) 'The teachers' lesson: collective bargaining and the courts', *Industrial Law Journal*, vol. 16(4).

Fredman, S. and Morris, G. (1989) *The State as Employer*, London: Mansell.

Gibberd, K. (1967) 'Teachers in revolt', *The Statesman*, 21 July.

GMB (1991) *Local Management of Schools: a New Threat to Jobs?*, London: GMB/Apex.

Gomberg, W. (1948) *A Trade Union Analysis of Time Study*, New York: Prentice Hall.

Goodrich, C. (1920) *The Frontier of Control*, London: G. Bell and Sons.

Gosden, P. (1972) *The Evolution of a Profession*, Oxford: Basil Blackwell.

Gramsci, A. (1920) *Selections from the Prison Notebooks*, 1970 edn, London: Lawrence & Wishart.

Greenhalgh, V. (1968) 'The movement of teachers' salaries 1920–1968', *Journal of Educational Administration and History*, vol. 1(1).

Greenwood, A. (1923) 'Education', *The New Leader*, 8 June.

Griffiths, T. (1970) *The Teachers' Strike*, London: NUT.

Griffiths, W. (1993) 'A leaner, fitter future for HR?', *Personnel Management*, October 1993.

Guest, D. (1991) 'Personnel management: the end of orthodoxy?', *British Journal of Industrial Relations*, vol. 29(2).

Hakim, C. (1990) 'Core and periphery in employers' workforce strategies: evidence from the 1987 ELUS survey', *Work, Employment and Society*, vol. 4(2).

Hammer, E. (1953) *Teachers' Salaries*, Washington DC: World Organisation of the Teaching Profession.

Hannington, W. (1937) *The Problem of the Distressed Areas*, London: Victor Gollancz.

Harris, N. (1990) *The Law Relating to Schools*, London: Fourmatt Publishing.

Harris, N. (1992) *The Legal Context of Teaching*, Essex: Longman.

Hastings, O. (1978) *In Retrospect or Reminiscence*, London: AAM.

Hayek, F. (1984) *1980s Unemployment and the Unions*, London: Institute of Economic Affairs.

Heywood, J. (1992) 'School teacher appraisal', in H. Tomlinson (ed.) *Performance-Related Pay in Education*, London: Routledge.

HMI (1992) *The Implementation of Local Management of Schools: a Report by HM Inspectorate 1989–92*, London: HMSO.

Horn, C. and Horn, P. (1979) 'Aspects of the development of teacher trade unionism in Britain 1860–1919', *Journal of Further and Higher Education*, vol. 3(2).

Houghton, D. (1974) *Report of the Committee of Inquiry into the Pay of non-University Teachers*, Cmnd 5848, London: HMSO.

Hughes, J. (1967) *Trade Union Structure and Government*, Research Paper 5(1), Donovan Commission, London: HMSO.

Hughes, J. (1980) 'Repeat Performance: Clegg and Houghton', *Times Educational Supplement*, 2 May, page 4.

Hughes, J. (1985) *Education: Investment or Impoverishment?*, London: NUT.

Hume, C. (1990) *Grievance and Discipline in Schools*, Harlow: Longman.

Hyman, R. (1972) *Disputes Procedure in Action*, London: Heinemann Educational Books.

Hyman, R. (1975) *Industrial Relations: a Marxist Introduction*, London: Macmillan.

Hyman, R. (1989) *Strikes*, London: Macmillan.

Incomes Data Service (1994) *Pay in the Public Services*, London: IDS.

Interim Advisory Committee (1988) *Report on School Teachers' Pay and Conditions*, Cm 363, London: HMSO.

Interim Advisory Committee (1989) *Second Report on School Teachers' Pay and Conditions*, Cm 625, London: HMSO.

Interim Advisory Committee (1990) *Third Report on School Teachers' Pay and Conditions*, Cm 973, London: HMSO.

Interim Advisory Committee (1991) *Fourth Report on School Teachers' Pay and Conditions*, Cm 1415, London: HMSO.

International Labour Organisation (1967) *Examination of Grievances*, Recommendation, no. 130, Geneva: ILO.

Ironside, M., Seifert, R. and Sinclair, J. (1993) 'Change in the teachers' unions', paper to University of Wales College of Cardiff Employment Research Unit Conference.

IRS (1994) 'Union derecognition and personal contracts', *Industrial Relations Review and Report*, 553.

James, C. and Newman, J. (1985) 'Staff appraisal schemes in comprehensive schools', *Educational Management and Administration*, vol. 13.

Jesson, D., Mayston, D. and Smith, P. (1987) 'Performance assessment in the education sector: educational and economic perspectives', *Oxford Review of Education*, vol. 13(3).

Johnson, S. (1980) 'Performance-based staff layoffs in the public schools: implementation and outcomes', *Harvard Educational Review*, vol. 50(2).

Johnson, S. (1983) 'Teacher unions in schools: authority and accommodation', *Harvard Educational Review*, vol. 53(8).

Johnson, S. (1984a) *Teacher Unions in Schools*, Philadelphia: Temple University Press.

Johnson, S. (1984b) 'Merit pay for teachers: a poor prescription for reform', *Harvard Educational Review*, vol. 54(2).

Joseph, K. (1984) 'Catastrophe or watershed?', *Oxford Review of Education* vol. 10(2).

Kelly, J. (1988) *Trade Unions and Socialist Politics*, London: Verso.

Kerchner, C. and Mitchell, D. (1988) *The Changing Idea of a Teachers' Union*, Lewes: Falmer Press

Labour Research Department (1991) *Women in Trade Unions*, London: LRD.

LACSAB (1990) *Performance Related Pay in Practice: a Survey of Local Government*, London: LACSAB.

Lambert K. (1982) 'Micropolitics, industrial relations and the school', *Education Management and Administration*, vol. 10.

Latta, G. (1969) 'The NAS: historical analysis', unpublished MA thesis, University of Warwick.

Lawrence, I. (1992) *Power and Politics at the Department of Education and Science*, London: Cassell.

Lawton, D. (1988) 'Teacher education', in M. Morris and C. Griggs (eds) *Education – the Wasted Years: 1973–1986*, Brighton: Falmer Press.

Lenin, V. (1902) *What Is to Be Done?*, 1963 edition, Oxford: Oxford University Press.

Luxemburg, R. (1906) 'The mass strike, the political party and the trade unions', in *Rosa Luxemburg Speaks*, 1970 edn, New York: Pathfinder Press.

Lyons, G. and Stenning, R. (1986) *Managing Staff in Schools*, London: Hutchinson.

Lyons, G. and Stenning, R. (1987) 'Some legal aspects of employment in schools' in A. Hoyle and A. McMahon (eds) *World Year Book of Education*, London: Longman.

Management Panel (1984) *Submission to the Arbitral Body on Teachers' Pay from 1st April 1984*, London: Burnham Primary and Secondary Committee.

Manzer, R. (1970) *Teachers and Politics*, Manchester: Manchester University Press.

Marchington, M. (1987) 'A review and critique of research on developments in joint consultation', *British Journal of Industrial Relations*, vol. 25(3).

Margerison, C. and Elliot, C. (1970) 'A predictive study of the development in teacher militancy', *British Journal of Industrial Relations*, vol. 8(3).

Marland, M. (1986) 'Appraisal and evaluation: chimera, fantasy, or practicality?', *Educational Management and Administration*, vol. 14.

Marsden, D. and Richardson, R. (1991) *Does Pay Motivate? A Study of the Inland Revenue Staff*, London: London School of Economics.

Marsden, D. and Richardson, R. (1994) 'Performing for pay? The effects of "merit pay" on motivation in a public servce', *British Journal of Industrial Relations*, vol. 32(2).

Marx, K. (1887) *Capital: A Critical Analysis of Capitalist Production*, London: Swan Sonnenschein, Lowrey and Co.

McCarthy, W. (1966) *The Role of Shop Stewards in British Industrial Relations*, Research Paper 1, Donovan Commission, London: HMSO.

McCarthy, W. and Parker, S. (1968) *Shop Stewards and Workshop Relations*, Research Paper 10 for the Royal Commission on Trade Unions and Employers' Associations, London: HMSO.

Megaw, J. (1982) *Report of an Inquiry into Civil Service Pay*, Cmnd 8590, London: HMSO.

Millward, N. and Stevens, M. (1986) *British Workplace Industrial Relations 1980–1984*, Aldershot: Gower.

Millward, N., Stevens, M., Smart, D. and Hawes, W. (1992) *Workplace Industrial Relations in Transition*, Aldershot: Dartmouth.

Moser, C. (1993) 'New deal', *Times Educational Supplement*, 12 November 1993.

Morris, G. and Rydzkowski, S. (1984) 'Anatomy of a dispute', *Health and Social Services Journal*, 12 April.

Morris, M. (1978) 'Teachers in action against unemployment', *Labour Monthly*, March.

Napier, B. (1993) *CCT, Market Testing and Employment Rights: the Effects of TUPE and the Acquired Rights Directive*, London: Institute of Employment Rights.

NAS (1974) 'Commission of inquiry into teachers' salaries', *The New Schoolmaster*, September.

NASUWT (1992a) *LMS: a Guide for Governors*, Birmingham: NASUWT.

NASUWT (1992b) *Coping with Appraisal*, Birmingham: NASUWT.

NUT (1931) *The Union and the Crisis*, London: NUT.

NUT (1972) *The Origin and Work of the Burnham Committee*, London: NUT.

NUT (1974) *NUT Submission to the Houghton Committee*, London: NUT.

NUT (1979a) *Teachers' Pay: the Fight For Houghton*, London: NUT.

NUT (1979b) *Submission to the Clegg Commission on Pay Comparability*, London: NUT.

Ozga, J. and Lawn, M. (1981) *Teachers, Professionalism and Class*, Lewes: Falmer Press.

Page Arnot, R. (1955) *A History of the Scottish Miners*, London: George Allen & Unwin.

Page Arnot, R. (1979) *The Miners: One Union, One Industry*, London: George Allen & Unwin.

PAT (1994) *Members' Handbook*, Derby: PAT.

Peters, T. and Waterman, R. (1983) *In Search of Excellence: Lessons from America's Best Run Companies*, New York: Harper & Row.

Phelps Brown, H. (1977) *The Inequality of Pay*, Oxford: Oxford University Press.

Price, M. and Glenday, N. (1974) *Reluctant Revolutionaries: a Century of Head Mistresses 1874–1974*, London: Pitman.

Price, P. (1970) 'The teachers' strike', *Trade Union Register*.

Priestley, R. (1955) *Royal Commission on the Civil Service*, Cmd 9613, London: HMSO.

Purcell, J. and Ahlstrand, B. (1994) *Human Resource Management in the Multi-Divisional Company*, Oxford: Oxford University Press.

Purcell, J. and Sisson, K. (1983) 'Strategies and practice in the management of industrial relations', in Bain, G. (ed.).

Reid, K. (1983) 'The management of decline: a discussion paper', *School Organisation*, vol. 3(4).

Reilly, R. and Chao, G. (1982) 'Validity and fairness of some alternative employee selection procedures', *Personnel Psychology*, vol. 35.

Report of six teacher organisations (1992) *Appraisal*, London: AMMA, NAHT, NASUWT, NUT, PAT, SHA.

Reynolds, D. (1987) 'Teacher appraisal and development: a review of the key issues', *School Organization*, vol. 7(2).

Riches, C. and Morgan, C. (eds) (1989) *Human Resource Management in Education*, Milton Keynes: Open University Press.

Robertson, I. and Makin, P. (1986) 'Management selection in Britain: a survey and critique', *Journal of Occupational Psychology*, vol. 59.

Routh, G. (1980) *Occupation and Pay in Great Britain 1906–1979*, London: Macmillan.

Roy, W. (1968) *The Teachers' Union: Aspects of Policy and Organisation in the NUT 1950–1966*, London: Schoolmaster Publishing Company.

Saran, R. (1985) *The Politics Behind Burnham*, Sheffield: Sheffield Papers in Education Management no, 45, Sheffield City Polytechnic.

Saran, R. (1989) 'The new teacher contract: changing power relations', *Educational Management and Administration*, vol. 17.

School Teachers' Review Body (1992) *First Report*, Cm 1806, London: HMSO.

School Teachers' Review Body (1993) *Second Report*, Cm 2151, London: HMSO.

School Teachers' Review Body (1994) *Third Report*, Cm 2466, London: HMSO.

Seifert, R. (1984) 'Some aspects of factional opposition: Rank and File and the NUT 1967–1982', *British Journal of Industrial Relations*, vol. 22 (3).

Seifert, R. (1987) *Teacher Militancy: A History of Teacher Strikes 1896–1987*, Lewes: Falmer Press.

Seifert, R. (1989) 'Industrial relations in the school sector', in R. Mailly, S. Dimmock and A. Sethi (eds) *Industrial Relations in the Public Services*, London: Routledge.

Seifert, R. (1990) 'Prognosis for local bargaining in health and education', *Personnel Management*, June 1990.

Seifert, R. (1991a) 'The conflict potential', *Managing Schools Today*, vol. 1(1).

Seifert, R. (1991b) 'Managing the conflict', *Managing Schools Today*, vol. 1(2).

Seifert, R. (1992a) 'Changing role of union reps', *Managing Schools Today*, vol. 1(6).

Seifert, R. (1992b) *Industrial Relations in the NHS*, London: Chapman and Hall.

Seifert, R. and Ironside, M. (1993), 'Industrial relations in state schools', in G. White (ed.) *Public Sector Industrial Relations in the 1990s*, University of Greenwich Business Paper no. 19.

SHA (1993) *Members' Yearbook 1993–4*, Leicester: SHA.

Sigurjonsson, K. (1976) 'Teachers and the Labour Movement in England', unpublished MSc. thesis, London School of Economics.

Simon, B. (1974) *The Politics of Educational Reform 1920–1940*, London: Lawrence & Wishart.

Simon, B. (1991) *Education and the Social Order*, London: Lawrence & Wishart.

Sinclair, J., Ironside, M. and Seifert, R (1993a) 'Classroom struggle? Market orientated education reforms and their impact upon teachers' professional autonomy, labour intensification and resistance', paper to International Labour Process Conference.

Sinclair, J., Ironside, M. and Seifert, R. (1993b) 'The road to market: management and trade union initiatives in the transition to school level bargaining under LMS', paper to BUIRA.

Sinclair, J. and Seifert, R. (1993) 'Money for value?', *Managing Schools Today*, vol. 2(9).

Sisson, K. (ed.) (1989) *Personnel Management in Britain*, Oxford: Basil Blackwell.

Smith, A. (1776) *The Wealth of Nations*, 1910 edn, London: Everyman.

Smith, K. (1984) *The British Economic Crisis*, Harmondsworth: Penguin Books.

Smyth, J. (ed.) (1993) *A Socially Critical View of the Self-Managing School*, London: Falmer Press.

Spoor, A. (1967) *White Collar Union*, London: Heinemann.

Stenning R. (1989) 'The conduct of industrial relations in schools: from collectivism to laissez-faire?', *Educational Management and Administration*, vol. 17 (4).

Stenning, R., Lyons, G., McQueeney, J. and Webster, R. (1984) 'The conduct of employment relations: interface between LEA and school', *Educational Management and Administration*, vol. 12.

Stenning, W. and Stenning, R. (1984) 'The assessment of teacher's performance: some practical considerations', *Abstracts*, Oxford: Journals Oxford.

Storey, J. (1992) *Management of Human Resources*, Oxford: Blackwell.

Storey, J. and Sisson, K. (1990) 'Limits to transformation: human resource management in the British context', *Industrial Relations Journal*, vol. 21(1).

Storey, J. and Sisson, K. (1993) *Managing Human Resources and Industrial Relations*, Buckingham: Open University Press.

Taylor, F. (1911) *Scientific Management*, New York: Harper & Bros.

Taylor, K. (1983) 'Heads and the freedom to manage', *School Organization*, vol. 3(3).

Teachers' Panel (1984) *Submission to the Board of Arbitration on the Salaries of Teachers from 1 April 1984*, London: Burnham Primary and Secondary Committee.

Terry, M. (1983) 'Shop steward development and managerial strategies', in G. Bain (ed.) *Industrial Relations in Britain*, London: Blackwell.

Theodossin, E. (1987) 'Quality control in education: the use of performance indicators', *Coombe Lodge Report*, vol. 20(1).

Thomas, H. (1984) 'Teachers in decline? The quality consequences of the management of changing rolls', *Educational Management and Administration*, vol. 12(1).

Thorold Rogers, J. (1891) *Six Centuries of Work and Wages*, London: Swan Sonnenschein.

Tomlinson, H. (ed.) (1992) *Performance-Related Pay in Education*, London: Routledge.

Tomlinson, H. (1992) 'Performance-related pay in the 1980s: the changing climate', in H. Tomlinson (ed.) *Performance-Related Pay in Education*, London: Routledge.

Torrington, D. and Hall, L. (1987) *Personnel Management: a New Approach*, London: Prentice Hall.

Tropp, A. (1957) *The School Teachers*, London: Heinemann.

Tuck, D. (1988) 'Local financial management', *Educational Management and Administration*, vol. 16.

Turnbull P. and Williams G. (1974) 'Sex differentials in teachers' pay', *Journal of the Royal Statistical Society*, Series A, vol. 137(2).

Turnbull P. and Williams G. (1975) 'Supply and demand in the labour market for teachers: qualification differentials in teachers' pay', *British Journal of Industrial Relations*, vol. 13(2).

Turnbull P. and Williams G. (1976) 'Teachers' pay: how and why men and women's earnings differ', *Employment Gazette*, September.

Turner, H. (1962) *Trade Union Growth, Structure and Policy*, London: George Allen & Unwin.

TURU (1992) 'Report on performance related pay for the National Union of Teachers and the National Association of Schoolmasters Union of Women Teachers', in NASUWT and NUT (1992) *Performance Related Pay: Submission to the School Teachers' Review Body*, Birmingham: NASUWT and London: NUT.

Unwin, B. and Weeks, J. (1991) *Managing Procedures and Pay*, Leicester: SHA.

Varlaam, A., Nuttall, D. and Walker, A. (1992) *What Makes Teachers Tick? A Study of Teacher Morale and Motivation*, London: LSE.

Waddington, J. (1992) 'Trade union membership in Britain 1980–1987', *British Journal of Industrial Relations*, vol. 30(2).

Walsall LEA (1992) *Manual of Personnel Guidance*.

Walsh, K., Dunne, R., Stoten, B. and Stewart, J. (1984) *Falling Rolls and the Management of the Teaching Profession*, Windsor: NFER-Nelson.

Walton, R. and McKersie, R. (1965) *A Behavioral Theory of Labour Negotiations*, New York: McGraw Hill.

Warwickshire LEA (1992) *LMS Personnel Guidelines*.

Way, P., Duncan, J. and McCarthy, W. (1981) 'Official pay inquiries: the Houghton Committee on teachers' pay', *Industrial Relations Journal*, vol. 12(1).

Webb, B. (1915) 'English teachers and their professional organisations' *The New Statesman*, vol. 5 (129).

Webb, B. and Webb, S. (1917) 'Professional associations', *The New Statesman*, vol. 9 (212).

Webb, S. and Webb, B. (1894) *History of Trade Unionism*, first edition, London: Longman.

Webb, S. and Webb, B. (1897) *Industrial Democracy*, 1920 edition, London: Longmans Green & Co 1920.

Wedderburn, W. (1986) *The Worker and the Law*, third edition, Hardmondsworth: Penguin Books.

Whitley, J. (1917) *Interim Report on Joint Standing Industrial Councils*, Cd 8606, London: HMSO.

Wilby, P. (1986) 'Teacher appraisal', *Journal of Education Policy*, vol. 1(1).

Winchester, D. (1983) 'Industrial relations in the public sector', in Bain, G. (ed) *Industrial Relations in Britain*, Basil Blackwell, Oxford.

Woodhouse, G. and Goldstein, H. (1988) 'Educational performance indicators and LEA league tables', *Oxford Review of Education*, vol. 14(3).

Wootton, B. (1962) *The Social Foundations of Wage Policy*, London: Unwin University Books.

Author index

Subject index

The following abbreviations have been used in the index:

ACAS	Advisory, Conciliation and Arbitration Service
ATL	Association of Teachers and Lecturers
HRM	Human resource management
IAC	Interim Advisory Committee on Schoolteachers' Pay and Conditions
LEA	Local Education Authority
LMS	Local management of schools
NAHT	National Association of Head Teachers
NAS	National Association of Schoolmasters
NASUWT	National Association of Schoolmasters and Union of Women Teachers
NUT	National Union of Teachers
PAT	Professional Association of Teachers
PRP	Performance-related pay
STRB	School Teachers' Review Body